The Taos Indians
and the Battle for Blue Lake

The
TAOS INDIANS
and the
BATTLE FOR
BLUE LAKE

by R.C. Gordon-McCutchan

Foreword by Frank Waters

RED
CRANE
BOOKS

For my parents Tom and Freddie,
From whom I learned the joy of knowledge.

Library of Congress Number: 90-61680

ISBN 1-878610-12-0
ISBN 1-878610-11-2 'p.

First Edition

Printed in the United States of America

Jacket Design by Joanna Hill
Text Design by Jim Mafchir

Title Page: San Geronimo Day at Taos Pueblo, c. 1925. Photo by George L. Beam. Courtesy Museum of New Mexico. Neg. No. 86294.

Red Crane Books
826 Camino del Monte Rey
Santa Fe, New Mexico 87501

Contents

Foreword by Frank Waters vii

Acknowledgments xiii

Chronology of the Fight for Justice xvi

Taos Pueblo Area Maps xviii

  1 Polarities: The Cacique and the Forester 3

  2 John Collier to the Rescue 23

  3 The La Farge Era 44

  4 The Tribe Assumes Control 64

  5 The First Hearing 85

  6 Things Turn Sour 107

  7 The Tide Begins to Turn 128

  8 Hemingway Luck 148

  9 Year of Decision 172

10 The Moment of Truth 194

Epilogue 214

Obituary 220

Notes 222

Resources and Bibliography 230

Index 232

Outflow of Blue Lake, the most sacred shrine of the Taos Indians, set in the majesty of the Sangre de Cristo Range of the Rocky Mountains, c. 1970. Photo by Dan Budnik.

Foreword

THE TAOS INDIANS AND THE BATTLE FOR BLUE LAKE by R.C. Gordon-McCutchan recounts Taos Pueblo's sixty-four year fight to gain restoration of its sacred Blue Lake and surrounding wilderness. The history of the mountainous area is given from 1551 when King Charles V of Spain claimed New Mexico as a Spanish province and gave Taos Pueblo first title to its grant of land. With thorough research, Dr. Gordon-McCutchan, for four years the Taos Pueblo planner, includes every public statement and action made by the host of the Pueblo's supporters to achieve victory on 15 December 1970.

The comments made here are chiefly about a book of my own written fifty years ago. It seems to me that they might more properly be included as a concluding footnote to this impressive book rather than as a foreword. It explains how I happened to share a little in the fortunes of Blue Lake and the Pueblo.

The first place where I lived when I came to Taos was Spud Johnson's house in Placita, which I rented for the summer of 1939. When he returned home, he took me to meet Mabel Dodge and Tony Luhan. They owned a small empty house near Spud's which they offered to let me live in if I would fix it up a bit. The house was an adobe, and was most comfortable after a few repairs. One of its great advantages was its location outside commercial Taos and at the junction of a dirt road leading through the reservation to Taos Pueblo.

The ancient town stood at the foot of its Sacred Mountain and, with its setting, was to me the most beautiful of all pueblos. There were two buildings, both terraced pyramids, one of five stories, the other of four. Through the great plaza between them ran the mountain stream which supplied the Taos people with water. The tribes of all the Rio Grande pueblos were believed to have been

Anasazis who had migrated to this region during the Long Drought in the thir-teenth century. Three major Tanoan dialects were spoken between them: Acoma, Zia, San Felipe, and Cochiti speaking Keresan; San Ildefonso, San Juan, Santa Clara, Nambe, and Tesuque speaking Tewa; and the three Tiwa pueblos of Taos, Picuris, and Sandia. Taos is the most northern of all pueblos, and the most distinctive for the dress of its people. Both men and women wear blankets in the winter and white sheets in the summer. The men are the only puebloans to wear their hair in two long pigtails, Plains fashion. Like the pueblo itself, Taos people had been for years the popular subjects for paintings and tourist photog-raphers.

I loved the Pueblo; it was so peaceful and quiet. I went there often to visit the first friends I made—Joe Sun Hawk Sandoval, Albert and Clara Martinez, and their families. The Pueblo, for all its earthy homeyness, somehow gave an other-worldly air of being oriented to the rhythms of sun, moon, and stars, the forces of the earth and the waters around them, rather than the cash-register life of the town plaza. The people were poor, but seemed somehow enriched by inner self-assurance.

One day, months after fixing up the house, I happened to wander into the county courthouse where a hearing was being held for a young Indian who had killed a deer out of season in the Carson National Forest. I thought nothing of the incident at the time, and walked home. Tony and Mabel had sold the house in which I had lived that winter, and I was now living in the big studio room above the garage of the "Tony House." It was called that because it stood on Tony's land on the Pueblo reservation. Dorothy Brett occupied a small house nearby, and we both shared the same outdoor privy.

While I was shaving a few days later after the hearing, three figures seemed to be reflected from the washbowl—the old governor of Taos Pueblo; Pascual Mar-tinez, local head of the Forest Service; and an Anglo whom I identified as the Indian trader Ralph Myers. They were evidently discussing the hearing I had observed at the courthouse. Right then the idea of the novel *The Man Who Killed the Deer* came to me. So, after washing the breakfast dishes, I settled down here on Indian land to write my first Indian novel.

The story didn't need to be contrived. It unfolded, like a flower, in its own inherent pattern. The words came easily, unbidden, as the flow of ink from my old red Parker.

The Man Who Killed the Deer is the story of Martiniano, a young Taos Pueblo Indian, who as a child had been sent away to a white man's school instead of being taught at home the traditional religious beliefs of his people. Upon his return he finds himself an outcast, constantly breaking Pueblo customs. Then he kills a deer out of season in the Carson National Forest. For breaking this law, he is arrested and fined. He has also violated a stricture of Indian religion by not obtaining the deer's ritual consent to its sacrifice.

To repay the money loaned him, by the trader Byers to pay his fine, he has to work at odd jobs all winter. The deer he has killed also exacts a penalty by haunting him. The story then, as later regarded by reviewers, developed as "a timeless story of Pueblo Indian sin and redemption."

But as Martiniano was arrested on the mountain watershed surrounding the tribe's Dawn (Blue) Lake, the presence of forest rangers stimulates the Pueblo to renew its efforts to regain control of its sacred wilderness.

This, of course, threw into focus the continuing controversy over the ownership of the Blue Lake wilderness. For in 1906, Pres. Theodore Roosevelt had established the Carson National Forest, taking for it fifty thousand acres of the Pueblo's wilderness without payment to them. In the years since, Spanish and Anglo newcomers had been coming in and preempting land, settling modern Taos, Ranchos de Taos, and a half dozen small villages.

A Pueblo Lands Board, after a lengthy investigation, prepared a bill for Congress which offered to pay the Pueblo $297,684.67, the 1906 valuation of the land in Taos taken from it. The Pueblo, however, waived compensation in return for a clear title to the fifty thousand acres of the Blue Lake wilderness.

On 4 October 1940, after a long delay, Congress passed a bill containing the Pueblo Lands Board offer, but in a much-amended form. It gave the Pueblo only a fifty year use-permit for thirty thousand acres.

The novel ended with the Pueblo's acceptance of this use-permit. I completed it in Los Angeles, where I had gone to work. The manuscript was sent to the New York publisher Farrar & Rinehart, and at Stephen Vincent Benet's insistence not a word was changed before it went to the printer.

Published on 11 June 1942, the book was a complete flop. The nation was preoccupied with the war effort. People were not interested in a book about an obscure Indian Pueblo in the mountains of New Mexico, or, for that matter, about Indians any time. Prejudice against them was still prevalent. The book quickly went out of print, and I entered the army and was then transferred into the Office of Interamerican Affairs in Washington, D.C.

I finally returned to Taos, editing the Spanish-English weekly newspaper *El Crepusculo*. Here I learned that the Forest Service had not been observing the terms of the Pueblo's fifty year use-permit for the Blue Lake area. It had cut trails into the area, and made it available to campers and tourists, who littered the ground with refuse and beer cans. Moreover, it had built a cabin for use of its rangers. Fisherman were coming in, further desecrating the area. It became quite clear to the Tribal Council that the Pueblo's 1940 use-permit was worthless. To preserve their wilderness area, they would have to gain full trust-title to it.

Things had been going a little bit better for *The Man Who Killed the Deer*. The novel, after going out of print, had become something of a collector's item. Alan Swallow of the University of Denver Press then reissued the book in a small edition. Soon beginning a new publishing venture under his own name, "Alan Swallow, Publisher," he began issuing other printings periodically. Operating a small one-man press, he became the only publisher west of the Mississippi to break the monopoly of the Eastern publishing establishment which looked down its nose at Western writers and books, regarding them as provincial. *The Man Who Killed the Deer* owes him its long life.

The fictional Martiniano grew less shy and unsociable. He and his wife farmed a few acres outside the Pueblo itself, but they had made friends in the Pueblo whom they frequently visited; and Martiniano especially loved to mix with the crowd in the plaza on the days when ceremonial events were open to the public. The rites in the underground kivas were secret but those held outside were exciting events. Townspeople, dressed in their fiesta best, swarmed in the plaza and perched on the Pueblo terraces and rooftops. On these days, the Pueblo showed all its warmth and hospitality. After each ceremonial, whatever it was, doors were open to anyone for a hearty meal of chile, lamb stew, vegetables, bread-pudding, and bread from the outdoor ovens. All this was good for Martiniano, for unlike individualistic Anglos, Indians were communal by nature, and he was losing his feeling of alienation and isolation.

I saw much of another Martiniano, for I had bought a dilapidated adobe with fields and pastures on the mountain slope above the little Spanish village of Arroyo Seco adjoining the Pueblo reservation. To help us work on the house, I hired a young Indian. He happened to be Martiniano—the man who under his own name Frank Zamora had killed the deer that instigated so much trouble. He was a fine workman, a skilled hand with my few horses, and a close friend. Throughout the many years we worked together, neither of us ever mentioned *The Man Who Killed the Deer*, although I'm sure he knew what the book was about if he hadn't read it. This was just as well. For Frank, the real Martiniano, never questioned what the fictional Martiniano had done or felt.

The water question in this little Spanish village on the northern boundary of the Indian reservation was always acute. Most of Arroyo Seco's water for irrigating its fields came from the Rio Lucero, which poured down from the Blue Lake watershed and then was divided between the Pueblo and Arroyo Seco. I was the only Anglo living in this village and soon became drawn into its affairs.

The general attitude in New Mexico toward Indians was not too favorable. In 1950, New Mexico representative A.M. Fernandez proposed to introduce into Congress a "Bill of Rights" for the Indians of Taos Pueblo, asserting that the Tribal Council took children out of school to carry on religious duties, interfered with their right to vote, refused freedom of worship, and did not permit farm improvements. The "Bill of Rights," in short, was aimed at destroying the Pueblo's traditional right to local self-government guaranteed it by the federal government.

I finally secured an appointment with Fernandez in Santa Fe, and took to see him Governor Star Road Gomez, influential Seferino Martinez, Pat and Abe Romero, and publisher Ted Cabot of *El Crepusculo*. After being kept waiting four hours, we were ushered into politico Fernandez's presence. The interview was a farce which I reported in full the following week, mailing copies to leading members of the state legislature and Congress. The "Bill of Rights" was never introduced, but strong opposition developed to the Pueblo's efforts to regain title to the Blue Lake watershed.

The spokesmen generating adverse publicity were George Proctor, the supervisor of the Carson National Forest, of course; and senior Sen. Clinton P. Anderson of New Mexico, a state that held nineteen Indian pueblos which needed his consideration. Anderson, however, claimed that the fifty thousand acres were properly in the public domain and should therefore be administered by the Forest Service under its "multiple-use" policy. The popular slogan voiced the exploitation policy of Europeans since they had first arrived in America. It now included the cutting of virgin timber, running roads through wilderness areas, leasing sites for ski resorts, camping grounds, stores and filling stations. Senator Anderson drew up an alternate bill, providing the Pueblo be given only 3,150 acres.

The most serious threat was that the Pueblo would shut off the water to downstream users if it gained control of the watershed. Jim Colgrove, editor of the *Taos News*, and the Town Council of Taos itself, supported this allegation. To discuss ways to counteract the adverse publicity the Pueblo was receiving, a small group of Anglos met frequently with members of the Tribal Council at the home of Mary Goodwin. The group included Joan Reed, Charlie Brooks, John Collier, Oliver LaFarge, and myself. One helpful step we took was drawing up a long petition urging the return of the watershed to the Pueblo.

The fear of losing water was as strong in Arroyo Seco as elsewhere. It must have seemed strange to my neighbors that I was helping the Pueblo to gain control of the source of our own water. But they did not protest my efforts. They were loyal, loved friends who always took good care of me.

The fight for Blue Lake grew into national proportions. Support for the Pueblo came from other Indian tribes, churches, schools, civic organizations, and thousands of individuals throughout the country.

This support came slowly. The general American public at the time knew almost nothing of Indian religion. The quest for Blue Lake brought Indian religion to the forefront of national consciousness. And it was crucial to the Indians' success that they convince the general public that religion lay behind their claim.

The Man Who Killed the Deer, with its wide distribution, made people aware that the whole natural landscape, the entire fifty thousand acres, contained innumerable shrines where the Indians would go to pray and hold ceremonies. It was important that the public understand that the struggle for Blue Lake concerned not just one pilgrimage or one location, like a kiva, but the whole watershed as the Pueblo's "church."

One of the key things brought out in the novel is that nature, for the Indians, is their sanctuary and altar. The man who killed the deer had violated one of the strictures of Indian religion, of failing to get permission from the deer to accede to its sacrifice. The belief that man should not kill needlessly, for fun or profit or sport—is not only a Taos Pueblo belief; it is common throughout all of Indian America. It is based on the understanding that all forms of life are alike, having an inner essence as well as an outer physical form.

In other Pueblos, especially the Hopi, the Kachina is the inner essence which always accompanies the outer form. But white America does not grant any inner essence to a rock, a mountain, a bird, an animal, or a tree, whereas Indian America does. Indians believe that there is no such thing as inanimate matter; all matter is imbued with life energy, although it may be in a very low form. While animals have not developed to the same point as human beings, nor have plants reached the state of animals, yet everything, the earth and mountains, is imbued with energy, with life in some degree. This kind of mysticism is a natural part of Indian culture. Indians believe in the intangible as strongly as whites believe in the tangible.

I am convinced that we must learn from the Indians this holistic way of thinking. We must realize our relatedness to all other forms of life, as I tried hard to bring out in *The Man Who Killed the Deer.*

Another thing that helped the Indians in their quest for Blue Lake was the growing public understanding of the concept of ecology. As the tenets of ecology became more widely appreciated, beginning in the early 1960's, so too did an understanding of the relationship between ecology and the basic principles of Indian religion. The public began to grasp the fact that ecology is the basis of Indian religion.

Blue Lake challenged the federal government to choose between adhering to its national materialistic policy or giving Indians the freedom of religion promised them by the Constitution.

Martiniano had taken me up there several times. The trip was a steep climb over six thousand feet in twenty miles. The trail led up the dark forested canyon, through groves of aspen, over high ridges, up the steep frost-shattered granite slope of Wheeler Peak, more than thirteen thousand feet high, the highest peak in New Mexico. But just below its summit, you saw it deep in the forest below. The little blue lake of life, clear turquoise blue as the sky above, dark purplish blue as the depth of the enclosing forest. The ancient lake, the place of Emergence.

One could envision the hundreds of fires, the tents and shelters around the lake, the welling chorus of song that filled the hours of the night. What happens up there that night in August no outsider may ever know. It may be no more— nor no less—than the spiritual communion that comes to a people who submerge for a moment their individuality in the collective unconscious which is not only tribal but universal.

Years ago, as I remember, girls and women returning from the pilgrimage came back with garlands of blue "Flowers of the Night" and garlands of bright yellow "Flowers of the Sun," but I haven't seen them since.

R.C. Gordon-McCutchan, Doroteo Samora, and Frank Waters in the aspen grove at Frank Waters's Taos home, 1990. Photo by Bill Davis.

In the late 1960's, the U.S. Indian Claims Commission decided that the Pueblo had proven title to the full fifty thousand acre watershed, and a bill confirming the commission's decision cleared the House of Representatives with a unanimous vote. There remained only one more barrier to pass.

There is no need to relate here the dramatic hearings it was given in the Senate. The exciting events are described in detail in R.C. Gordon-McCutchan's present book. Sen. Clinton P. Anderson continued to the last to oppose the bill by offering his own. The highlight of the hearings was the appearance of ninety year-old Juan de Jesús Romero, the Cacique, or religious leader of the Pueblo, who had been brought to testify to the religious importance of Blue Lake.

Finally, on 15 December 1970, the Senate passed the bill by an overwhelming vote of nearly six to one for Pres. Richard M. Nixon to sign into law. It was the first land claims case settled in favor of an Indian tribe based on the freedom of religion.

Taos Pueblo today, commemorating the twentieth year of its victory, has undergone many changes as it enters a new phase in its long life. *The Man Who Killed the Deer* also has much to celebrate. It has been in print for nearly fifty years, has sold one million copies, and is still selling in domestic and foreign translation editions. A second French translation is now in preparation, the first one having been issued in 1964.

For this half-century the novel has portrayed Taos Pueblo as an Indian village of multi-storied adobe buildings whose Native American residents carried on a simple life of earthy homeyness nourished by their strong religious feelings and a holistic worldview. This picture is no longer true. The poor and peaceful Pueblo Martiniano knew, has changed completely. I have never revised the book, and won't after all these years. It may be that the Pueblo still maintains its holistic viewpoint despite all the changes.

Anyway, I'm glad to leave *The Man Who Killed the Deer* the way it was written. After all, the book was not my creation. It was born in a washbowl.

—Frank Waters

Acknowledgments

PRIMARY THANKS for the existence of this book go to Michael and Mari-
anne O'Shaughnessy, whose financial and emotional support made this
project possible. Patrons, benefactors, and friends, they demonstrated
courage and commitment when unforeseen problems arose, and gave me the
resolve to press ahead. Thanks also to Paul J. Bernal, whose initial backing of the
book enabled me to obtain approval from the Taos Pueblo Tribal Council, and
the full cooperation of the Indian people who carried on the struggle for
decades. I am especially grateful to Joe Louis Mirabal, the Taos Pueblo war chief
in 1988, who stood unwaveringly behind the book from the outset. Much
appreciation goes to Douglas Schwartz, president of the School of American
Research, under whose auspices this book was written. And thanks also to my
parents Tom and Freddie, who in ways great and small undergirded the creation
of this moving story.

Many individuals contributed directly to amassing the voluminous information which went into the writing of the saga of Blue Lake. Chief among them is
Alfred Bush, curator of the Western Americana Collection at Princeton University. Not only was Mr. Bush most cooperative in making available to me the original documents concerning Blue Lake, but he also provided me with helpful
bibiliographic suggestions and scholarly contacts. In addition, he gave sage
counsel respecting myriad other matters.

Sincere thanks also are due to Mr. Richard Salazar, Chief of Archival Services
for the New Mexico Records Center and Archives, and to his able assistants
Alfred Aragon, Al Regensberg, and Ron Montoya. They proved unfailingly helpful in giving me access to the extensive Paul J. Bernal Blue Lake Papers.

Additional information concerning the Blue Lake story came through the good offices of Barbara Johnson, curator of the Clinton P. Anderson Papers at the University of New Mexico. Thanks also to Mr. Bennie Salas, real property officer for the Northern Pueblos Agency, who helped me gather information on Blue Lake from the files of the Bureau of Indian Affairs in Santa Fe. Another appreciated contributor is Mr. William Moehn, staff member at the Carson National Forest Headquarters in Taos, who helped me sort out matters pertaining to boundaries in the Blue Lake area and who allowed me to copy valuable maps in the possession of the Forest Service.

An especially important source for telling this story from the tribal perspective was the Taos Pueblo War Chief's Office. I am grateful to War Chief Bennie Martinez for permission to have access to the files, and to Bernie Cordova for her cheerful assistance in gathering the informative documents in the office of the war chief. Thanks also to Mr. Vicente Lujan, the Taos Pueblo real property officer, who helped me better understand complicated matters pertaining to boundaries and ownership questions.

Fellow historian Myra Ellen Jenkins contributed many helpful insights as well as documents and two important unpublished manuscripts. Neil Poese of the Kit Carson Historic Museum made available to me hundreds of photographs, some of which appear in the book. Thanks also to his assistant Victor Grant. David Witt of the Harwood Foundation helped me with their excellent collection of photographs. Thanks to him, as well. Paul O'Connor deserves praise for the reproduction of photographs from sources in Taos.

Heartfelt appreciation goes to Taos Pueblo Governor Mike Concha and tribal secretary Nelson J. Cordova for their review of the manuscript, assistance in gathering information, and smoothing the occasionally troubled political waters. Sen. Pete Domenici of New Mexico and his assistant, Paul Gilman, helped in many ways with matters relating to the Washington political scene.

Harriet Slavitz, my editor and friend, deserves the warmest of thanks for her painstaking reading of the manuscript. She helped me avoid contradictions, add needed explanations, and in every way contributed to the language of the book's final version. Working with her was both instructive and pleasurable.

A final thanks to Suzie Poole, through whose foresight the Blue Lake Papers were brought together and donated to Princeton University, and through whose efforts invaluable interviews with chief protagonists in the struggle were taped. To her goes much of the credit for the very existence of this book.

R.C. Gordon-McCutchan
Broken Arrow Ranch
Taos, New Mexico

CHRONOLOGY OF THE FIGHT FOR JUSTICE

1300

Taos Pueblo Indians occupy their present homeland and establish the central village as their permanent residence.

1598

Spanish rule is established, under laws recognizing Indian possessory rights to territory used and occupied.

1821

Mexico assumes sovereignty and confirms Indian possessory rights to occupied territory under treaty of Cordova and Mexican Declaration of Independence.

1848

Sovereignty passes to the United States under the Treaty of Guadalupe Hidalgo, which guarantees protection of all property rights recognized by Spanish and Mexican law.

1906

United States government appropriates Blue Lake area and makes it a part of the Carson National Forest.

1926

The Pueblo offers to waive compensation awarded by the Pueblo Lands Board for Indian lands settled by non-Indians, if it can acquire title to the Blue Lake area, but it receives neither compensation nor title.

May 31, 1933

Senate Indian Affairs Committee recommendation that title be restored results in diluted act providing for a permit to protect Indian use-rights. Permit not issued by the Department of Agriculture until 1940.

Aug. 13, 1951

Pueblo files suit before the Indian Claims Commission, seeking judicial support for the validity of its claim.

Sept. 8, 1965

Indian Claims Commission affirms that the U.S. government took the area unjustly from its rightful Indian owners.

March 15, 1966

S. 3085, legislation to return the sacred area to the Pueblo, is introduced in Congress by Sen. Clinton P. Anderson of New Mexico "by request," to indicate his lack of support. The bill dies without action in the Senate Interior and Insular Affairs Subcommittee.

May 10, 1968

H.B. 3306, to restore the sacred area to the Pueblo, is introduced in 1967 by Rep. James A. Haley, chairman of the Subcommittee on Indian Affairs. It passes the House of Representatives unanimously, but dies again in the Senate Interior and Insular Affairs Subcommittee.

Jan. 3, 1969

The Blue Lake bill is reintroduced by Rep. James A. Haley as H.B. 471 on the first day of the Ninety-first Congress.

Jan. 26, 1970

National Congress of American Indians Executive Committee endorses H.R. 471 and calls for presidential support as the cornerstone of a new Indian policy.

July 8, 1970

President Nixon announces support for H.R. 471 as the first element of his new Indian policy.

July 9, 1970

Hearings open before Senate Subcommittee on Indian Affairs on H.R. 471 and Senator Anderson's alternative, S. 750.

Aug. 27, 1970

Senate subcommittee favorably reports to full Committee on Interior and Insular Affairs both H.R. 471, which grants trust title to 48,000 acres comprising Blue Lake and access routes from the Pueblo, and S. 750, which grants an exclusive-use area of 1,640 acres around Blue Lake, but without exclusive access thereto.

Sept. 30, 1970

Full Senate committee meets with majority favoring H.R. 471, but adjourns before vote is taken.

Oct. 6, 1970

Full committee approves a substitute measure which would deprive the Pueblo of control of its sacred lands and undermine its water rights.

Nov. 19, 1970

Committee amends its substitute measure to eliminate threat to Pueblo's water rights, but retains other unacceptable provisions.

Dec. 2, 1970

Senate kills substitute measure, 56 to 21; approves H.R. 471, 70 to 12.

Dec. 15, 1970

President Nixon signs H.R. 471 into law.

Map on left shows the Blue Lake acreage returned to the Tribe (Area 1) minus the 2,000 acres in the Wheeler Peak Wilderness (Area 2).

Map on right depicts the various tracts into which the Federal and State government had divided the sacred watershed.

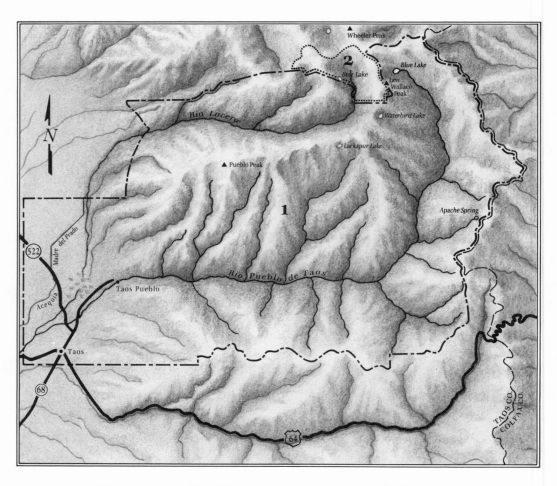

——— · ——— · **1** 48,000 acres covered by Public Law 91-550

·············· **2** Wheeler Peak Wilderness Area

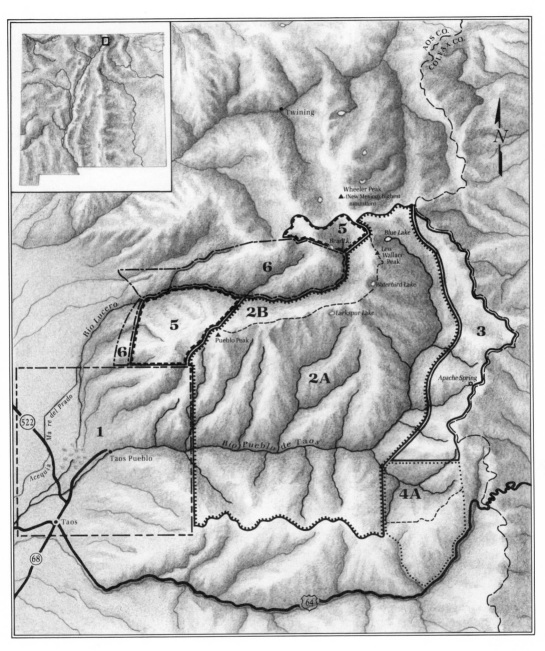

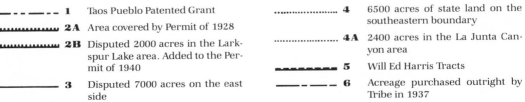

▬ ▬ · ▬ · ▬ · **1**	Taos Pueblo Patented Grant	
▬▬▬▬▬ **2A**	Area covered by Permit of 1928	
▬▬▬▬▬ **2B**	Disputed 2000 acres in the Lark- spur Lake area. Added to the Per- mit of 1940	
▬▬▬▬▬ **3**	Disputed 7000 acres on the east side	
·············· **4**	6500 acres of state land on the southeastern boundary	
·············· **4A**	2400 acres in the La Junta Can- yon area	
▬ ▬ ▬ ▬ **5**	Will Ed Harris Tracts	
▬ ▬ · ▬ · ▬ **6**	Acreage purchased outright by Tribe in 1937	

The afternoon passes, the light fades, and evening is coming when we are upon the cold, treeless ridges in austerity and awe, utterly removed from everyday life and everything we are used to in light and sound. As we top the last bleak, shale-covered edge we see below us Blue Lake. Bottomless, peacock blue, smooth as glass, it lies there like an uncut, shining jewel. Symmetrical pine trees, in thick succession, slope down to its shores in a rapid descent on three sides.

This Blue Lake is the most mysterious thing I have ever seen in nature, having an unknowable, impenetrable life of its own, and a definite emanation that rises from it. . . . It has never been surprising to me that the Indians call Blue Lake a sacred lake, and worship it. . . . The Indians begin to chant, at first in faint, humming tones, that gradually grow strong and full. They look over to the lake and sing to it. Their faces show they are deep in communion with the place they are in. They experience it and adore it as we do not know how to do. . . .

Most of us are used only to the awesome holiness of churches and lofty arches, cathedrals where, with stained glass and brooding silences, priests try to emulate the religious atmosphere that is to be found in the living earth in some of her secret places. . . .

Mabel Dodge Luhan
Reprinted from *Winter in Taos*
1982 by permission of
Las Palomas de Taos, New Mexico

The Taos Indians
and the Battle for Blue Lake

"Cui Bono" shows painting of Taos Pueblo, c. 1913. Photo by Gerald Cassidy. Courtesy of and on permanent exhibit in the Museum of New Mexico. Neg. No. 20794.

1

Polarities: The Cacique and the Forester

RUNNING SOUTH FROM THE BROOKS RANGE in Alaska, the great Rocky Mountains stretch all the way to Mexico. Their main body, however, rises 400 miles north of the Canadian border in Jasper National Park and descends to the plains at Santa Fe in central New Mexico. Traversing that distance, one crosses some of the most beautiful mountains on earth—the Wind River Range, the Medicine Bow, the Bugaboos, the Tetons, the Bighorn peaks, the Absarokas, the Sangre de Cristo, the Sawatch, and the Grenadiers.

Imagine, if you will, that these Rockies are some great dragon, its tail in Canada and its snout hundreds and hundreds of miles south in Santa Fe. This beast reaches maximum height in Colorado, where more than fifty of the spikes on its massive back tower above 14,000 feet. It then slopes gradually downward as it stretches south, rising abruptly at Taos where Wheeler Peak, New Mexico's highest mountain, forms the dragon's single great horn. And just below that horn is its one eye—a perfect circle of the deepest blue, perhaps the most beautiful alpine lake in all of the Rockies. Called Blue Lake by the Indians who worshipped there for centuries, around it centers our tale.

Hidden at 11,000 feet in a glacial cirque of the Sangre de Cristo, this cobalt blue mountain tarn has been the focus of furious national debate and a great congressional battle. Hundreds of articles and editorials on the controversy it aroused have appeared in newspapers from the *New York Times* to the *Times* of Los Angeles. Just before the long-awaited showdown finally took place in the United States Senate in 1970, President Nixon gave a dramatic policy speech which made the return of Blue Lake to the Taos Indians the symbol of his "new

3

deal" for tribes throughout the country. Firmly backing the Indians, the *New York Times* editorialized that "the Senate now has a rare chance to do justice and perhaps to start the country back on the long road toward regaining the trust of the first Americans." The lead editorial for the *Washington Post* agreed, calling the Blue Lake vote "an acid test of the policy of respecting the Indians' rights and allowing them the cultural freedom that other ethnic groups in the country enjoy."

On one side of the debate, in support of Nixon and the Taos Tribe, was the unlikely coalition of Senate majority whip Robert Griffin, Ted Kennedy, Fred Harris, and Barry Goldwater. On the other, in grimly determined opposition, were Senators Clifford Hansen, Henry Jackson, Clinton Anderson, and Lee Metcalf. And high up in the Senate gallery sat four old Indians, intensely making medicine.

Emerson said that an institution is the lengthened shadow of one man, an observation borne out by this conflict. In the battle over Blue Lake, each side had at its center the will and inspiration of a single individual. The background of these two men could not have been more different.

One was a young Indian born into a small tribe in the remote mountains of northern New Mexico. Unable to read or write, poor and unworldly and without political connections, this young man would, after decades of persistence, finally lead his people to an extraordinary victory. The other protagonist was a young white from a wealthy and politically powerful eastern family. With every material advantage, he attended the best schools, wielded great power, and could say in later life that he personally had known every president from Ulysses S. Grant to Harry S. Truman. Yet the institution which was his lengthened shadow proved the loser in the coming clash of forces. To better understand these forces, we must understand the men who represented them.

Juan de Jesús Romero was born into the Taos Tribe of Indians, inhabitants of the northernmost of the nineteen native pueblos or villages still in existence in New Mexico today. They are directly descended from the great Anasazi Indian culture which flourished from A.D. 100 to A.D. 1200 in the Four Corners area of the southwest where Utah, Arizona, Colorado and New Mexico join. Mesa Verde and Chaco Canyon are the most famous Anasazi sites, where thousands of native people lived in settled communities with well constructed "apartment houses" and carefully irrigated fields.

For reasons not entirely clear, but probably as a result of drought, the Anasazi abandoned their settled communities, and by 1300 these once-teeming cities stood empty. Archaeological evidence indicates that the first Anasazi migration into the Taos area occurred as early as A.D. 900. Some five hundred years later, Taos Pueblo looked much as it does today, with five-story mud and straw buildings surrounded by extensive fields watered by an elaborate hand-dug irrigation system.

The Tribe's spiritual leader, the Cacique Juan de Jesus Romero (right), with Teofilo Romero, a Tribal elder, c. 1950. Courtesy of William P. Martinez.

Taos Pueblo is one of the Southwest's most famous places. The oldest continuously inhabited structure in North America, it is a National Historic Landmark. Recently the U.S. government paid Taos Pueblo the high tribute of nominating it as a World Heritage site. Set at the foot of the Sangre de Cristo, the ancient pueblo looks out to New Mexico's high desert mesas and the Rio Grande Gorge beyond. In this beautiful mountain setting, the remote ancestors of Juan de Jesús Romero developed the unique culture which remained little changed down to his own time.

However, the march of history did not leave the Taos Indians untouched. In 1540, the Spanish explorer Francisco de Coronado led the first expedition up the Rio Grande Valley. Admiring the great southern chain of the Rockies bathed in the red of a spectacular sunset, the conquistadores named the range Sangre de Cristo— or Blood of Christ.

The local Indians, initially friendly to the newcomers, soon came bitterly to resent the *encomienda* system of forced taxes imposed upon them. Worse still was the brutal suppression of native religion carried out by the Franciscans. Sent to convert the Pueblo Indians, the Franciscans set about their task with a will. Decreeing an absolute prohibition on native religious dances, they raided the *kivas* (ceremonial rooms), persecuted native religious figures, and gathered up and destroyed the sacred masks and fetishes.[1] As a result, native religion went underground. The Indians hid their religious practices from the oppressive Franciscans in order to preserve them.

In 1680, smoldering tribal resentment became violent opposition. Inspired largely by religious ideals, the Indians all along the Rio Grande, in a concerted and well-planned uprising, attacked the Spanish settlers and drove them from New Mexico. The Spanish returned in force in 1693, and soon succeeded in subduing the rebellious tribes. Eventually both sides settled into an uneasy alliance against the marauding Apaches, Comanches, and Navajos.

Spain lost control of the Rio Grande Valley following the Mexican Revolution of 1821. After just twenty-five years of sovereignty, the new government of Mexico was embroiled in boundary disputes with the rapidly expanding United States. In the ensuing war, the Mexicans were routed and, with the signing of the Treaty of Guadalupe Hidalgo in 1848, New Mexico came under the control of the U.S. government. Some thirty years later, Juan de Jesús Romero was born in a simple mud and straw building like those that had housed his people for centuries. Romero belonged to the family from which the Tribe draws its most important member. This leader, the Cacique, is the highest authority in both religious and secular affairs. In time, Juan de Jesús became Cacique, and events were soon to provide him with a trying test of his endurance, will, and leadership.

Gifford Pinchot's world differed radically from that of Romero. Born on the elegant Connecticut estate of his grandparents at the close of the Civil War, young Pinchot grew up with every possible advantage. Governesses waited on him as a child, he went to preparatory school at prestigious Phillips Exeter Academy, and then on to the privileged world of Yale.

Just before he left for college, his father suggested to him that forestry might offer a challenging and worthwhile career. Despite the existence of millions of forested acres, however, there was at that time neither a profession of forestry in the United States nor a place where one could train for such work. So Pinchot crossed the Atlantic to study European methods of timber management. Of greatest interest to him was the principle of sustained yield. Through careful planning and management, French and German forests yearly produced as much timber as they had been yielding for centuries. Europeans regarded forests as good farmers would their crops—tending and harvesting them carefully to ensure provision for future needs. They understood the importance of forests as a renewable resource.

The American attitude could not have been more different. For the early colonizers, forests represented a foe to be felled and conquered. The settlers equated the march of civilization with the clearing of land. Even when, by the nineteenth century, this attitude softened, little concern was given to the preservation of forests, which still were regarded as inexhaustible resources. The government gave away forest lands for token fees, or else timber companies simply moved into the public domain and took what they wanted. Loggers clear-cut vast areas and then moved on to do the same elsewhere.

Through their writings, the Transcendentalists Emerson and Thoreau began to change this attitude toward wilderness. They saw nature as esthetically and spiritually necessary. People began to take seriously Thoreau's belief that "in wilderness lies the preservation of the world." In 1872, protection of large forested areas began with the creation of Yellowstone National Park, and later Yosemite. The closing of the American frontier in 1890 constituted an acknowledgement that the continent's natural resouces were not infinite. By that time three-fourths of the forests were gone, much of the mineral wealth had been wasted, and the soil was eroding at an alarming rate.

Congress addressed this growing national concern by passing the Forest Reserve Act of 1891. The act gave the president the power to withdraw land in the public domain from private sale and designate it a public reservation. The following year John Muir, inspired partly by the Transcendentalists, founded the Sierra Club. One of its purposes was to have acreage withdrawn under the Reserve Act treated as national parkland, protected from all uses other than light recreation.

Pinchot, meanwhile, had put his European-inspired principle of sustained use into practice on the Vanderbilt family estate in North Carolina. In so doing he demonstrated that this method both protected the forests from destruction and returned a profit. Now widely recognized as America's chief forester, Pinchot clashed with Muir over the issue of public land use. Muir supported unconditional protection and Pinchot controlled production. Congress agreed with the professional forester, and in 1897 passed the Forest Management Act, which mandated grazing and scientifically guided production of raw materials from forested land. The following year, when Pinchot became head of the Agriculture

Gifford Pinchot, the father of the Forest Service, whose belief in the scientific production of raw materials from forested land, expressed in the policy of "multiple use," conflicted with the Indians' need for privacy in the practice of their religion. Drawing by Chuck Asay, c. 1980. Courtesy of the Carson National Forest Headquarters in Taos.

Department's Division of Forestry, he began a vigorous campaign to bring management of all forest reserves under his office's direction.

Pinchot's efforts gained from the assassination of President McKinley in 1901 for McKinley's successor, Theodore Roosevelt, was perhaps the nation's most conservation conscious president. Like Pinchot, Roosevelt belonged to the wealthy American elite and his heritage allowed him the leisure to spend much of his youth sporting in the wilds of the West. Over time, he became deeply attached to the grandeur of its mountains. Pinchot had met Roosevelt some years before he became president, and encouraged his belief in the wisdom of preserving the nation's forests. By the time Roosevelt reached the White House, the two were close personal friends and Pinchot had ready access to the president. This personal connection did much to promote the cause of conservation. In fact, Roosevelt's first message to Congress identified forest and water issues as America's most important internal problems.

A man of action, the president quickly put his beliefs into practice. Using the Forest Reserve Act, he set aside 150 million acres of land as a forest reserve and withdrew from public entry another 85 million acres in Alaska and the Northwest. He also assisted Pinchot's efforts to have the forest reserves transferred from the Department of the Interior to the Department of Agriculture (since trees were a crop) and renamed National Forests. Pinchot and his growing band of professional foresters then began applying sustained-yield policies to these millions of acres. They also worked hard, in keeping with the "Progressive" political principles ascendant at the time, to convince the American public that such policies were for the long-term good of all the people. The Progressives believed that human betterment lay in the application of scientific principles through federal control. It was precisely this approach that characterized Pinchot's policies for the developing National Forest Service. While Pinchot himself had only a small role in the coming battle over Indian lands, his ideals were to be at its heart for decades. To better understand that conflict, it is necessary to go back in time to the late nineteenth century.

Prior to European expansion, Taos Pueblo had a recognized homeland encompassing some 300,000 acres. It stretched over much of present day Taos, Colfax, and Mora counties, and Blue Lake was its sacred center. After the arrival of the Spanish, the Tribe's acreage began to be reduced, both through large grants made by the Spanish crown and appropriation of small acreages by squatters. This loss of land accelerated under Mexican sovereignty, when corrupt administrators were bribed to produce fradulent titles. At the same time, disease and political oppression reduced the Tribe's population from an estimated 20,000 when the Spaniards arrived to a meager 400 or 500 souls in 1900.

While the Indians vigorously attempted to retain their land, their dwindling numbers made use of all of the 300,000 acres less necessary. Also, while the land lost was important to them, it did not include the sacred center of their tribal life, which comprised the 50,000 acre watershed immediately surrounding Blue Lake. This watershed was literally the Tribe's source of life; the people used its waters both for drinking and irrigation of crops. Spiritually, too, it was the heart of Indian worship. As the Tribe's attorney eloquently said:

> The watershed creates the Rio Pueblo de Taos. Blue Lake and the numerous sacred springs are the sources of the stream. The waters of the Rio give life to the watershed and to the Indians who dwell therein . . . .Blue Lake, as the principal source of the Rio Pueblo is symbolically the source of all life; it is the retreat also of souls after death, the home of the ancestors who likewise gave life to the people of today. . . .Blue Lake, therefore, symbolizes the unity and continuity of the Pueblo; it is the central symbol of the Indians' religion as the cross is in Christianity.[2]

Thus, while the Tribe had by 1900 lost tens of thousands of acres of its aboriginal holdings, it had until that time steadfastly resisted any intrusion into the sacred Blue Lake area.

In the 1890s, however, a legend began to spread that there had been extensive gold mining around Taos during the Spanish period. The story was told of the Indians throwing vast quantities of gold and silver into one of their lakes to safeguard it from the Spaniards. Further, it was widely believed that gold could be found in the Blue Lake area itself, since there were already several mines in operation not far from the Pueblo's sacred center.[3] The result was that prospec-

The Rio Pueblo de Taos has long furnished water for crop irrigation, the watering of horses and cattle, and domestic needs. Courtesy of New Mexico Records Center and Archives, Dept. of Development Collection No. 2237.

tors in ever-increasing numbers began to explore the mountains of Taos.

The Tribe began to be alarmed at the possibility of intrusions into their sacred area. They also were concerned about the inevitable pollution of their water source by mining. As a Taos old-timer, Bert Phillips, recalled:

> In 1898, my first year at Taos, Manuel Mondragon, a member of the Pueblo now still alive, talked to me of the Indians' fear that non-Indians would move up the Rio Pueblo canyon and settle above Taos Pueblo, thus contaminating Pueblo water and taking over lands used only by the Pueblo as far back as any man knows.[4]

Some years later, Phillips met Vernon Bailey and C. Hart Merriam, both employed by the Bureau of Biological Survey to report on the Taos area. Phillips got his Indian friend Manuel Mondragon a job working for Bailey as a guide. Mondragon proved such an invaluable assistant that Bailey asked Phillips what he might do to help the Indians. Phillips says:

> . . .I reminded him of the Indians' fear that they might lose this land and asked him whether it could not be made into a National Forest. Mr. Bailey was very much in favor of this idea, saying that he recognized there was

Mining operations at Twining, a few miles northwest of Blue Lake, caused the Indians to fear the invasion of their sacred watershed, c. 1906. Courtesy of the New Mexico Records Center and Archives, Adella Collier Collection No. 32016.

Indian use as far back as was known; he told me he would take the matter up with Theodore Roosevelt personally, and that he was sure the president would share his enthusiasm for the idea of protecting this area for continued exclusive Indian use in its natural condition.[5]

Phillips remembers that "the Taos Indians were very pleased with the whole plan."[6]

The process of bringing the Blue Lake area into the forest reserves began in 1903. The Secretary of Agriculture petitioned the Department of the Interior, which then had jurisdiction, to have the Blue Lake area and adjacent townships "temporarily withdrawn from settlement, pending an examination as to their suitability for the purposes of a forest reserve."[7] While the Tribe was exclusively using the area in question, for legal purposes the government considered it "vacant public land." At this time, the Tribe had established legal rights only to their original Spanish league grant, some 17,000 acres which included only the village itself and the immediately surrounding agricultural plots. The United States government patented this area to the Tribe in 1864. While Spanish and Mexican law recognized Taos Pueblo as the owner of all of the lands which it exclusively used and occupied, the United States government at this time considered Taos Pueblo the owner only of their 17,000 patented acres. Legally, then, the sacred Blue Lake area was part of the public domain, and, as such, it could be brought within the forest reserves.

The Department of the Interior, as requested, withdrew the land from all use pending completion of the suitability assessment. When the Tribe learned of the withdrawal and the proposed study, they drafted a letter to the Interior Secretary explaining the area's importance to them. And they asked him, "when the proper time arrives, to issue to us an exclusive permit to the use of said area."[8] This letter makes clear that the Indians were not concerned about establishment of a forest reserve, only that they be given exclusive use of the area when a forest reserve came into being.

The United States Geological Survey sent Theodore F. Rixon to Taos to carry out the suitability study and he filed his report in 1905. It is especially noteworthy because of its praise of the Tribe's conservation practices:

> The whole watershed of the Pueblo is well stocked with a luxuriant growth of forage grasses, being the only area met with in New Mexico where the pasturage was plentiful. The reason for this is that the Pueblo Indians of Taos . . . have prohibited all outsiders from grazing within its confines, and especially the Mexicans from driving therein their herds of sheep and goats. Besides preserving the grasses they do not allow even one of their own tribe to cut or remove any of the down or standing timber within one hundred yards of either side of the river, a regulation that has preserved the water supply and prevented the sudden rush of waters down the stream . . . .This tract is worthy of examination showing what can be done towards the preservation of pasturage and water by a little care and attention.[9]

As a result of Rixon's report and another submitted by F.G. Plummer, the Department of Agriculture recommended creating the Taos Forest Reserve. Indeed, Gifford Pinchot himself told the Interior Department that "this reserve should, I think, be created without delay."[10] Shortly thereafter, on November 7, 1906, President Roosevelt signed a proclamation establishing the Taos Forest Reserve. Although they were not aware of this at the time, the proclamation stripped the Tribe of aboriginal title, gave their sacred land to the federal government, and made it subject to the policies of the Forest Service. The seeds had now been sown for a conflict that was to last for decades.

The protracted controversy that followed was rooted in opposing philosophies with regard to nature and its uses. Central to Forest Service policy is the concept of "multiple use." According to this principle, the forests under its jurisdiction are for recreational purposes, for the production of resources, and for grazing. In providing for these uses, the Forest Service has the authority to stock lakes with fish, to cut roads and trails, to authorize mineral extraction and timbering, to manipulate vegetation to improve water yield, and to issue grazing permits. Central to the Taos Indians' way of life is the belief that in the beginning Mother Nature imparted to their ancestors proper and perpetual modes of behavior. Departure from these established patterns is considered sacrilegious. A key tenet of the ancestors was the interrelationship of the people and the land. The people, through their prayers and religious ceremonies, give homage to and fructify the land. The land, in turn, nourishes and sustains the people. Land and people, therefore, are joined in a sacred, symbiotic bond; and any alteration of the land directly threatens this bond. For this reason, the Indians look upon preservation of their wilderness as a sacred obligation. It is easy to understand how this belief came inevitably into conflict with the Forest Service policy of multiple use, which permitted timbering, cutting roads, and manipulating the vegetation.

Another key teaching of the ancestors was the necessity for keeping tribal religious knowledge secret. To reveal it to outsiders is to weaken it. As a tribal member said, "People want to find out about this Pueblo but they can't. Our ways would lose their power if they were known . . . ."[11] Similarly, sacred rituals performed in the presence of non-Indians are thought to lose their power. Franciscan repression of native religion even further intensified the need for secrecy. As the anthropologist John Bodine, a close student of Pueblo culture, expressed it:

> The priests of the various religious societies at Taos must go into the area in question and to Blue Lake time after time during the year. They go alone or in small groups to perform the special rituals with which they have been charged and to train their successors. Outsiders, including Forest Service personnel, constitute a great threat to the proper performance of these duties. Their very presence, even if they observe nothing, is contaminating. It constitutes a serious invasion of religious privacy. . . .[12]

Given their need for religious privacy, we can appreciate the Indian reaction to the presence of Forest Service personnel and to recreational use of their sacred area by outsiders. As long as the Forest Service permitted such intrusions, the Indians felt their religious life threatened. Problems between the Forest Service and the Taos Indians were, however, still some years away at the time that the Taos Forest Reserve was created. This was largely due to the fact that their friend Bert Phillips became the first forest ranger for the newly established reserve. He tells us that:

> In 1906 I was employed as the first ranger in the new Forest. I went into the watershed surrounding country regularly. I saw that there were good homestead sites in the Forest, but because of the Indians' prior use and the whole intention of setting this area aside, I refused to give any permits to applicants anywhere in the watershed.
>
> At the time I was working in the Forest, 1906-1910, there were no permits for non-Indians and no non-Indian livestock anywhere in that Rio Pueblo watershed, because I knew the Indians' use rights and President Roosevelt's purpose in establishing this forest reserve. Any permitting came after my time and I believe considerably after my time.[13]

The first sign of trouble came in a 1909 letter from the Forest Service supervisor, Ross McMillan, to the Taos Pueblo governor. McMillan was replying to the Tribe's request, made five years earlier, that at the creation of the reserve they be assured of exclusive use. McMillan tells them that their request is "immaterial," since the Forest Service will protect their interests.

It is significant that McMillan did not respond to the Taos Indians' request for exclusive use. He told them only that the Forest Service would protect their grazing and irrigation rights. His letter in subtle fashion opened a heated debate that continued unresolved for decades: whether the Blue Lake watershed should be for exclusive Indian use, or whether the Forest Service's "multiple-use" policy, disregarding the Indian claim, should prevail.

The key fact in the debate is that the friends of the Tribe worked to put the watershed into the forest reserves in order to preserve it for exclusive Indian use. Bailey and Hart Merriam told the Tribe that "the purpose of such a forest reserve including the watershed would be to protect the entire watershed for the exclusive Indian use as always in the past."[14] The Tribe's 1904 letter also specifically made this point. Testifying before a Senate hearing decades later, Stewart Udall noted that if Roosevelt had known how the Forest Service would treat the Indians, he would never have put their land in the forest reserves. Certainly this is true. Phillips tells us that Bailey promised personally to raise the question with Roosevelt and that,

> later Mr. Bailey wrote back to me from Washington, telling me that the land would be so reserved, with the entire watershed for exclusive Indian use, and President Roosevelt did actually make it a National Forest.[15]

It is clear, then, that if the Indians and their supporters thought reserve status meant anything less than exclusive use, they would never have proposed it. Forest Service representatives, on the other hand, unaware of early understandings between the Tribe's friends and President Roosevelt, maintained that the land should be open to multiple uses by the general public. They were fighting for Pinchot's ideals as they had come to be embodied in the Forest Service bureaucracy.

The inclusion of Indian land in the forest reserves was by no means a problem exclusive to Taos. It happened to Indians all over New Mexico. By 1910 the situation was serious. The Indians, accustomed to grazing their cattle on ancestral land which now belonged to the Forest Service, suddenly were required to pay grazing fees which they could not afford. Many were forced to sell their stock and the Tribes' economic base rapidly eroded. At Santa Clara Pueblo in 1910, this led to a dramatic incident: "Indians fully armed seized cattle, arrested officers of the law, defied Federal officials, and ignored the orders of the courts."[16] The cattle seized, grazing under Forest Service permits, had strayed onto their land. This incident underscores the "new limitations, new expenses, and additional perplexities"[17] placed on the Indians by the inclusion of their aboriginal lands in the forest reserves.

F.H. Abbott, the assistant commissioner of Indian Affairs at that time, was sent to New Mexico to handle the explosive situation, and proposed a practical remedy:

> If a portion of the several Forest Reserves adjacent to or near these Indians' land, free use of which the Indians have enjoyed for centuries, could be reserved by the President for their use and occupancy, it would seem that ample provision might be made for the needs of these Indians.[18]

The Indian Affairs Office, displaying genuine concern for the plight of their charges, made every effort to have such executive order reservations created for the New Mexico Indians. Only by doing so, these enlightened bureaucrats believed, could the government halt the Indians' increasingly rapid slide into federal dependence. Further, they said, "The Pueblo Indians were the ancient owners of all of these lands and the question involved is largely one of restoring to them a part of the domain which they formerly held."[19]

Under this plan, Taos was to be given 3,200 acres of public land and an additional 41,440 from the Carson National Forest, acres representing most of the sacred watershed. As an executive order reservation, it would be exclusively for their use. But the Forest Service callously declined to give up any land now under its jurisdiction. Obviously disappointed, those working on the Indians' behalf concluded that "the case should be closed and all interested therein notified."[20]

Taos, however, refused to let the matter rest. Two years later, through their superintendent, they again requested that the commissioner of Indian Affairs put their sacred watershed in an executive order reservation. The superintendent, in a prophetic statement, worried that "if the land is not reserved for them now it will be impossible to obtain it later on."[21] His superiors failed to accept his counsel, arguing that the Forest Service would never consent to return the land since "such a reservation would divide the forest reserve into two parts and probably seriously interfere with the administration of said forest."[22] And so the initiative died.

In 1916, the same year that the Tribe received this rejection, something even worse happened. Elliott Barker became supervisor of the Carson National Forest. Determined that the Indian land should be used like other national forests, he set about opening it up to outsiders. First, he cut trails into the Blue Lake country to make it more accessible to recreation. And then, to make the area more inviting, he carried thousands of fingerling trout in ten-gallon cans on horseback into the wilderness. For the first time fish now swam in the sacred Blue Lake and outsiders cast baited fishing lines into its hallowed waters. Not stopping there, Barker, with the needs of World War I as justification, pressured the Tribe into allowing non-Indian cattle to graze the east side of the sacred watershed. In the three short years of his superintendency, Barker personally oversaw the destruction of the Indians' centuries-old exclusive-use rights. And he

The sleepy Plaza of the town of Taos, c. 1920, when serious infringements of the Tribe's rights in the sacred watershed began to occur. Courtesy of State Records Center Archives, Adella Collier Collection No. 32002.

was to be one of their chief opponents in the congressional battles fifty years hence. The man who attacked the Tribe's exclusive use prior to World War I remained implacably one of their main foes after men had gone to the moon.

The revocation of their exclusive rights opened a decade of problems for Taos Pueblo. One of the most threatening was the attack on Pueblo religion started by the United States government in 1921. Using the recently passed Religious Crimes Act as its chief weapon, the government made the practice of Indian religious ceremonies a punishable offense. At the same time, the government launched a public campaign to vilify native religion. Directed by the commissioner of Indian Affairs, Charles Burke, the campaign gave wide circulation to lurid reports of immorality and debauchery at Indian ceremonials; and also claimed that native religion was largely responsible for the Indian failure to assimilate into the cultural mainstream. For Indians to rise above their "savage" state, so the argument ran, it was necessary to destroy their pagan worship.

The campaign against Taos was particularly ugly. Commissioner Burke personally went to Taos, invaded the Tribal Council chamber, and denounced the tribal elders as "half-animal" for their religious beliefs. He insisted that the council renounce their ancient religion "within a year." He further demanded that they end the practice of having children temporarily withdrawn from school for religious instruction. When the Tribal Council refused, Burke had the old men arrested and transported to jail in Santa Fe. This in a country which had as one of its founding principles freedom of worship! The Indians all along the Rio Grande steadfastly resisted these illegal pressures. In a united manifesto of 1924 they declared:

> Our religion to us is sacred and is more important to us than anything else in our life. . . .Our happiness, our moral behavior, our unity as a people and the peace and joyfulness of our homes, are all a part of our religion and are dependent on its continuation. To pass this religion, with its hidden sacred knowledge and its many forms of prayer, on to our children, is our supreme duty to our ancestors and to our own hearts and to the God whom we know.[23]

While engaged in this struggle for religious freedom, the Indians also had to fight to protect their land, threatened by the infamous Bursum Bill. In the nineteenth century the Pueblo people were not under federal jurisdiction and trusteeship as were the Indians who had been confined to reservations. It was not even clear if, for legal purposes, they should be considered to be Indians. Because of this uncertainty, the Pueblo Indians, including those of Taos Pueblo, did not have the protection of the laws which regulated the dealings of reservation Indians with outsiders.

In 1913, in the important case of *United States v. Sandoval*, the courts decided that Pueblo people were indeed Indians. As such, they were entitled to federal protection and services. This decision directly threatened the 12,000 or so squatters on Indian land, who would now face federal eviction proceedings if they could not prove title. Alarmed and angered, the Anglo and Hispanic citizens of New Mexico clamored for an anti-Indian solution. Sen. Holm O. Bursum of New Mexico was glad to oblige. He drafted a bill which, in essence, would have put the burden of proof on the government rather than the squatters. Studied closely, the bill amounted to nothing more than a quick and easy way for squatters to obtain clear title to their stolen Indian land. The Pueblo people, in concerted and vigorous action, waged a nationwide campaign against this destructive legislation.

Aiding their efforts was a coalition of nationally prominent artists and writers which brought the issue to the awareness of the American people with the wide publication of "The Artists and Writers Protest," a caustic denunciation of the Bursum Bill. Signed by creative luminaries such as Zane Grey, D.H. Lawrence, Vachel Lindsay, Edgar Lee Masters, Maxfield Parrish, and Carl Sandburg, "The Protest" awakened public indignation and popularized the Indians' cause. Through the combined efforts of the Indians and their many non-Indian supporters, the Bursum Bill was defeated.

While pernicious in its intentions, the Bursum Bill at least awakened Congress to the land ownership problems facing many New Mexicans. To resolve them,

Congress passed the Pueblo Lands Act in 1924. That act established a Lands Board whose duty it was to investigate all private claims to Indian land and determine authenticity of title. The Lands Board was to consider title established if the claimant could show continuous occupancy since 1902 "under color of title" with payment of taxes, or continuous occupancy since 1889 with payment of taxes but without color of title. If the Lands Board confirmed the title of a claimant, the board then had to determine the amount to be paid to the Tribe for the land lost.

The Lands Board began work in Taos in 1926, and a majority of the Pueblo's Tribal Council members attended the opening hearing. They presented to the Lands Board a proposal which they had made to Commissioner Burke five years earlier. Recognizing that the town squatters would in most cases meet title requirements, the Tribe was prepared to yield on the 200 or so claims in question. But, in return, they asked again that the sacred watershed be transferred from Forest Service jurisdiction to the Interior Department as an executive order reservation. If the Lands Board would make this recommendation, the Tribe offered to concede that the town settlers had held their land long enough to qualify for title. If the Tribe then actually did get the sacred watershed, they would also agree to waive all right to be compensated for the land lost in the town of Taos.

The Tribe understood that while the Lands Board did not have the power to return their land to them, a recommendation from the Lands Board to that effect would greatly assist their effort to regain control of the sacred watershed. Since law now prohibited creation of executive order reservations by the president, return of Blue Lake would depend upon passage of an act by Congress.

H.J. Hagerman, head of the Lands Board, favored the transfer, but not out of affection for the Indians. In the campaign against Indian religion, the Taos Pueblo's annual August ceremonies at Blue Lake came in for particularly lurid publicity. Accounts of communal nudity and the deflowering of young virgins by tribal elders circulated widely. Hagerman pointed out to Burke that if the watershed came under the control of the Interior Department, then so would the tribal ceremonials. Interior could then "adopt whatever policy it determined upon as wise or necessary in respect to these ceremonies, and enforce such policy. . . .This age-long discussion about the ceremony, with all its accompanying gossip, rumor, dark hints of murder and other things, could be settled."[24] Despite this tempting advantage, Burke cautioned the board not to make recommendations outside of its jurisdiction. He advised Hagerman not to mention the Blue Lake transfer, and Hagerman agreed. The Lands Board then proceeded to double-cross the Indians. While the board made the Tribe's waiver of its claim in the town of Taos a matter of official record, it said nothing about the waiver's contingency upon the return of Blue Lake. Hagerman simply pressured the others on the board into remaining silent about the Blue Lake "deal."

With the failure of this initiative, the Tribe decided to take their case directly to

Commissioner Burke. They wrote to complain that prospectors were once again trespassing into the wilderness, threatening the purity of the water and the sanctity of their rituals, and appealed to him to help them get title so that they would have undisturbed possession. They explained, "This region is like a church to us, and if you look at it in that way you will understand how deeply we feel."[25] Burke passed the Tribe's request on to the secretary of the Interior, Hubert Work. Work in turn wrote to the secretary of Agriculture, saying that Interior would like "to do anything that is practicable" to protect the Tribe's religious interests. He asked if "there would be serious objections to the elimination of the Blue Lake region from the Forest, for the purpose of adding it to the Taos Land."[26] Agriculture quickly let it be known that they did object, not only because the "area involved is chiefly valuable for forestry purposes,"[27] but also "because it is quite foreign to the policies of the Department of Agriculture, when once some land has been set aside as a National Forest, to allow it to be withdrawn completely and donated to a private purpose."[28] This argument was to be repeatedly revived in the coming legislative battles.

At the same time that the Tribe was seeking title, their attorneys were working on another strategy to protect Indian interests—a Cooperative Use Agreement between the Tribe and the Forest Service. In the spring of 1927, the Forest Service sent a draft of such an agreement to Taos. The related correspondence conveys the strong impression that the Forest Service thought of the sacred watershed as their domain, that the Indians had no rights to it and should be grateful for any Forest Service concessions. Congratulating themselves on their magnanimity, the Service clearly felt that the terms of the agreement were more generous than any granted to previous applicants. After a period of unequal negotiation, the Tribe and the Department of Agriculture signed the agreement on September 28, 1927.

The provisions of this agreement formed the basis for much misunderstanding and conflict in the years to come. The Forest Service pledged itself to protecting the water supply from pollution, while reserving the right to employ any necessary measures to care for the forest. These included road/trail construction, timbering, and manipulation of the vegetation. It was agreed that non-Pueblo members would be admitted into the watershed "only under written permits issued by the Forest Supervisor."[29] The Tribe, in turn, was to patrol the area and report any violations, to provide salt for grazing animals, and to assist in any necessary fire suppression. Both parties had sixty-day termination rights.

The agreement clearly satisfied the Pueblo's advisors. Their government attorney, Walter Cochrane, felt that it "effectively disposes of a long-standing grievance" and "meets nearly every reasonable requirement that the Indians can have." He went on to note that while some in the Tribe felt that they should have gotten the land without restriction, "the more intelligent of them realize that this agreement is the most that they could hope for and are satisfied to have it so."[30] Cochrane's words, "the most that they could hope for," are illuminating.

They underline the point that the Forest Service controlled the watershed and that any Indian usages were not enjoyed by right but were a matter of bureaucratic largesse.

While working out the terms of the Cooperative Agreement, the Tribe was also taking further steps to protect the watershed from potential mining. Prospectors had once again begun threatening to stake mineral claims in the Blue Lake area. Concerned about the purity of their water, the Tribe asked the Interior Department to draft a bill prohibiting mineral entry, and Congress passed Public Law 194 in March of 1928. It authorized the president to withdraw "from all forms of entry" 30,000 acres within the Rio Pueblo basin. President Calvin Coolidge issued an executive order of July 7, 1928, based on this law, withdrawing the 30,000 acres. This action finally ended any threat of mining in the sacred watershed.

With the signing of the Cooperative Agreement and the executive order withdrawal, the Tribe's earliest efforts to protect their religious heartland drew to a close. While those working with the Tribe felt that it now had all the protection it needed, a strong faction at Taos Pueblo still wished to have title to the Blue Lake area. Further, the Cooperative Agreement itself was seriously flawed, containing as it did provisions respecting timbering, visitors, and administrative control that were inimical to the religious interests of the Pueblo. The negative consequences of these provisions became ever more apparent as the Tribe and the Forest Service put the Cooperative Agreement into practice, and led to progressively deteriorating relations between them. For, in fact, while the Forest Service piously expressed concern for Indian religion, their actual intention was to administer the watershed much like any other national forest, giving little consideration to the area's religious importance to the Tribe.

Over time, the bureaucratic arrogance of the Forest Service intensified. The Forest Service considered the sacred watershed theirs, and demonstrated little respect for tribal authority. A memorandum from the Forest supervisor, C.R. Dwire, to the district forester illustrates this. It refers to an issue that was to have a long and contentious history—the issuance of visitor permits.

In the late twenties, commercial operators from Therma and Red River took campers into the watershed, entering from the east side. "To save the public inconvenience," the Forest Service allowed the tour guides to themselves issue visitor permits, which then were simply mailed to the Forest Service ranger in Taos. While this was convenient for the Forest Service, the tour guide, and the public, the practice was seriously disruptive to the Indians. They had no way of knowing when visitors might be coming into the sacred area, possibly interrupting their religious observances. To protect the secrecy of their rituals, the Tribe asked the Forest Service to issue permits only in Taos, and to have them countersigned by the Pueblo governor. The attitude of the Forest Service to Indian authority and religious needs is summed up in Dwire's reply: "To have the permit countersigned by the Indian governor is entirely unnecessary, as the Blue

This postcard photograph of Blue Lake was taken by a commercial intruder in the early decades of this century. Courtesy of State Records Center and Archives, Alice Duffey Collection No. 4387.

Lake area is Forest land and administered by the Forest Service."[31] Dwire both dismisses Indian authority and makes clear that recreational use of the area by outsiders should take precedence over religious use by the Indians.

Nothing better symbolizes the Forest Service's heedlessness and disrespect for the Tribe's concerns than an outrage which occurred in 1928. In the sacred Blue Lake basin, the pristine heart of tribal spirituality, sounds of sawing and hammering arose. To the profound horror of the Indians, forest rangers were constructing a cabin, an outhouse, garbage pits, and horse corrals within a stone's throw of the sacred Blue Lake. In a perfect wilderness setting, unmarred by human artifice for centuries, the sacred center of tribal existence, the Forest Service had chosen to erect tangible evidence of their authority over the watershed. With thousands of acres of building plots available, the Forest Service sited their cabin at Blue Lake, and rangers began periodically to live there. The perfect, round, cobalt blue eye of the great Rocky Mountain dragon had been contemptuously violated.

The construction of this cabin at Blue Lake marks the nadir of tribal fortunes, and symbolizes the terrible travail of the twenties. First there was the Indian Bureau's attack on their religion; then the Bursum Bill's attack on their land base; followed by the Lands Board's perfidy; and the signing of a Cooperative Agreement destructive of the Tribe's religious interests.

While the Cooperative Agreement's provisions regarding timbering and watershed manipulation were bad enough, the permitting of visitors posed the

The Forest Service cabin whose construction in 1928 outraged the Taos Indians. Courtesy of Charlotte Trego.

most serious problem. In 1928 alone, nearly 100 different recreational parties were allowed to enter the watershed. Since these incursions were concentrated during the summer months, a recreational group was in the watershed virtually every day. Additionally, the Taos forest ranger stayed at the cabin about thirty days out of the ninety days of summer. Religious rituals requiring absolute secrecy were, therefore, continually being threatened by the presence of outsiders. Happily for the Tribe, their fortunes were soon to improve, with the appointment of John Collier as commissioner of Indian Affairs.

2

John Collier to the Rescue

I N HIS MEMOIRS *From Every Zenith*, John Collier tells us that his love for northern New Mexico began in 1920 when he received an invitation from Mabel Dodge Luhan to visit Taos. Mabel Dodge, a wealthy New York socialite, had come to Taos four years earlier seeking spiritual renewal. She found it in the beauty of the landscape and the culture of the Indians (she married Taos Pueblo Indian Tony Luhan), and quickly became an apostle for the new world she had discovered, drawing to northern New Mexico such literary and artistic luminaries as Mary Austin, D.H. Lawrence, Willa Cather, and Georgia O'Keeffe.

Collier was among those swept up in Mabel Dodge's enthusiasm. They had been friends in New York where he worked on behalf of The People's Institute, an organization devoted to helping immigrants and the poor. When he received her invitation he readily accepted and spent nine months in Taos, devoting much of the time to camping with his family. He, too, was greatly moved by the culture of the Taos Indians, especially their connection to the primordial religious tradition of their ancestors. Mabel Dodge's invitation began Collier's lifelong involvement with the Indians of Taos Pueblo.

Collier first became concerned about Indian political issues in 1922 when Albert B. Fall, Interior secretary to President Harding, "declared that the Indian title to the lands reserved to them by Executive Order was no title."[1] Since more than half of all Indian land was held under executive order, Collier realized that if Fall's declaration was applied, Indians throughout the country would lose millions and millions of acres. Fall also was a supporter of the Bursum Bill, which would not only strip the Pueblo Indians of their land and water, but also allow any citizen to "pull the Pueblo religions into court and force the revealing of secret disciplines and religious faiths."[2]

Mabel Dodge Luhan c. 1930, whose enthusiasm for Taos drew many creative individuals to New Mexico. Photo by Will Connell. Courtesy Museum of New Mexico, Neg. No. 16755.

A festive group of artists and literary luminaries gather at the Taos home of Mabel Dodge Luhan and her husband Tony Luhan, c. 1939. Front row (left to right): John Young-Hunter, Angelo Ravagli, and Eve Young-Hunter. Back row (left to right): Tony Luhan, Mabel's Cousin, Mabel Dodge Luhan, Frieda Lawrence, Frank Waters, Leon Gaspard, Evelyn Gaspard, and Malcom Groefflo. Courtesy Kit Carson Historic Museums.

Collier was at this time living in California. He had moved there in 1919 to head up an adult education program sponsored jointly by the Regents of the University of California and the State Board of Education. In this capacity, he traveled throughout the state leading forums which discussed many of the significant issues of the day. Controversy about the "radical" content of his talks forced his resignation, however, and he then became director of social science training at the San Francisco College, where he served during the academic year of 1921 to 1922. During this period of time his interest in Indian affairs intensified.

When the implications of the government's Indian schemes became clear, wealthy Californians whom Collier had come to know through his teaching experience there offered to pay his expenses for two years if he would work with the Indians in New Mexico to fight Fall's potentially devastating policies. Collier promptly accepted and moved to New Mexico where, with Mabel Dodge's husband Antonio, he visited all of the Pueblo Indians of the area to acquaint them with the threat to their land and religious culture posed by the Bursum Bill. Collier helped the Indians organize the All-Pueblo Council, widely considered the oldest mutual defense league in the western hemisphere, to coordinate

John and Lucy Collier in California with tribal leaders from the New Mexico Pueblos during the national tour to enlist opposition to the Bursum Bill, c. 1922. The feathered headresses, not worn by Pueblo Indians, were obviously borrowed for dramatic effect. Courtesy of Mary and John Collier, Jr.

opposition to Bursum. He was also instrumental in enlisting the active support of the creative Anglo community. To popularize the Indian cause and raise money to fight the bill, Collier took seventeen Pueblo leaders on a national tour. The group also testified before the relevant House Committee and succeeded, through their own eloquence and with the help of outside pressure, in killing the bill.

Shortly thereafter, Collier helped form the American Indian Defense Association, chartered in 1923 to protect the rights of the native peoples. As its executive secretary, he traveled throughout the United States to acquaint himself at firsthand with the situations and living conditions of Native Americans. Appalled by what he saw and heard, Collier in 1927 persuaded the U.S. Senate to create an Indian Investigating Committee. After diligent research, the committee published in 1928 a shocking report which revealed the degradation of Indian life. These investigations suggested a program to improve the Indians' lot, a program which Collier had the opportunity to implement when he became commissioner of Indian Affairs in 1933 under Harold Ickes, President Franklin Roosevelt's secretary of the Interior. Through the determined efforts of Ickes and Collier, the Indian New Deal gave the tribes much greater control over their own affairs and culminated in passage in 1934 of the Indian Reorganization Act. Especially important to Collier were the IRA's provisions, which took away the governmental repressions of Indian ceremony and ritual, and abolished the Indian Bureau's power to suppress or interfere with Indian freedom of religion, speech, and association.[3]

Collier's appointment as Indian Affairs commissioner, while beneficial to all tribes, was of special significance for Taos Pueblo. Even before he entered government service, Collier, in his capacity as executive secretary of the Indian Defense Association, had been active in Senate investigations which had a direct impact on Taos Pueblo and the fate of Blue Lake. His commissionership then gave him the power to act upon what he had learned.

Senators from the committee on Indian Affairs held New Mexico hearings in May of 1931 to learn how effectively the Pueblo Lands Board Act was resolving land title problems. The senators soon understood that there had been serious difficulties with the act's implementation. The duty of the Lands Board was to investigate all private claims to Indian land, establish title, and then appraise the value of the land lost by the tribes and non-Indian settlers.

In the course of its research, the Senate committee learned that, after appraising the parcels in dispute, the Lands Board paid non-Indian claimants the fair market value of the land they had lost while paying Indians only about one-third of market value. Because they felt cheated, the New Mexico tribes began filing suits of ejectment to remove white settlers from disputed lands. The committee realized that if these suits were brought to judgment, the work of the Lands Board would have been for nothing.

To solve this problem, the committee recommended that additional funds be appropriated to compensate tribes for the actual value of the lands they had lost. New Mexico Senator Bronson Cutting then introduced Senate Bill 2914 (all Senate bills will hereafter be styled S. followed by the number of the bill) which authorized additional payments to Indian tribes to bring their financial compensation up to fair market levels. The following year, on May 31, 1933, Congress voted in favor of the House of Representatives Bill 4014 (all House bills will hereafter be styled H.R. followed by the number of the bill), essentially the same as Cutting's Bill but introduced in the House. This legislation, popularly known as the "Pueblo Relief Bill," appropriated for the tribes the additional money requested by the Senate Investigating Committee.

What then happened at Taos Pueblo is a good example of the impact of this legislation. The Senate hearings revealed that while professional estimators appraised the Pueblo's adverse claims at $458,520, the Lands Board approved payments to Taos amounting to only $99,890, and actually paid the Tribe $76,128—$382,000 less than what they were owed. Collier, who had been present with the Pueblo representatives at the Lands Board hearings in 1926, brought to light the reason behind this enormous disparity—the Lands Board's failure, at Hagerman's urging, to record the Tribe's proposal that they be given the Blue Lake watershed in exchange for the money owed them for their land claims in the town of Taos. As mentioned earlier, the Lands Board had accepted the Tribe's waiver of its right to be compensated for the town land, but failed to note the contingency of the waiver upon the return of the sacred watershed. The Senate report concluded that either the Tribe should be paid the money owed them, or the Blue Lake area should be restored to the Tribe.

When the actual funds were appropriated to the tribes, the Taos claim was divided into two parts. It was determined that the Tribe was owed $298,000 for the land lost in Taos itself and $160,000 for land lost outside the town boundaries. The Tribe was given an additional $84,000, effectively resolving its claim for the land lost outside of the town. However, the Tribe was still owed nearly $300,000 for the town claim, and Section 4 of the act of 1933 authorized the secretary of Agriculture to grant the Pueblo a fifty-year use-permit for the sacred area as compensation. As Ickes explained in a letter to Sen. Burton K. Wheeler, chair of the Senate Committee on Indian Affairs, Section 4 of the act

> authorizes the segregation for 50 years or longer of a certain mountain tract, lying within the boundaries of the Kit Carson National Forest, for the use and benefit of the Indians of the Pueblo of Taos . . . . Section 4 is in effect a substitution of an award of land tenure, in the case of this pueblo, for an award of money. It is desired by the Tribe.[4]

While apparently a solution to the Taos problem, Section 4 in fact laid the basis for a forty-year conflict between the Tribe and the Forest Service. In their quest for the return of the watershed, the Tribe wanted a patent to the area as well as administrative control. Under the terms of Section 4, however, they merely received the right to apply for a conditionally renewable fifty-year use-permit, which left authority for managing the watershed in the hands of the Forest Service. Thus conflicts of authority became inevitable. However, Section 4 did at least address the Tribe's main objection to the permit of 1927—its permission of the entrance of outside visitors into the sacred area with its attendant threat to the privacy and sanctity of the Tribe's religious observances. As Collier, who took a direct hand in drafting Section 4, commented in a letter to Agriculture secretary H.A. Wallace:

> Congress enacted at the last session a bill . . .whose Section 4 dealt with a subject of deeply human interest. This section of the bill provides that the Department of Agriculture may enter into a 50-year lease-contract with the Pueblo of Taos. Under this contract, the pueblo would have the exclusive use of an area of about 30,000 acres of canyon land, high in the Rockies, at the top of which area is situated Blue Lake. Blue Lake . . .is the shrine of the pre-Columbian religion of the Taos Tribe. It is sacred and taboo. . . .The contract would insure the exclusive use of the area by the Tribe . . . .Tourists have been too freely permitted to visit the lake and camp on its banks, with sanitary conditions not at all good. The Indians are aggrieved and troubled.[5]

Shortly after passage of the 1933 act, the Tribe applied for the permit authorized by Section 4. In the course of negotiating its conditions, the Pueblo realized for the first time that neither the cooperative agreement of 1927, nor the

Blue Lake surrounded by pine forest, with a dreamy vista of mountain ridges in the background. Photo by Dan Budnik.

executive order withdrawal of 1928, nor the act of 1933 applied to all of the acreage within the Blue Lake watershed.

Of initial concern were 2,000 acres on the west side in the Larkspur Lake area. When the Tribe learned that this land did not fall under the protection of Section 4, it immediately suspended permit negotiations and launched a determined effort to add this acreage to their protected area. Taos Pueblo and the local Forest Service signed an agreement in the fall of 1933 which added the 2,000 acres to the executive order withdrawal of 1928. While the validity of the agreement was questioned in 1934—on the grounds that the 1928 order authorized withdrawal only of land in the Rio Pueblo watershed and not the watershed of the Rio Lucero where the Larkspur Lake area was located—it remained in force at least down to the late 1940s.

Also of great concern to the Tribe was the disposition of 7,000 additional acres on the east side, which had been left out of the Cooperative Agreement of 1927. The Indians had thought that the agreement covered the entire watershed, but they now learned that their eastern boundary extended only one-half mile from the Rio Pueblo. In fact, the eastern boundary of the watershed was nearly three miles from the Rio Pueblo, and this left 7,000 acres, which had been leased to white cattlemen, still outside the permit boundaries.

As commissioner of Indian Affairs, Collier took a direct role in attempting to have the 9,000 acres added to the Pueblo's protected zone. Legislation to that effect was introduced in 1934, 1935, and 1938, but none of the bills passed. In 1936, however, the Tribe did succeed in having the 7,000 acres added to the executive order withdrawal of 1928. Under the terms of this order, the land was protected from the threat of mining, but it was not a part of the watershed protected by the Cooperative Agreement of 1927.

In addition to its efforts to reclaim the overlooked 9,000 acres, the Tribe also undertook measures to purchase approximately 6,500 acres of state land on their southeastern boundary. Despite warnings from the Indian bureau that such a purchase was economically unsound, the Tribe persisted because, as bureau attorney William Brophy wrote Collier, they "attach a prodigious sentimental value to the lands and want to own the same."[6] These efforts, however, met with no more success than did those directed towards acquiring the other 9,000 acres.

Frustrated in their legislative attempts to amend the 1933 act to include the desired acreage, in 1939 both the Tribe and the Indian Bureau reluctantly agreed that they ought to apply for the exclusive-use permit that it authorized. Accordingly, on behalf of the Tribe, Interior sent the Agriculture Department exactly the same application that they had developed in 1933 but had not acted on pending the outcome of efforts to expand the acreage protected by the permit. This application now touched off a year of bitter wrangling between Interior and Agriculture over the meaning of the 1933 act and the terms of the use-permit that it authorized.

The 1933 act provided for two things. One was the development of a segregation order that prevented acquisition of title by outside entities to any of the acreage covered. On this there was no disagreement, and it was signed in 1939. The other was the use-permit itself, and Agriculture took strong exception to the terms proposed by the Tribe and Interior. They felt that Interior's proposal "seems to go further than it is believed the Department would be warranted in going under the provisions of the Act in issuing the permit contemplated."[7]

Agriculture's objections centered on three issues, explained in a letter from Acting Secretary of Agriculture Harry Brown to the secretary of the Interior. First, Brown denied that the act provided for the Tribe the exclusive benefit of the watershed's resources. He insisted that while the Tribe did have the right to graze animals and take wood, any surpluses of forage or timber could be disposed of by Agriculture "under the regular regulations relating to the administration of the national forest . . . ."[8] He also denied that the Tribe had exclusive rights to mineral extraction. Second, he maintained that the watershed should be subject to the regulations of the state of New Mexico that covered hunting and fishing. And third, he held that the act did not give the Tribe exclusive use-rights to the area, and that visitors should be permitted during times of non-ceremonial observance. Brown sent the Interior Department a counterproposal embodying these positions.

Interior officials in Washington sent Brown's draft to New Mexico for comment. In their reply, Brophy and bureau superintendent Sophie Aberle objected strongly to the limitations placed by Agriculture on the terms of the permit, especially since "the Pueblo of Taos obtained the use of these lands, not by any grace, but because the pueblo relinquished very valuable claims that it had to certain parcels of land in the Village of Taos . . . ."[9] Stressing the act's requirement that the permit must safeguard all rights and equities previously enjoyed by the Tribe, they insisted that the watershed must be exclusively for Indian use. As they wrote to the assistant commissioner of Indian Affairs:

> The real intent of the act, in the light of the facts as they existed when the act was approved, is to give exclusive use of the land to the Indians, together with all of the natural resources of the area, if such resources are needed by Taos.[10]

They then proposed four changes that needed to be made to Agriculture's draft. These included removing any limitation on the Tribe's exclusive use of the area; striking the paragraph giving the Forest Service the right to dispose of forest resources not needed by the Indians; eliminating the provision that placed the area under state game laws; and giving the Tribe the right to make improvements to the forest without requiring that such improvements be mandatory. Extensive consultations with John Collier concerning the intentions of the act supported all of these positions. Interior then unequivocally advised rejecting Agriculture's proposal.

Oscar Chapman, assistant commissioner of Indian Affairs, so informed the

Department of Agriculture. He told them that a close reading of the act and a study of its historical background "compels the belief that Congress had no intention of relegating the Indians to a position of having to share the resources of the area with others on an equal footing. . . ."[11] He also took exception to imposing state game laws on the watershed, an especially touchy point with the Pueblo. As Brophy, who had just had an extensive conversation with the tribal elders on the permit situation, explained the matter to Collier:

> In order to carry on the ceremonies properly it is necessary to take certain game at a time when it is not permitted to take game under the State laws of New Mexico. Therefore, the least that should be included in the permit is that nothing shall prevent the Taos people from taking ceremonial game at such times as they traditionally use the said game.[12]

He emphasized the outrage of the councilmen that Agriculture "should even consider restricting the rights that the Pueblo has in the Blue Lake area,"[13] and reiterated "that the Indians bought the use of the Blue Lake area, and insofar as it is within their power they will not permit any restriction of their use."[14]

By the summer of 1940, Collier and representatives from Agriculture had nearly completed the final form of the permit. In early fall it was polished and then signed on October 24, 1940. Brophy made it clear that he felt Interior had largely buckled under to Agriculture: "The permit seems satisfactory inasmuch as it apparently is the best that can be obtained, and I suppose that it will have to do."[15] A reading of the permit's terms reveals the reasons for Brophy's disheartenment.

The permit of 1940 gave the Tribe fifty-year use rights to 30,000 acres for grazing, obtaining water, wood, and timber, and for ceremonial religious observances. It had seven basic provisions:

- The first gave the Tribe exclusive use of the area for three days during the latter part of August, with notification of the dates to the forest supervisor ten days in advance. However, it allowed persons other than tribal members or forest officers to use the area recreationally through "written permits issued under authority of the forest supervisor and concurred in by the governor or his designated representative."[16]

- The second granted the free and exclusive use of timber, wood, and grazing to tribal members for personal purposes. It also gave them the right to buy and then resell forest products commercially according to normal Forest Service regulations.

- The third directed the Forest Service to "improve" the forests in the area, using accepted methods of silviculture and forest management.

- The fourth allowed the Tribe, provisional on the forest supervisor's written consent, to construct and maintain such improvements and facilities as they desired or were needed to protect the forest and the water supply.

- The fifth authorized the Tribe to patrol the watershed to prevent permit violations, suppress fires, and maintain sanitary conditions.

- The sixth required tribal members to assist, uncompensated, in fire suppression.
- The seventh entitled the Tribe to renew the permit at its expiration.

Clearly, the permit did not give the Pueblo what it requested in its original application. It restricted exclusive religious use to three days in late August, and it allowed visitors to enter the area, provided they had written permission from both the Forest Service and the Pueblo. It gave the Forest Service the right "to extend and improve the forest," thereby potentially violating the religious integrity of the forest vegetation. It required the permission of the forest supervisor to construct facilities and make improvements. Finally, it left unclear in whose hands rested administrative authority for the watershed—the Tribe or the Department of Agriculture.

However, the Forest Service had made some concessions. The permit did not impose state game laws; require the Tribe to make improvements; or give the Forest Service the right to cut and sell timber not needed by the Indians. Further, it permitted visitors only with the concurrence of the Pueblo governor.

The interesting fact is that henceforward the Forest Service now began to move inexorably toward administering the Blue Lake area according to the principles laid down in their first draft of the fifty-year permit, while the Tribe now acted as if the forest were governed by the principles enumerated in their initial draft application of 1933. These conflicting interpretations produced clashes between the Tribe and the Forest Service which continued to intensify over the next thirty years.

Forecasting these troubles is the objection made to Brophy by three Taos Pueblo councilmen when they visited his office in December of 1939. One of these men was Seferino Martinez, a spirited and determined Pueblo leader. Brophy told Collier that the three councilmen "are disturbed that the Department of Agriculture should even consider restricting the rights that the Pueblo has in the Blue Lake area."[17] From this time forward, Martinez did all that he could to make life miserable for Forest Service personnel employed in the watershed. Through his opposition, he made clear that the Indians would not be ruled by outsiders' policies. As a close student of this period in tribal history observed:

> Certainly of unique spirit was the fiery Seferino Martinez, whose actions kept the Forest Service in the Blue Lake area in almost constant turmoil. This spirit prevailed during his many years as pueblo governor and council member. . . .[18]

One of the most contentious issues during the forties was that of grazing. Prior to 1935, the Pueblo had run very few cattle and these were concentrated almost exclusively in the lower reaches of the canyons, where they posed no threat to the sacred watershed. In the late thirties, however, the Bureau of Indian Affairs purchased nearly 500 head of prime cattle for Taos Pueblo. When these were added to the existing herds, grazing use suddenly exceeded the

Seferino Martinez, c. 1960, the fiery councilman who for many years led the Tribe in its opposition to Forest Service control of the sacred lands. Courtesy of Saki Karavas.

land's carrying capacity by 1,000 animal months. By 1940, 700 cattle were graz-ing a range which could accommodate only about 500. Inevitably, too, the cattle began drifting higher and higher into the watershed in search of forage. The Indians exacerbated the problem by failing to dispose salt strategically, leaving some areas badly overused while others remained relatively lush. Overgrazing became a serious problem.

By 1946, bureau officials were holding meetings with Pueblo officials and stockmen to discuss the worsening situation. The BIA obtained approval to do a livestock tally, anticipating that it would justify significant reductions in the numbers of horses and cattle grazing the watershed. Because of the cattlemen's resistance, however, the program failed.

The BIA then tried another approach. Rather than simply reducing the num-ber of cattle, BIA fieldmen sought to convince the Tribe to cull out the "broom-tails" (poorer quality stock) and introduce good quality bulls, thereby reducing quantity while improving quality and profit. This measure, too, met with opposi-tion, since Indians in part measured wealth according to numbers of animals owned, with little consideration for quality. Especially vocal in his opposition was Seferino Martinez, who even defied his own leaders. Brophy reports that the issue grew so heated that it led Taos Pueblo governor Antonio Mirabal to resign his position in 1948, because "he as Governor ordered the broomtails taken off the grazing lands and Severino [*sic*] did not want to remove his broom-tails."[19]

Also problematic in the forties was cattle trespass. Because of inadequate fenc-ing along the Pueblo's boundaries, cattle belonging to the Tribe often trespassed onto rangelands leased to white ranchers, and non-Indian cattle often strayed into the Tribe's sacred watershed. As the administrative authority in charge, the Forest Service was saddled with the task of adjudicating disputes and imposing penalities. As a result, cattle trespass produced considerable rancor among the Tribe, its neighbors, and the Forest Service.

The issue grew serious enough by 1949 to cause the Forest Service to call a meeting with the Tribe to try to reach an understanding about range management. The BIA once again proposed that all stock be ear-tagged and marked, the more easily to identify trespassing animals. If violations occurred, the Forest Service was to invoke rule T-12, which allowed them to impound trespassing stock and fine the owner or sell the stock for damages.

The Tribe agreed, but the program enjoyed only limited initial success because a few of the major Pueblo stock owners refused to comply. Again, Seferino Martinez headed the opposition. Five months after the program began, only 125 head had been tagged. When the Forest Service began rounding up untagged cattle, most were discovered to belong to Martinez. When the Forest Service began imposing fines on untagged cattle, Pueblo opponents of tagging argued that such fines violated the terms of the special use-permit. They contended that Forest Service had no right to impose fines since the Tribe enjoyed free and unencumbered grazing privileges.

The Indians also complained that the Forest Service did little to keep out non-Indian stock, did nothing when some were found, and yet were all too ready to impose sanctions on Indian cattle in violation. Despite these problems, the situation eventually improved. By the summer of 1950, Carson supervisor Louis Cottam felt that the trespass problem was under "fair control." Two years later the Indians, after an inspection tour of the watershed with BIA officials, remarked that non-Indian stock trespass had been greatly reduced and the condition of the forage much improved. The range management procedures were having the desired effect.

Over time the Tribe gradually reduced the numbers of cattle grazing in the Blue Lake watershed to zero, shifting ranching operations to vast tracts of land west of the Pueblo proper. They preferred to keep the watershed in its pre-Columbian natural condition. Overgrazing and Indian cattle trespass were problems no longer. However, non-Indian cattle continued to stray into the Blue Lake watershed, proving a source of ill-feeling as late as the congressional battles of the sixties.

The Indians perceived another threat from the timbering in the La Junta Canyon area on the Tribe's southeastern boundary. Owned by the state of New Mexico, these 2,400 acres fell outside the use-agreement of 1940 and were therefore eligible for timbering contracts. The Tribe became concerned when the state decided to issue timber contracts for La Junta in the forties, since laws controlling cutting were minimal. The Indians were worried about pollution of the river and desecration of the vegetation.

In 1948, the Forest Service renewed efforts to obtain the state land through exchange. They promised the Tribe that if the deal went through they would recommend assigning the area to the Tribe for its use. The state land commissioner did all he could to carry out the exchange, but "cattle interests balked the deal."[20] Shortly thereafter, the state sold the timber in La Junta Canyon and the BIA worked to minimize the impact, "trying for an arrangement whereby the State will control the cutting so that the watershed will not be damaged too much."[21] In the fall of 1948, the OK Lumber Company began timbering La Junta Canyon.

In January of 1949, New Mexico representative A.M. Fernandez introduced in the House a bill that would transfer the state land to the Carson National Forest. The bill passed and an agreement was struck transferring the La Junta area to the Carson in exchange for other Forest Service land. Unfortunately, the Forest Service could not assume immediate control of the exchanged tracts because of existing timbering contracts which ran until the end of 1956. By 1950, timbering in the La Junta was in full swing, and it was a good example of clear-cutting at its worst. The land was ravaged. The BIA met with Forest Service representatives in 1952 in an attempt to curtail the extent of the cutting to reduce fire danger and pollution. Their efforts were unsuccessful, and it became clear that they were going to have to wait until the timbering contracts ran out in 1956 to try to repair the extensive damage.

Twenty years later the Indians were still furious about this development. Seferino Martinez testified before the Senate committee in 1968 that

> a desecration has been done by these people, tremendous damages have been done . . . . In this area the land looks to me to be almost beyond recovery. The watershed is damaged so badly that it is going to take a long time to bring it back to its natural form.[22]

Although the timbering was on land outside Forest Service control, the Tribe nevertheless blamed the Forest Service for the destruction of La Junta. They became convinced that it was only a matter of time until the Blue Lake watershed itself was timbered. This belief contributed significantly to deteriorating relations between the Tribe and the Forest Service.

Another continuing cause of conflict remained the old issue of tourist use, including fishing. Brophy set forth the Tribe's concerns to his superior, L.G. Boldt:

> Another complaint that the Indians have is that the Forest Service has stocked Blue Lake with fish. They don't think that a stream which is used for human consumption ought to have that many fish. Moreover, they say that because there is fish there and because it is such a beautiful spot hundreds of tourists go up there with pack horses and that they are the ones who have overgrazed around the lake and have torn down some of the trees, which damaged not only the beauty but the utility of the lake. Furthermore these tourists, the Taos people say, have littered the place up with all sorts of rubbish, camp fires, tin cans and junk so that it looks more or less like a dump. The Taos people think that this is a disgrace and an abomination. They want you to take steps to keep all tourists out of the place.[23]

Tourism, with its attendant problems of fishing and litter, exacerbated the bad feelings between the Tribe and the Forest Service. Fortunately, the stocking of fish in Blue Lake ended in 1953, when the Tribe's old nemesis, Elliott Barker, retired as head of the state Game and Fish Department after more than twenty years of service. But tourists continued to angle for the remaining fish, and the issue agitated relations between the Tribe and the Forest Service for the next two decades.

A further source of tribal discontent was the inaccuracy of the boundary for the permitted area. This issue flared in the late forties when investigations revealed that the 7,000 east side acres desired by the Tribe had been lost through the perfidy of the Forest Service.

The facts came out as the result of Brophy's determined probing. He learned that the Tribe's loss resulted from a deliberate "switcheroo" on the part of the Forest Service. As discussed earlier, when the Tribe surrendered their claims to the land in the town of Taos, they thought they were getting as compensation the entire watershed up to the ridge of La Junta Canyon, a distance of some three miles from the Rio Pueblo. After the agreement had been signed, however, the Tribe discovered to their dismay that their eastern boundary was only one half mile from the river, a difference of some 7,000 acres. Naturally they were angry: "When the boundaries in the 1933 statute and in the permit failed to take their use up to the ridge, they felt aggrieved and, they have had that feeling ever since."[24]

To better understand the situation, Brophy held discussions with members of the Tribal Council who had assisted in developing the draft of the 1927 Cooperative Agreement. They "insisted that they were told the east line would be three miles east of the creek (this is approximately right for the summit line and the watershed boundary)."[25] At the time the agreement was developed, the Tribe had their attorney, Dudley Cornell, prepare a draft which specifically identified their land rights as comprising the entire watershed. But the Forest Service amended the draft to include only a portion of the watershed, cheating the Tribe out of 7,000 acres in the process. As Brophy's co-worker, R.M. Bunker, informed him:

> The switcheroo is obvious between Cornell's draft and the final agreement presented for Taos' signature. Cornell's draft left blanks for an exact description of the land involved, but went on to say that those 'described sections . . . form *the watershed* from which the water supply for said Pueblo of Taos is obtained.' The signed version says 'form *a portion* of the watershed from which etc.'[26]

Most damning to the Forest Service was evidence which indicated that the 7,000 acres had been left out to protect the grazing interests of white cattlemen who had had permits to the area. These acres were permitted to outsiders beginning in 1918, although the Tribe never gave permission for such leases. When it came time to describe the land to be covered by the Cooperative Agree ment, the Forest Service simply left out the 7,000 acres used by white cattlemen in order to protect "the accrued rights of non-Indian permittees in the Forest."[27] This boundary, violating the terms requested by the Indians, was then perpetuated in the 1928 executive order withdrawal as well as the act of 1933.

During the forties and early fifties, the Tribe made repeated attempts to regain the lost 7,000 acres, as well as to add to its permitted area other tracts of land belonging to the Rio Pueblo watershed. On May 7, 1943, Representative O'Connor introduced H.R. 2656 on behalf of Taos Pueblo. The bill would have amended the 1933 act to include the 7,000 acres as well as the 2,000 acres in the Larkspur Lake area. The bill failed to pass, but the Tribe remained committed to recovering this acreage.

During this same period of time, another opportunity arose for the Tribe to acquire additional acreage. It began with an offer by Will Ed Harris to exchange 6,700 acres of land owned by him for national forest land. Located in the northern region of the Pueblo's permit area, the acreage was divided into two tracts. Both tracts were virtually unusable by anyone but the Tribe, since their land almost entirely surrounded them. When the exchange went through in 1950, the Forest Service began negotiations with the Tribe over grazing permits for the area. The Pueblo's long-term goal, however, was to have the Harris tracts added to their use-permit.

By 1952, the Tribe was actively seeking legislation which would add to their permit area nearly 20,000 additional acres including 6,680 in the two Harris tracts, 3,160 acres on the western boundary, 7,980 acres on the eastern boundary, and the 2,000 acres of land recently acquired by the Forest Service from the University of New Mexico. It appears that the Tribe, the BIA, and the Forest Service were all in agreement concerning this initiative. Brophy told BIA Area Director, C.L. Graves:

> The Carson National Forest Officers have indicated their willingness to have the five aforementioned units added to the Taos statutory permit if the non-Indian permits can be satisfactorily acquired and upon reaching an agreement with the Taos Tribe in the matter of cooperating in the management of the entire area which is to be used by the Taos people.[28]

While the Tribe was pleased with the initiative to add land to the permit area, in fact they were still vigorously opposed to Forest Service control of the watershed and hoped for a patent or title to the area. The various difficulties between the Tribe and the Forest Service—grazing, timbering, fishing, tourists, litter, and boundary disputes—made the Indians wary of continued outside control. BIA realty officer Dewey Dismuke told area director Graves that "dissatisfaction has been expressed in recent years by the officials of the Taos Pueblo with the manner in which the Forest Service is supervising the use of the Blue Lake area...."[29] Despite Brophy's warning that a patent attempt might bring out opposition from the Forest Service, conservation groups, cattlemen, and local interests, and despite his fear that they would not have the funds properly to administer the area and might even have to pay state taxes on it, the Indians insisted that "they wanted to get a patent to the whole area, that they didn't like a permit."[30]

Various elements emerged in the late forties and early fifties which began to make that dream a reality. The first of these was the return to Taos Pueblo in 1946 of a young tribal member, Paul J. Bernal. He had been serving aboard the U.S.S. Ticonderoga during World War II, where he polished his English and became familiar with the ways of the outside world. Impressed by his energy, intelligence, and language skills, the Tribal Council employed him as their general interpreter. In that position, Bernal soon became knowledgeable about all aspects of tribal affairs, and from the outset took a special interest in the return of Blue Lake. He dedicated himself to regaining the sacred watershed, and for twenty-five years carried the political load for the Tribe in its quest for the mountain shrineland.

Another contributing factor was the publication, shortly after Pearl Harbor, of an obscure little book called *The Man Who Killed the Deer*. While the book disappeared in the nation's mobilization for war, it began to sell at a slow but steady pace when brought out by a small publisher some years later. It is Frank Waters's dramatic rendering of the struggle of Taos Pueblo for the return of its sacred "Dawn Lake." He tells us that there was in its composition something of the miraculous:

> I remember that fall morning in Taos, sitting in front of the fireplace in the big room above the garage in back of Tony Lujan's house just inside the reservation. The story did not have to be contrived; it unfolded, like a flower, its own inherent pattern. The words came easily, unbidden, as the flow of ink from my old, red Parker. . . .It seemed impelled by the unconscious rather than by rational consciousness.[31]

Waters goes on to say that two incidents touched off composition of the book:

> I had strayed into the county courthouse where a hearing was being given an Indian for killing a deer out of season in the Carson National Forest. A few mornings later, when I was bending over the washbowl to shave, I envisioned reflected in the water three figures evidently discussing the incident and who bore striking resemblances to the old, blanketed governor of Taos Pueblo, Pascual Martinez in his Forest Service boots and whipcord and Ralph Myers, the Indian trader. Right then the idea of the novel presented itself, and after washing the breakfast dishes I sat down to write.[32]

Over the next twenty-five years, thousands read this charming little novel and were favorably influenced to support the Tribe's quest for "Dawn" or Blue Lake. It has been said of the book that it "was the single most potent outside force in Taos Pueblo's achieving its ultimate victory."[33] While that may be an exaggeration, it contains a grain of truth. Waters's book did make an important contribution to the Tribe's eventual victory.

Additional elements of great significance were the entrance of the writer

Paul Bernal (right), the key political point-man for the Tribe in its congressional battles, c. 1968. Courtesy of Dan Budnik.

Frank Waters (left) with Doroteo "Frank" Samora, the Indian whose courthouse hearing inspired The Man Who Killed the Deer. *C. 1950, courtesy of Frank Waters.*

Oliver La Farge and the Association on American Indian Affairs into the quest for Blue Lake. La Farge became interested in the Indians of the Southwest while on an anthropological expedition to Navajo country during his undergraduate days at Harvard. This began his lifelong commitment to Indian affairs. He received his M.A. in anthropology from Harvard in 1929, having written his thesis on *Derivation of Apache and Navajo Culture.* In that same year he won the Pulitzer Prize for his novel *Laughing Boy,* a moving love story set in Navajo country.

La Farge's involvement with the practical side of Indian affairs began in 1930 with his election to the Board of Directors of the Eastern Association on Indian Affairs, an organization dedicated to protecting Indian rights and to improving their living conditions. Three years later La Farge became president of the EAIA, and received an invitation from John Collier, now commissioner of Indian Affairs, to conduct field investigations in the Indian country of the Southwest. Despite an ongoing feud between Collier's Indian Defense Association and La Farge's EAIA, the two soon discovered that they "shared an identical concern in making practical application of social science to the problems of Indian affairs administration."[34] They worked harmoniously together, and in 1937 merged their once-competing organizations into a new group called the Association on American Indian Affairs, with La Farge as president. For the next twenty-five years La Farge worked unpaid in that capacity on behalf of America's native peoples. As La Farge saw it, AAIA's role was

to find the most effective ways of assisting Indians to advance themselves
. . .with a preference for achieving this end through causing the appropriate agencies of the federal government to do everything that they ought to
do.[35]

La Farge first became directly involved with Taos Pueblo in 1947 in conjunction with the Tribal Council's effort to evict non-tribal members from the reservation. While the situation proved unimportant, it brought La Farge into direct
contact with the elders of Taos. He learned from them of their dissatisfaction
with the administration of the watershed by the Forest Service, and of their
desire to reclaim the sacred land of their ancestors. From this time forward, La
Farge took a special interest in Taos Pueblo and played a key role in drawing
AAIA into the struggle to reclaim Blue Lake.

The following year, La Farge and AAIA spearheaded the effort to give New
Mexico Indians the vote. While Congress in 1924 had declared all Indians citizens of the United States and thus eligible to vote, the actual implementation of
such voting depended upon passage by the individual states of the required
legislation. Not surprisingly, the two states with the largest Indian populations,
Arizona and New Mexico, were the last states to permit Indian voting. When
Indian servicemen returned from World War II, they began agitating for suf-
frage. AAIA took up the cause, and played a key role in bringing to trial a test
case which resulted in a 1948 federal court decision granting New Mexico
Indians the right to vote.

In that same year, Felix Cohen, the great scholar of Indian law who had written both the Indian Reorganization Act of 1934 and the Claims Commission Act
of 1946, became general counsel for AAIA. One of his tasks was to address the
more traditional Indians' fear of voting. Older tribal members were concerned
that if they voted their lands would be taken away and their old ceremonies and
customs stamped out. Cohen, explaining that these fears were groundless,
argued that voting was the only means by which the Indians could protect their
land and culture. While some of the younger Indians then did vote, most continued to mistrust the ballot.

Opposition was especially intense at a traditional pueblo like Taos. When La
Farge sent AAIA field assistant Alison Stacey to meet with the Indians of Taos in
1948, she found that "they are avoiding the voting issue as if it were the
plague. . . ."[36] It was not until the late sixties, after the issue nearly tore tribal
goverment apart, that Taos Indians began to vote in any significant numbers.
Voting then, too, made its contribution to the eventual success of the quest for
the return of Blue Lake.

The final element which fell into place during this period was the establishment by the United States Congress of the Indian Claims Commission. Authorized by the Claims Commission Act of 1946, the Indian Claims Commission was
a special court to which tribes could present claims for land they had lost and
for which they had received inadequate compensation. Under the Claims Act,

The New Mexican author Oliver LaFarge was a selfless and stalwart supporter of the Tribe for many years until his last illness. Photo c. 1937, courtesy of Penn LaFarge.

such cases did not require special enabling legislation as had previously been the case. Considerations of justice as well as a desire to save time and money in adjudicating tribal claims motivated passage of the act.

The Taos Indians were aware of the possibility of filing a claim with the ICC as early as 1948. When they took the matter up with Brophy, he explained that the ICC was empowered only to award financial damages to tribes, but could not actually return disputed land. He reports, "They told me they wanted the land rather than money. . . ,"[37] and discussions of a possible ICC action were dropped.

Santa Fe attorney Henry Hughes reopened the issue two years later when he contacted several New Mexico tribes, including Taos, about taking advantage of the ICC legislation. He convinced them that they ought to file. The BIA opposed Hughes, however, and made it clear that they would not approve any contracts he might make with New Mexico Indians.

In addition to his work with AAIA, Felix Cohen was at that time general counsel to the All Pueblo Council, and in that capacity had contact with Hughes. Hughes asked Cohen for help in getting legal representation for the tribes. Since Cohen was also general counsel to still another entity, the Joint Efforts Group, a consortium of lawyers representing various tribes before the ICC, he naturally turned to them for recommendations. He learned that one of their member firms, Karelsen & Karelsen of Washington, D.C., would be willing to take the New Mexico cases. Cohen so informed Hughes, who in turn informed the Indians. The New Mexico Pueblos interested in filing ICC claims then retained Karelsen & Karelsen as their legal representatives, with Darwin Kingsley of that firm as lead attorney. In the event of a settlement, the tribes agreed to pay the attorneys 10 percent of the total amount recovered, with 65 percent of the fee going to the Joint Efforts Group, 17.5 percent to Kinglsey himself, and another 17.5 percent to his law firm.

By the time the tribes signed their contracts with Karelsen & Karelsen, it was already late in July of 1951; and the petitions had to be filed before the ICC by August 15. In less than two months, Cohen, as counsel for the Joint Efforts Group, drew the claims petitions for all of the New Mexico tribes and filed them just two days before the deadline. Taos Pueblo's grievance at losing control of the sacred watershed was now a matter of official record.

3

The La Farge Era

ROM THE OUTSET DIFFICULTIES BESET the Tribe's suit before the Indian Claims Commission. The first problem stemmed from factional infighting fostered by the meddling of Henry Hughes. While he had been instrumental in the retaining of Kingsley, Hughes became increasingly bitter at not being given the cases himself. As a close friend of Seferino Martinez, Hughes was able to circulate rumors about Kingsley through the fiery councilman. Chief among them was that Kingsley had drawn the ICC petitions to seek financial damages rather than return of the sacred watershed. Tribal sentiment quickly began to turn against him.

When Kingsley came to Taos in 1953 to gather information for the Pueblo's claim, Martinez tried to prevent his meeting with the council. Fortunately, Bernal intervened and saved the situation. As Kingsley said to La Farge of Bernal:

> He was the one who, when he heard the story from me, risked the wrath of Seferino and his clique and insisted that the Council meet with me. Without the resulting Council meeting . . . I could have gotten nowhere with Taos![1]

Two factions quickly developed in the Tribe: an anti-Kingsley group headed by Martinez, and a pro-Kingsley group led by Bernal. The dispute became so heated that the Indians turned to Oliver La Farge for mediation. He promptly wrote to Kingsley, telling him of the Tribe's fear that their petition sought money, not land. Kingsley replied that the petition as filed was rather general and deliberately vague with respect to the specific relief sought by each tribe. "It makes no mention of money or specific acreage. We have told each of the pueblos that we will do our darndest to get land rather than money. . . ."[2]

La Farge then explained to the Tribe that under the rules of the Claims Act they would be allowed to alter their petition only once. Kingsley's strategy was to see what form the government case against the Tribe took, and then amend the petition to meet that course. With respect to the land/money dispute, La Farge reassured them that

> the petition is written in such a way that the attorneys can ask either for title to the land or for compensation money, according to their instructions. You have instructed them to ask for title, and that is what they are going to do.[3]

Apparently satisfied with La Farge's explanation, Martinez dropped open opposition. The first hearings on the Tribe's suit went forward without mishap, and during 1953 and 1954 the tribal council willingly provided testimony which established their long-standing use of the entire area claimed. They hoped that the ICC would rule in their favor, and provide legal justification for their quest to reclaim all of the sacred watershed.

Unfortunately, the 1950s were not the best time for an Indian tribe to seek to expand its landholdings. From World War II onward, a movement had been growing among conservative congressmen to force the assimilation of Indians into the general population by ending the special relationship between tribes and the federal government. Known as "terminationists," these congressmen "advocated an end to trust arrangements and any remaining tribal sovereignty, the integration of Native Americans into the dominant culture, and federal withdrawal from all Indian affairs."[4]

Termination became official government policy in August of 1953, with the passage of House Concurrent Resolution 108. It made clear that the will of Congress was to terminate, as rapidly as possible, the special legal status of all Native Americans. In the context of this general policy, land tenure got special attention. A move was soon under way to end trust arrangements whereby the federal government protected Indian land held in community by tribes, and to open such land holdings to private ownership. Given the prevailing climate, the Taos Indians had little chance of getting Congress to increase the acreage held in trust for them.

Despite this unfavorable political atmosphere, the Taos Pueblo Tribal Council, led by Seferino Martinez, decided that problems with the Forest Service made it necessary to seek legislation which would better protect their rights in the Blue Lake area. As early as 1950, Martinez, Gov. Star Road Gomez and Bernal met with La Farge and informed him that they had chosen him to help them "get" Blue Lake. At the time, La Farge declined to become directly involved. In 1955, the council asked Martinez to once again approach his good friend La Farge for assistance. La Farge, although wanting to devote more time to his writing career, reluctantly agreed. As La Farge told AAIA staffer, William Zimmerman:

> It may seem peculiar that I should allow myself to be involved in this matter at all when I am crying to be let alone. It is partly a matter of Seferino's

remarkable personality, partly a matter of not betraying the confidence that the Taos Indians now seem to have in me, and partly that I do not think I shall be required to expend a very great amount of time.[5]

That last supposition was to prove unrealistic. However, La Farge's sense of justice drew him inexorably into the fray.

The claim is a strong one morally, probably strong legally, and has tremendous sentimental appeal . . . . As this matter develops I hope that the Association will give it active support both as a matter of justice to Taos Pueblo and for our own benefit.[6]

As the last phrase hints, La Farge was also aware of the issue's potential value to AAIA. This comes out plainly in the letter to Zimmerman:

The whole matter, with its strong character of old Indian beliefs and practices, is one that can be made most appealing to the public and used for the benefit of the Association.[7]

A week later, Richard Schifter, general counsel for AAIA as well as legal consultant to the Joint Efforts Group, pointed out to La Farge that this was not a favorable time to seek a bill to convey the watershed to Taos, in view of the strategy being pursued before the Indian Claims Commission. Kingsley and the other attorneys working on the claims case were seeking to secure from the ICC an interlocutory judgment on liability which would incontestably establish the Tribe's legal right to the area. They then wanted to take the matter to Congress, asking for a bill that would confirm the Pueblo's title to the watershed. This strategy was predicated on the belief that the Taos bill would stand a much greater chance of passage if it were supported by a judgment of the commission confirming the rights of the Pueblo to the area. Schifter told La Farge that the government attorney for the ICC, the commissioner of Indian Affairs, and the members of the New Mexico congressional delegation had already agreed in principle to the plan. For the Tribe to insist on introducing a bill now would upset this carefully conceived strategy. He conceded, however, that

the foregoing notwithstanding, I do not believe that any harm would come from initiating action at this time for the introduction of a bill.[8]

It seems clear that Martinez was behind the move to have a Taos bill introduced as quickly as possible because of lingering suspicions about the ICC. He was still concerned that the claims attorneys were asking for a monetary judgement and not the return of the watershed. Even if this were not so, Martinez feared that the ICC judgment might force the Tribe to take money and give them no opportunity to seek the return of the watershed. Although Kingsley assured La Farge that the ICC followed a two-step process, first ruling on the Pueblo's rights to the land and then moving on to a determination of the amount of money owed the Tribe—at which time the Tribe could refuse financial compensation and go before Congress to request the return of the land itself—Martinez and others were apprehensive that an ICC judgment would commit them to taking the money as the ICC legislation expressly provided. Therefore Martinez urged the introduction of a Taos bill as a safeguard against possible ICC duplicity.

Once the Tribe decided to seek legislation, what sort of legislation they ought to seek became the pressing question. Should they simply duplicate the effort of 1952 to have all of the acreage forming the watershed added to the use-permit of 1940? Should they seek fee-simple title, which would give them outright ownership and responsibility? Or should they seek trust title, which would leave ownership with the federal government? If they sought trust title, should they try to obtain all 50,000 acres forming the watershed; or should they seek trust title only to obtain the 33,000 acres presently under the permit and then try later to obtain the additional 17,000 acres? Further, under trust title should the administrative authority continue to be the Department of Agriculture or should authority be shifted to the Bureau of Indian Affairs and the Department of the Interior?

Early 1955 saw considerable discussion of these options among the BIA, La Farge, and the Tribal Council. Swayed by Martinez's strong opinion on the subject, the Pueblo initially wanted to try for fee-simple title. However, the prospects for this approach quickly dimmed when BIA real property officer Dewey Dismuke pointed out that the Tribe might have to pay taxes on the land, and that the Tribe lacked the resources properly to administer the area. He was also concerned about the attitudes toward such a proposal of both the Forest Service and the non-Indians who were dependent on the water flow from the sacred area. La Farge agreed with Dismuke's reservations and hoped to persuade the Tribe to seek a trust patent rather than fee-simple title. If they refused to take his advice, he felt that it would be impossible for him to support the measure.

When the Tribe had been convinced that a bill seeking fee-simple title would not receive the backing of the New Mexico congressional delegation, they shifted their efforts to securing trust title instead. Further, the Pueblo and its advisors decided that the proposed legislation should seek conveyance of the entire 50,000 acres in the watershed, since "to ask for less might make it impossible to recover the entire area for Taos later."[9] Now in agreement on their basic strategy, in the spring of 1955 La Farge and the Tribe began preparing a draft bill for submission to New Mexico's congressional delegation, led by Sen. Clinton P. Anderson.

Born in South Dakota in 1895, Anderson moved to New Mexico at the age of twenty-three to recover from tuberculosis. Restored to health, he became a reporter for the *Albuquerque Herald*, covering the legislature in Santa Fe. Thus began his lifelong interest in New Mexico politics as a member of the Democratic Party. Following his stint as a reporter, Anderson was employed in the insurance

The dubious distinction of the Tribe's most implacable foe must be awarded to Senator Clinton P. Anderson of New Mexico. Photo c. 1955, courtesy of the Center for Southwest Research, University of New Mexico. General Library Special Collections 000-020-0001

field, where he was so successful that he soon was able to buy the business for which he initially worked.

Anderson's serious involvement with public life began in 1933 with his appointment to the State Treasurer's office. His ability won him appointments to several other public positions during the thirties, culminating in his election in 1940 to the United States House of Representatives. There he served with distinction until 1945, when Harry Truman appointed him secretary of Agriculture. In 1948 Anderson won election to the United States Senate and soon became one of its most respected members.

Given Anderson's growing power and prestige, La Farge naturally turned to him for help with the Blue Lake legislation. After explaining the Tribe's suit before the ICC, La Farge confided to Anderson that if he were advising white men he would tell them to postpone legislative action until a decision by the ICC. "As it is," La Farge continued, "nothing will satisfy them but the knowledge that at least the bill has been introduced . . . ."[10] Sounding a positive note, he went on to suppose that

> many members of Congress would be sympathetic to the idea of awarding these Indians an area of land on much of which they already have an exclusive use-right, and is already Federal property, rather than a considerable sum of money.[11]

This proved to be true of the other members of the New Mexico delegation. Sen. Dennis Chavez and Reps. Antonio Fernandez and John J. Dempsey all assured the Tribe that they would assist in the effort to get trust title to the watershed. Anderson, however, demurred. As secretary of Agriculture, he had come to have great respect for the ideals of Gifford Pinchot as embodied in the policies of the Forest Service. As a result, he was now "opposed in principle to chopping away at the national forests . . . ."[12] He told La Farge that experience had taught him that small villages, both Indian and non-Indian, often damage rough mountain resources because they lack the financial wherewithal

> to administer it and perform the conservation work that is required from time to time. Therefore, I believe that the Taos Indians would derive more benefit from these areas under Forest Service management than they would under community management.[13]

Citing obstacles to the proposed legislation if existing non-Indian grazing permits were revoked, and past problems with Indian overgrazing in the Blue Lake area, he went on to praise the management of the watershed by the Forest Service and to urge the Indians to protect their ceremonials by working out some kind of permanent arrangement with the local Carson National Forest authorities. He felt the Indians would be better off abandoning their title quest and accepting a cash settlement, "because, quite frankly, I believe we would have a very slim chance of getting legislation of this type passed."[14]

La Farge did his best to persuade Anderson otherwise. While he agreed that it was best not to "chip away" at the national forests, he felt that the Taos case was unique.

> It was not the usual practice to set aside as national forest tracts of land to which private individuals had a strong claim and which they were actively using and had been using over an extremely long period of time. This was done only when the persons affected were Indians . . . this makes a special situation and indicates the propriety of creating a situation in which these Indians may state their claim, not to damages, but to title or some kind of special right to the land itself.[15]

La Farge then played the Tribe's trump card, telling Anderson that the Indians had a long list of people sympathetic to their claim whose political support they were going to seek if Congress did not cooperate. Anderson, unconvinced, refused to take any action that would remove the sacred watershed from the administrative authority of the Forest Service.

This Forest Service sign, posted c. 1950, directing campers to Blue Lake, graphically illustrates the callous disregard for the Tribe's requirement for privacy on its sacred lands. Courtesy of Charlotte Trego.

Given Anderson's opposition, the Tribe felt it had no choice but to bring its case before the tribunal of public opinion. Working closely with La Farge, they developed a moving petition setting forth their claim. After reviewing the legal situation respecting the area, they keyed their appeal to the religious significance of the watershed.

> Above all, that is the location of Blue Lake, the most important religious shrine to us, the Indians of the Pueblo of Taos, and a number of other shrines, sacred to us since long before the Spaniards came.[16]

They went on to complain that they had been told by the government

> that the purpose of putting all this area into a forest reserve would be to protect it for exclusive Indian use as always in the past. We believed these words, so we were happy until we found out that they were false.[17]

They expressed dismay that the use-agreement with the Forest Service did not recognize their rights within the watershed, especially because

> it permits tourists to enter our Blue Lake Area and defile it by leaving trash and cans in the vicinity of our shrines and disturbs us in our religious observance.[18]

They concluded their appeal by asking Congress to give them ownership rights to the watershed (for which they had given up hundreds of thousands of dollars) "so that our religion may be safe . . . ."[19]

Printed in the spring of 1955, the petition received widespread public notice through a tribal press release of May 16th. La Farge told Kingsley that Seferino Martinez was "putting his propaganda machine into operation,"[20] underscoring the critical role played by Martinez in the legislative battle. Martinez had pressured La Farge into taking up the Tribe's cause, he had initiated the "propaganda campaign" based on religious issues, and he had insisted that a bill be drafted and submitted to the congressional delegation even though the ICC had not yet handed down their decision.

Sadly, the Tribe's effort to obtain trust title failed. In early June, Senator Chavez wrote to La Farge saying that it was too late in the session for a bill introduced to receive consideration. A month later, Congressman Dempsey informed La Farge that he was now of the opinion that legislative action on Blue Lake ought to be postponed until after the ICC had handed down a decision. Anderson had made his unwillingness to assist in obtaining title quite clear.

With congressional support fast diminishing, La Farge decided to try another tactic. On July 12 he told Congressman Fernandez that

> I strongly feel that the reasonable and wise action at the present time would be to introduce a bill enlarging the mandatory permit area to include all of the land they are asking for, which forms a single, natural drainage unit. If this were done, I believe that I could convince them, and, equally important, the many non-Indians in New Mexico who favor their cause, that it was a real victory and an important step in the direction they desire.[21]

Fernandez, a long-time friend and supporter of Taos Pueblo, agreed with La Farge's idea of dropping the trust-title initiative in favor of a bill that would expand the Tribe's use-permit to the entirety of the watershed. On July 30th, he introduced H.R. 7758 which amended the act of 1933 to include all 50,000 of the acres desired by the Pueblo.

With the expansion bill already before Congress, La Farge had to convince Martinez, now governor of the Pueblo, of the wisdom of the idea. He likened the title quest to a war whose successful conclusion depends upon winning a number of different battles. The introduction of H.R. 7758 was one of those battles, and a "big step" toward eventually securing title. La Farge explained that it would strengthen their ICC case, enabling the lawyers to say that Congress had recognized the Tribe's special rights to the area. If the ICC then found for the Tribe, obtaining actual trust title would be made that much easier. La Farge "strongly urged" the Tribe to support the bill. Since the introduction of H.R. 7758 was a *fait accompli*, the Tribe had little choice but to go along. However, a shocking event a month later made it plain that the headstrong Martinez was anything but pleased with the tactics being pursued for recovery of the sacred watershed.

With the ICC case apparently stalled and the trust-title quest frustrated, Martinez's opposition to Kingsley resurfaced with a vengeance. The Tribe informed him that after "long and lengthy [sic] deliberation" they had decided to dismiss him as claims attorney

because you have repeatedly broken your promises to us. We are not
impressed with your ability or knowledge in general or as to Indian law and
we further strenuously object to the way you have handled our Blue Lake
Claim.[22]

Signed by most of the members of the Tribal Council, the letter was sent to
everyone connected to the Blue Lake claim.

Profoundly shocked and deeply concerned about the possible damage this
action might do the Pueblo's ICC claim and title quest, both La Farge and Kingsley tried to dissuade the Tribe from taking this precipitous action.

La Farge told them that their decision jeopardized the long-term plans that
they had laid for trust-title acquisition and threatened to "kill off everything that
has been done and everything that we have gained so far."[23] He expressed dismay
that they would have taken such an action without first informing him. Kingsley
explained that the responsibility for the delay of their ICC case rested not with
him but with the government. Indeed, while he filed their claim in the summer
of 1951, it was not until just a month earlier, more than four years after his initial
filing, that he finally received from the ICC an answer to the Taos petition. He
said he had been ready to try the case for more than a year, and was simply
awaiting ICC action. He also made evident to the council that, from the outset,
the attorneys understood that the Tribe wanted the land, not money, and had
developed the case accordingly.

In the meantime, La Farge made contact with friends of his in the Tribe in an
attempt to find out what had occasioned the council's action. He learned that the
dismissal letter had not even been discussed in a council meeting, but had been
drawn up for Martinez and kept at his office where he called council members in
one by one and had them sign it. Bernal was not able to take action because he was
in Arizona running a Caterpillar tractor. La Farge learned that the council was
considerably upset with the way Martinez had been operating, and felt he was
breaching their customary procedures for self-government.

Armed with this information, La Farge created a situation which brought him
together with Martinez, an old tribal councilman, Juan Cordova, and an interpreter. He patiently explained, "in terms even old Mr. Cordova could understand," the strategy for the title quest—to first obtain an ICC judgment and then
press for a legislative conveyance of trust title. Martinez became "astoundingly
mild," and defended his actions as the wish of the council. He knew he was "on
the hook" for having taken an action "detrimental to the recapture of the sacred
area." La Farge reassured the Indians that Kingsley was forgiving and would continue to work for them, that no permanent harm had been done. "This was an
enormous relief to them all, and doubly so to Severino [sic]."[24]

Shortly after this meeting, Bernal and Councilman Abe Romero paid La Farge
a visit.

I learned some curious ethnological items about Taos, most of which I shall
keep to myself. What is significant is that Paul is by birth a firmly established

official in the Taos politico-religious organization, while Severino [*sic*] is the classical picture of the man born without status and somewhat under a cloud, who by force of character and wiliness has been able to negotiate himself into a position that he should not properly occupy. This helps explain many things about him. It does also mean that he is more vulnerable than I had thought, and he knows it.[25]

La Farge then asked Bernal and Romero to do all they could to get it across to the Tribal Council "that they must stop rocking the boat, and above all must avoid any further action so perfectly aimed to foul up all our joint plans."[26] They readily agreed, and revealed to La Farge that there was at the Pueblo "a strong drive on to elect a new governor in January who really will be the governor and not be Severino's [*sic*] puppet."[27] They also told La Farge that Kingsley's old nemesis, Hughes, had been behind the dismissal letter.

Thinking he had defused the potentially explosive situation, La Farge later learned to his astonishment that the Tribal Council on December 20 had passed a resolution again dismissing Kingsley as counsel. Worse still, the resolution had been sent not only to Kingsley, as before, but also to the commissioner of Indian Affairs in Washington. It could therefore be acted on legally. The resolution itself once more charged Kingsley with working only to get a cash settlement for Blue Lake, and said he did so to obtain a higher fee. It listed various other complaints and concluded that the Tribe could no longer work with Kingsley as he had lost their "faith and confidence." The resolution asked the commissioner to let Kingsley's contract lapse and be replaced with one for Taos attorney Stephen A. Mitchell. On learning of this development, La Farge promptly contacted Bernal, who was "flabbergasted." He said he knew nothing about the resolution, "and the thought that the action could have been taken under his nose without his knowledge really hurt."[28]

At the beginning of 1956, Bernal's prediction about an "anti-Seferino" man being chosen governor came to pass. The Pueblo elders selected Geronimo Trujillo, with James Mirabal as lieutenant governor. Both were independent thinkers who could be counted on to buck Martinez if the situation called for it. With a favorable tribal administration now installed, La Farge urged Bernal to have the members look into the validity of the procedures that led to the December 20, 1955 resolution firing Kingsley. If the resolution did not stem from a "lawful" council meeting, then the Tribe needed to decide if they wanted to stand by the decision or repudiate it. La Farge stressed the importance of maintaining their traditions:

> You all want to keep your Taos way. The way you govern yourselves is part of that way. If the Taos people do not keep straight on that and do everything the way it is supposed to be done, then you will hurt all the rest.[29]

In late January, La Farge went to Taos to attend a Tribal Council meeting concerning the Pueblo's position on H.R. 7758, the bill introduced the previous summer by Congressman Fernandez expanding the area covered by the use-permit to the full 50,000 acres. Martinez stridently opposed the bill, while Bernal just as emphatically supported it. Significantly, Bernal guided the course of discussion. La Farge reports:

> Paul's control of the meeting was extraordinary. He can't have much status. He kept well within the Taos requirements of self-effacement and respect, but he did control.[30]

As a result, the council repudiated Martinez and approved H.R. 7758. La Farge observed that Martinez "had taken a real fall, and might yet fall further."[31]

Fall further he did, for the council then took up the firing of Kingsley. It turned out that there had been no proper meeting on the matter, and that Martinez had again simply called councilmen in one by one to sign what they thought was merely a strong expression of support for the return of Blue Lake. When Bernal read them the resolution of December 20, more than half of the members said they had not known its actual contents, and that Martinez had misled them.

So divisive was the issue that the council could not reach a consensus and had to call two more meetings on the subject. The second meeting was especially bitter. Martinez "addressed Paul in particularly violent terms and even told him that he was crazy."[32] But Bernal finally prevailed. By a vote of 28 to 8, the council rescinded the firing of Kingsley. The dissent of a minority is anathema to the Pueblo politics of consensus, and shortly after the meeting Martinez's seven supporters deserted him. They changed their votes and he now was the single dissenter. La Farge commented that Martinez "really has taken a tumble. . . . I honestly feel sorry for the old man."[33] The new governor, lieutenant governor and Bernal then made it a point to call on La Farge and assure him that they were "determined to get the Taos governmental system back completely on the right path."[34]

Despite his humiliation, Martinez was man enough to consider the quest for Blue Lake more important than his personal feelings. At the same time, Bernal recognized that he needed Martinez's experience and political influence. To meet their common objective, La Farge reported that

> a truce has been negotiated under which administrations are chosen alternately from what we might call the Severino [sic] Martinez group and the Paul Bernal group.[35]

Both factions had recognized that they had to put the conflict behind them. Tempers cooled, divisiveness faded, and the Tribe once again began working together to obtain the sacred watershed. It was not, however, the last time that Bernal and Martinez were to clash. This imbroglio remains significant insofar as it marks Bernal's assumption of control of the fight for Blue Lake. He was now the guiding force in council politics and had successfully blocked Martinez's opposition to H.R. 7758 and the retention of Kingsley as claims attorney.

The Tribe now focused its attention on the passage of the Fernandez expansion bill. While there were no new developments regarding the bill during the congressional sessions of 1956, the measure got a boost late that year when Anderson let it be known that he planned to introduce in the Senate a bill identical to the Fernandez bill in the House. Since the provisions of H.R. 7758 left the Forest Service in control of the watershed, Anderson felt he could in good conscience support it. He kept his word, introducing S. 48 in early January of 1957. Like the Fernandez bill, S. 48 put an additional 20,000 acres under the Tribe's use-permit.

Neither bill received congressional consideration, because of the determined opposition of the Forest Service. Its parent Department of Agriculture blocked action on both bills for four reasons: (1) passage of the bill did not seem vital to maintaining the Taos economy; (2) the timber resources in the area had not been utilized; (3) the bills would prevent "expansion of recreational use"; and (4) the Tribe did not have a valid claim to the additional 20,000 acres since much of the land had only recently been acquired from the state or private owners.

In 1958 the story was much the same. Anderson again introduced S. 48, and Agriculture again blocked congressional action, arguing that transfer of the 20,000 acres was not vital to the maintenance of the economy of the Taos Indians, while "public recreational use of the area is important and increasing."[36] As E.T. Benson of Agriculture summed up his department's opposition:

> S. 48 would give the exclusive use and benefits of publicly-owned timber and forage resources on the 20,000 acres of land to a limited group; extend to them privileges not available to other citizens; create a situation which potentially could interfere with recreational use of the lands by the general public; and possibly inhibit full utilization of the timber resource.[37]

Undaunted, the Tribe appealed to Anderson in 1959 to reintroduce the bill. He complied and introduced S. 903 on February 3rd. Shortly thereafter, Santo Domingo Pueblo succeeded in getting trust title to a desired tract of land. This inspired Taos to drop the initiative to expand the acreage under the permit and to seek trust title instead.

One of the first steps taken by the Tribal Council in this direction was to meet with BIA assistant secretary Roger Ernst and explain to him their need for control of the entire watershed. Immediately sympathetic, Ernst then conferred with La Farge and local BIA officials to discuss possible legislation for Taos. He agreed to try to get a bill introduced which would give Taos trust title to the entire 50,000 acres. He concurred with La Farge that it was Interior's duty to get the Tribe as much control as possible. By fall, Interior's preparation of the trust title bill was well under way and Ernst promised the Tribe that when it was ready Interior would request the withdrawal of S. 903 and its replacement with the trust-title bill.

The Tribe officially authorized Interior's initiative in March of 1960, when it passed a resolution asking Interior to withdraw S. 903 and replace it with a bill conveying trust title. The Pueblo's strategy had now formally shifted from seeking merely an expansion of the permit area to striving for conveyance of trust title to the entire 50,000-acre watershed.

In a follow-up letter, however, they insisted that Interior, in drafting the bill,

> should take into consideration their feelings that there should not be included in said proposed bill any references to the use of the area for the purpose of recreation or for the timbering of the land, as was included in S. 903.[38]

The Tribe was especially touchy about the timbering issue, since in the previous spring Interior had reported to the Senate that they would support S. 903 provided that the Forest Service had the right to "dispose" of the "over-mature" timber on all 50,000 acres. The Tribe upbraided Interior, saying that only people who look at forests through dollar signs think all "over-mature" timber needs to be cut down. They wanted neither timbering nor recreation in the sacred area.

Introduction of the trust-title bill proved difficult because of the strong opposition Ernst encountered from the Department of Agriculture. Both Schifter and La Farge finally concluded that the bill stood no chance of passage if supported only by Interior and opposed by Agriculture. They decided to try to break the log-jam by enlisting the support of the Department of Justice as part of the claims adjudication. Their strategy was to arrange an overall settlement under which the Pueblo's ICC claim would be dismissed if the government agreed to give the Tribe trust title to the watershed. Negotiations with Justice dragged on for months without result and there was no opportunity for congressional action on the Pueblo's bill. Agriculture had once again thwarted the Tribe's quest for title.

In the fall of 1960, the election of a new president, John F. Kennedy, gave the Pueblo renewed hope. The Tribe and its advisors felt that Orville Freeman, Kennedy's secretary of Agriculture, would be more sympathetic to their plea. Soon after the inauguration, Schifter set to work in Washington to get interdepartmental concurrence from Agriculture, Interior, and Justice on a trust-title bill for Blue Lake. La Farge urged him to settle the matter as quickly as possible because the Tribe was growing ever more restive:

> These people know that we have a favorable administration and they are straining at the leash. I don't just mean Severino [sic] and Paul, but the whole Tribe . . . . I hope that before long we can give them some indication of progress.[39]

Agriculture continued to be unresponsive, however, and Martinez and Bernal decided to take matters into their own hands. In conjunction with a visit to the East Coast in the spring of 1961 to speak at the annual AAIA meeting, they traveled to Washington to confer directly with Richard E. McArdle, chief of the United States Forest Service. They bluntly told him that the Tribe wanted an end to Forest Service supervision of the Blue Lake area. McArdle responded that if the decision were left up to him he would gladly transfer the area to the Indians.

Impressed by McArdle's sympathy, Martinez and Bernal left Washington feeling he would assist their cause.

Two months later, however, McArdle backed down, saying he thought his Forest Service and the Tribe could work things out in a way that would make transfer of the ownership of the sacred area to the Tribe unnecessary. Martinez and Bernal were furious. They felt betrayed, and Martinez, now governor, threatened to refuse to sign any visitor permits for the Blue Lake area. He also wrote Agriculture secretary Freeman directly, telling him the Tribe

> [did] not wish further supervision of the area by the Forest Service. . .inasmuch as the Pueblo is now seeking to return the area to its original trust status befitting a place of worship.[40]

When Freeman took no action, Martinez made good his threat. In July of 1961 he flatly refused to sign visitor permits. George Proctor, supervisor of the Carson National Forest, countered by insisting that even if the Tribe refused to sign them, his office would continue to issue permits. So intense was Martinez's rage at this affront to tribal rights that La Farge became seriously concerned. He told Schifter of the old councilman's anger:

> He has had this bottled up in him since he was a young man. (I believe that when Leo Crane was superintendent of the northern pueblos, Severino [*sic*] was one of a number of young Taos Indians who were briefly put in jail for adherence to some of their religious practices.) Now he has blown the cork out of the bottle, at least part way, and if we don't watch out, there will be fizz all over the place.[41]

Agriculture and the Forest Service were unimpressed. They steadfastly maintained that the present arrangement protected the interests of everyone, both Indian and non-Indian. They also argued that their continued supervision was necessary for proper conservation of a critical water-production area. While they agreed to work with the Tribe the better to protect its religious needs, they unequivocally refused to consider transferring title to the Pueblo.

The closing of the Blue Lake area set off a storm of protest throughout the non-Indian community in New Mexico. The newspapers took the line that the Tribe was trying unlawfully to seize a large area of federal property by force. Hostilities increased dramatically in Taos when the Tribe cut off the water to the El Prado and Arroyo Hondo ditches. The situation eased somewhat when Martinez met with the affected users and explained that the cut-off was inadvertent, but tensions still ran high. La Farge described the situation as "explosive" and commented, "It is a complex situation, involving three races, four cultures, and a number of fools. We must walk on eggs."[42] He counseled the Tribe to take no further action on Blue Lake until all tempers had cooled.

In a conciliatory gesture, Agriculture suggested that they might be willing to transfer trust title to the area immediately surrounding Blue Lake, some 3,000 acres. Agriculture under-secretary Charles Murphy told Philleo Nash, the commissioner of Indian Affairs, that

Paul Bernal, on the rim of "The Bowl," above Blue Lake and its surrounding 50,000-acre sacred watershed. C. Mid-1960s. Photo by Dan Budnik.

> it [is] easier to understand how a relatively compact area could be of religious significance. It is more difficult to subscribe to the thought . . . that 50,000 acres constitute a religious shrine.[43]

The Tribe refused to consider the proposal, since they looked upon the entire watershed as an indivisible organic whole. As La Farge explained to Schifter:

> The Indians have a name for the entire area, the English translation of which is 'The Bowl.' I gather that they are and always have been conscious of its unity, which helps to explain why they seem determined to obtain such a large area.[44]

With their attempt to obtain trust title once again frustrated by Agriculture, and with public sentiment running against them, the Tribe and its advisors decided late in 1961 to drop their legislative initiative and focus on their most immediate problem: the entrance of outsiders into "the Bowl" under Forest Service permits. The contention of the previous summer over the Pueblo's refusal to sign permits brought into the open a question that was now to occasion months of bitter wrangling. This was whether the permit of 1940 gave the Tribe the right to refuse to sign visitor permits and thereby prevent the entry of outsiders.

Fortunately for the Pueblo, John Collier was now a resident of Taos. Since he sheperded both the act of 1933 and the permit of 1940 through official channels, he was in a better position than anyone to know what was intended by these documents. Collier provided the Tribe with an affidavit which made manifest that it was the purpose of the permit to "insure to the pueblo the exclusive use of the Sacred Area, the year-round exclusive use, identical with that which a trust patent might insure."[45] Outsiders were to be permitted in the area "only through the joint assent of the Forest Service and the Pueblo."[46] Collier stressed that the Pueblo would never have signed the agreement if it gave them anything other than exclusive use, including the right to keep out non-tribal members.

Schifter conducted exhaustive research which brought him to the same conclusion. He determined that the "concurrence" clause in the permit gave the Tribe the absolute right to bar outsiders from the watershed simply by refusing to sign the Forest Service permits. The Forest Service took the view that the Pueblo could refuse to sign permits only if it gave a valid reason for declining to do so. Collier was quick to point out that such a requirement was an infringement of the Tribe's right to religious privacy. The Tribe might refuse to sign a permit, he hypothesized, giving religious privacy as the reason. The Forest Service might then decide that they were lying and

> the determination that such a lie might exist would entail a probing by the Forest Service into the structures of religious authority within the Pueblo; and to such a possible probing, the Pueblo never could consent.[47]

When local Forest Service authorities refused to concede the point, the Tribe took the matter all the way to Washington. The solicitor of the Department of the Interior sided with them, and opened discussions with the Department of Agriculture in an attempt to negotiate an agreement. As a result, Agriculture gave assurance that no permits would be issued without tribal signature. However, they did not concede, as a matter of law, that permits *had* to have a signature. As Schifter explained to La Farge: "We are still in a situation where Agriculture feels that it is according the Pueblo a privilege rather than recognizing a right."[48] Although the issue was not resolved with the clarity desired by the Tribe's legal advisors, in a practical sense the Pueblo had achieved what it wanted: agreement by the Forest Service that no permits would be issued without Pueblo concurrence.

During the course of the permit negotiations, the Tribe sought to reduce the anti-Pueblo sentiment occasioned by the closing of Blue Lake by developing a local support group in Taos. In August of 1961, La Farge met with a group of pro-Pueblo Anglos (including "former Commissioner John Collier, very deaf, greatly aged and shrunken, but making excellent sense"[49]) and concluded that there "was plenty of local friendship for the Indians that could be drawn upon if it was gone about correctly."[50] Key supporters were Charles and Mary Brooks, novelist Frank Waters, and Joan Huggins Reed, who was chosen to chair the group. They developed a petition backing the Tribe's title quest which they began to circulate in Taos and Santa Fe. They turned it over to La Farge the following spring with more than 400 signatures.

The Tribe itself commenced a public relations campaign in the fall of 1961,

The aged John Collier, Sr., shown here in retirement in Taos (c. 1960), was for many decades one of the Tribe's most dedicated and effective supporters. Courtesy of Mary and John Collier, Jr.

which they kicked off with a long article in the *Taos News* setting forth various aspects of the Blue Lake quest. They pointed out that their acquisition of title would threaten no one's water rights (a major local fear) and that increasing recreational use of the area imperiled their spiritual integrity. In another move to neutralize local opposition, the Tribe's claims counsel hired Taos attorney Stephen A. Mitchell to work as community liaison.

Just when it appeared that the animosities of the previous summer were beginning to abate, an episode of the television program *Accent* devoted to the Tribe's title quest was shown nationally in March of 1962. An article in the Santa Fe newspaper, the *New Mexican*, titled "TV Show Brings Cries of Anger from Taos," detailed local reaction. The article said that the non-Indian population of Taos felt that the program told only the Indian side of the story and that they were "in an uproar" over the "great injustice" of the presentation:

> Immediately after the show, a wave of complaints swept the town of Taos, and many residents and organizations fired off wires or began penning letters to CBS and their Congressmen.[51]

Not only did the locals complain about the accuracy of the program, they also demanded equal time for rebuttal, believing that the nine million people that viewed the show nationally had been given a biased and slanted presentation. Shortly after the program, Carson National Forest supervisor George Proctor went on KKIT radio in Taos to denounce both the Indians and the *Accent* show. His strident words further inflamed local passions.

La Farge, who had been prominently featured in the telecast, became alarmed at the possible consequences of the "violent opposition" generated by the program. He understood that it threatened the Tribe's title quest in two ways: it would stiffen the opposition of the secretary of Agriculture, who was receiving a great deal of anti-Tribe mail on the subject; and it would undermine the support of the New Mexico congressional delegation, which would "be governed by the votes to be won or lost in the matter." He knew that the screams of the opposition were "bound to be alarming to key people in the Washington political scene."[52]

The furor brought up once again for the Tribe and its advisors the question of Indian voting. It was an issue of considerable concern during the early sixties. As Schifter commented,

> It is difficult to see the New Mexico delegation taking a stand in favor of legislation requested by non-voting Indians and opposed by voting non-Indians.[53]

Anderson himself had earlier put the question directly to the Tribe when he asked

> how could he support legislation which was vigorously opposed by a number of his supporters when the proponents of the legislation simply did not vote.[54]

In the elections of 1960, of the seventy-five tribal members registered, only thirty voted, hardly an impressive number to election-conscious representatives. La Farge and claims counsel continually pressed the Tribe to improve upon this dismal showing. They were only too aware that "unless Taos Pueblo begins to vote and the town drops its opposition to the bill, there is simply no chance for the Blue Lake legislation."[55]

The Tribe had to confront the voting issue because it was becoming ever clearer that pressure was increasing to expand recreational uses of the watershed. If this occurred, protective legislation would be more necessary than ever. Intrusion of outsiders into the sacred area had prompted the Tribe to seek greater control of the watershed in the first place. The Tribe returned to this point again and again during the early sixties. For example, a promotional pamphlet issued by the Tribe in the spring of 1961 complained:

> Under the administration of the Forest Service the use of this area for hunting, fishing and camping has steadily increased to the point that the religious feelings of the Pueblo are grossly affronted. The only solution is the total exclusion of non-Indians from the area.[56]

The Tribe tried to persuade the Forest Service to stop permitting visitors into the sacred watershed, but George Proctor, the Carson supervisor, simply wouldn't listen. As La Farge told Schifter,

> I want to repeat to you that much of the existing conflict comes from the position taken by the Carson National Forest Supervisor that he must pro-

mote the recreational use of the Blue Lake area, even through the lake itself
is protected from actual camping.[57]

Committed to the policy of "multiple-use," Proctor felt it was his duty to make the
watershed available to the non-Indian population.

The Pueblo took the view that both the act of 1933 and the permit of 1940
were developed precisely to ensure their exclusive use of the area. John Collier
cut through to the heart of the matter:

> The general question is—is it not?—whether, on the one hand, the land will
> be treated as National Forest Land, with particular Indian privileges in use
> of forage and timber and during the ceremonial; or, on the other hand, the
> land will be treated as Indian Land, with joint Pueblo and Forest Service
> responsibility for conservation.[58]

It is highly likely that had the Forest Service acceded to the Tribe's request that
tourism be banned, the Pueblo would not have pushed their quest for title. They
probably would have been satisfied with legislation that brought the entirety of
"the Bowl" under the protection of the 1940 permit, provided, of course, that
they had absolute assurance that the timbering that had desecrated La Junta
would never be allowed to occur anywhere within the confines of the
watershed.

The threat of timbering remained very much in the minds of the Pueblo
leaders, because both Anderson and the Forest Service kept asserting the need
to harvest the "overripe" timber in "the Bowl." They criticized the Tribe for its
failure to "harvest" this valuable resource. La Farge told Schifter:

> As to the harvesting of overripe timber, the Forest Service has been crying
> about this for quite a long time. The Indians answer that there has been
> overripe timber in the area for thousands of years and no harm has
> resulted. I find the answer difficult to refute. The Forest Service's craving
> for harvesting timber sometimes strikes me as an occupational disease. The
> alleged necessity would apply equally well to wilderness areas.[59]

Quite simply, the Tribe regarded the forest as an integral part of their sanctuary, and to cut it down would violate deeply held religious principles. As Martinez movingly said:

> We don't have beautiful structures and we don't have gold temples in this
> lake, but we have a sign of a living God to who [sic] we pray—the living trees,
> the evergreen and spruce, and the beautiful flowers and the beautiful rocks
> and the lake itself. We have this proof of sacred things we deeply love,
> deeply believe.[60]

As long as the threat of timbering remained, the Tribe felt constrained to continue to strive for trust title to the sacred watershed.

Unexpectedly, John Collier himself now dealt the title quest a serious blow,
and in the process occasioned a heated exchange with La Farge. In the summer
of 1963, Collier became convinced that seeking trust title was not in the Tribe's

Oliver LaFarge, c. 1955, at the time of his early commitment to the trust-title fight. Courtesy of Penn LaFarge.

best interest. Further, he accused the attorneys of paternalism, and maintained that they, and not the Tribe, were behind the title initiative; and that the Indians had been sold on the idea by their legal counsel. La Farge testily replied that:

> We shall never cease to have misunderstandings unless you accept the idea that the initiative in the present drive to obtain title to the Blue Lake and as much of the Blue Lake area as is possible originated with Taos Pueblo and has been maintained consistently by it.[61]

La Farge went on to explain that since his earliest involvement in the matter in 1950, the Tribe had made clear that their goal was acquisition of title, a point they had emphasized to the claims attorneys a year later, when the ICC suit began. La Farge then remarked:

> In the course of the past thirteen years a number of occurrences have led me to conclude that the Indians are right in desiring outright title. . . . The governing fact is that this is what the Taos Pueblo Council wants. On this matter I do not think that the Council is the least confused. Nor have I been able to find any indication that the Council was sold on this idea of obtaining title by any non-Indian.[62]

It is sad that enmity marred this exchange between these two old friends of Taos Pueblo, for it proved to be their last. La Farge had been seriously ill since 1962, and his health took a turn for the worse in the spring of 1963. On June 6, breathing oxygen from a cylinder, he was transported to Taos to attend what was to be his final meeting with the Indians who had come to mean so much to him. On August 2 he died, leaving the Tribe bereft of one of its staunchest defenders. Bernal, weeping profusely, served as pallbearer at the funeral. La Farge's part-time secretary, Corinne Locker, tried to console Bernal by promising that AAIA would continue to stand by the Tribe in its quest for the return of Blue Lake. But the death of La Farge and the opposition of Collier derailed that quest for nearly two years.

4

The Tribe Assumes Control

ROM THE LATE FORTIES DOWN TO 1963, John Collier and Oliver La Farge had exerted enormous influence on the Tribe in its quest for trust title. With the death of La Farge, Collier's influence on tribal politics grew even stronger, intensified by his close friendship with Seferino Martinez. Martinez's son remembers:

> John Collier used to come to the house all of the time. . . . John was very paternalistic—I don't mean that in a negative sense but he was genuinely concerned about what was going on, and he would express his feelings on what strategy to follow, and I think my late father took a lot of advice from him because he knew the ins and outs of the bureaucracy, the system, and he was very helpful in that respect. . . . He had a lot of connections with Washington and elsewhere.[1]

Collier's adamant opposition to the trust-title initiative caused the Tribe to re-examine the whole question, and conclude that a strictly observed use-permit would be more advantageous than a trust title.

Collier backed the use-permit because it would advance his two objectives. He wanted to see the Tribe's exclusive use-rights protected; and he also wanted to see the watershed itself protected—through the resources and knowledge of the Forest Service. Collier favored retaining the permit of 1940, which he believed accomplished both objectives. It may also be true, as Schifter thought, that Collier had a personal stake in seeing the permit retained:

> Let me add, at this point, that I feel that one of our problems here is that John Collier is personally responsible for the 1933 Act and the forest per-

mit. I think he feels that he got for the Pueblo the best possible deal and simply rejects the thought that anyone can do better.[2]

Be that as it may, it is evident that Collier sincerely trusted that all would be well
if only the Indians and the Forest Service adhered to the intentions of the 1940
permit.

Collier now pushed the Tribe to abandon the quest for title and to direct its
efforts instead toward getting the Forest Service to administer the watershed
exclusively for the benefit of the Indians. Martinez urged the Tribal Council to
follow Collier's advice. Bernal, demoralized by the death of his friend La Farge,
had lost heart for the title fight and supported Martinez.

A document prepared for the Tribe shortly after the death of La Farge is revealing. Written in conjunction with Bernal by a local agitator and reputed com-
munist, Craig Vincent, the document reviews the Blue Lake situation and points
out that under the permit the Tribe has the use of the 30,000 acres for religious,
water, timber, and grazing uses: "We have, in fact, everything but the *name* of
trust title."[3] It goes on to say that the permit offers even more than would a trust
title because the permit gave them joint conservation responsibility with the
Forest Service, while under the provisions of the trust-title bill the Forest Service would have complete conservation control. It then proposes that the attorneys "drop their activities . . . to obtain the introduction of a bill to give trust
title,"[4] and concentrate instead on winning a favorable judgment before the ICC.
It concludes,

> Of course, we must be prepared, now as always, to continue to struggle for a
> correct interpretation of the permit and to struggle against any effort to
> amend the act of 1933.[5]

In addition to Collier's objections, two other factors contributed to the abandonment of the title quest. One was the issue of Indian voting, and the other was
the local non-Indian opposition. With respect to voting, we have already seen
that the Tribe's advisors linked voting with the title quest. For the title bill to
receive congressional support, the Indians would have to become a politically
significant group through voting. Many in the Tribe, however, remained fearful
of voting, and the effort to encourage it was having severely divisive effects
within the Pueblo. As a result, both Bernal and Martinez made it clear that

> the explosiveness of the voting issue has caused them to accept assurances
> of local white friends that the Forest Service permit is adequate protection
> of their interest in the Blue Lake area . . . .[6]

With respect to local opposition, it flared up once again during the summer of
1963. At his last meeting with the council on June 6th and 7th, La Farge encouraged the Tribe to re-open the quest for trust title, dormant for over a year
because of the local furor raised by the *Accent* television program in 1962. At the
behest of the council, and in perhaps his last act on their behalf, La Farge
drafted another trust-title bill and sent it to New Mexico Congressman Tom

Morris for review. Morris sent the draft to the Department of Agriculture for comment and Agriculture sent it to the Forest Service in Washington, which in turn sent it to George Proctor, who then made it public in Taos. Proctor's revelation touched off another wave of "fierce" local opposition. The editor of the *Taos News* noted that when they broke the story,

> both sides fell to with a will, and the feathers flew for about three weeks. When everybody had had their say, the issue was dead. Undoubtedly, the Indian's land request will come up again from time to time, and local reaction will remain the same.[7]

By July of 1963, Collier's influence, the voting controversy, and local furor caused the Tribe to postpone, if not entirely to abandon, the quest for title, and concentrate instead on protecting their rights under the 1940 permit. As Corinne Locker told Schifter of a meeting she had with Martinez and Bernal:

> In the ensuing discussion, it became clear that the Indians were still thinking principally in terms of relying on the use-permit, and on the Association to protect it for them. They asked twice that we give priority to working out a strategy to counter any attempt to modify the application of the use-permit. At no time did they suggest that we work on ways to obtain title, speaking of it always as a vague future goal.[8]

It is significant that from this time forward Locker essentially assumed La Farge's role with the Tribe. She was well prepared for the job, having worked as his part-time secretary for nearly fifteen years. At the time of La Farge's death, she remembers, she had little interest in the matter. But when Bernal and a tribal delegation asked her to help them with the issue, she agreed and her interest began to grow.

> I began to wear the hat . . .and when you're working on something you tend to magnify its importance and it began to take on much greater significance after I started working on it.[9]

In the summer of 1963, Locker began to write to the officers of AAIA in New York and to the claims attorneys in Washington, keeping them informed of local developments within the Tribe as well as in the town of Taos. Further, she now worked with officials in the Tribe, especially Bernal, in the development of policy and strategy.

Like La Farge, she was committed to the idea of trust title, and during the several months after his death she invested a great deal of effort in urging the Tribe to reverse its abandonment of that objective. For example, in the fall of 1963 she wrote to Schifter to say she believed that the Tribe had been misinformed as to the desirability of title, and thought it AAIA's responsibility to "attempt to convey to them directly—as well as to their misguided friends—the reasons why acquisition of title to the area is desirable."[10] Two months later, with the Tribe still unconvinced, she wrote to Schifter again, telling him that they should contact the Tribe once more with assurances of AAIA's continued support, and "to dispel the impression they have been given that the use-permit is as good as title."[11] Two weeks after this, she reported to Schifter that she had met with Martinez and Bernal and attempted

> to disentangle their thinking about the value of the use-permit as against title, which, as you know, had been thoroughly confused by their reaction to the voting issue.[12]

Locker had in Schifter a strong ally in the effort to persuade the Tribe to re-open the title quest. In his view, with the permit

> the Pueblo is the beneficiary of an act of grace of the United States. Such rights as it now has in the Blue Lake area may be terminated by Congress at will. The Pueblo is not protected by the Constitution of the United States. The rights which would vest in the Pueblo under our proposed law, by contrast, would be fully protected by the Fifth Amendment.[13]

He also noted that several conditions and contingencies were attached to renewal of the permit at the end of its fifty-year duration, and pointed out that the present agreement had done nothing to prevent conflicts between the Tribe and the Forest Service. He believed it was in the Indians' best interest to seek title: "There is no doubt that the rights which the Pueblo would derive if our bill were enacted into law would be far greater and more secure."[14] However, in the fall of 1963, he agreed with the Indians that the initiative should be deferred at least until local opposition "simmered down" and the ICC reached a decision.

Locker, however, refused to let the matter rest. She favored pressing for title immediately, since it put the Tribe on the offensive. However, she perceived two problems that would need to be solved if the original plan to get title were to be revived.

> One was to convey to the Indians the insecurity of their right in the Blue Lake area, and the other to persuade them of the necessity that they take action themselves.[15]

Her strategy with respect to the first problem was to collect information about the tourist boom in New Mexico, hoping that it "would impress upon the tribe the potential threat to its continued exclusive use of the Blue Lake area."[16] Concerning the second problem, she was not optimistic about the Indians' ability to act independently. She told AAIA executive director William Byler that

> even if we succeed in stimulating the Indians into initiating some action on their own, it will be a long time before they are confident enough to follow through a sustained action without the reassurance of personal consultation with V.I.P.'s (to us provincials, you and Mr. Schifter.)[17]

Nevertheless, she sought to provoke the Tribe to an action which she presented in such a way that they would think the idea was their own. In explaining her plan to them, she was careful "to avoid the appearance that it was a well-worked out proposal already discussed and approved by their advisors and presented to them in predigested form."[18]

Locker's idea was to have Taos Pueblo convene a meeting of the New Mexico tribes and invite candidates for political office to address them. In presenting the idea to the Pueblo's leaders, she first emphasized the flimsiness of their protections under the use-permit and then revealed New Mexico's plan for a statewide tourist promotion effort. She told them that this plan was the "real reason" for Proctor's opposition to their obtaining title, and that he would use it to convince the people of New Mexico "that the Pueblo's exclusive use-permit was standing in the way of the economic progress of the whole area."[19] She next presented the Tribe with a "sheaf" of newspaper clippings on the promotion of tourism in New Mexico, and then "went into the importance of action by Indians themselves. . . ."[20] Her strategy was to combine in the minds of the Indians the three issues of recreational development, the weakness of the permit, and the need for political action.

To Locker's surprise, her tactics had an immediate effect. The Tribe began preparations at once to secure the involvement of the All-Pueblo Council in planning for the candidates' forum. While the forum would not deal with the Blue Lake issue directly (except, perhaps, through a question planted in the audience), she considered that this experience of direct participation would favorably improve the Tribe's attitude toward political action, and encourage their further efforts to obtain the sacred watershed. As she explained her thinking about the forum to Schifter,

> Any benefits to Taos' cause would be indirect and incidental, the most important being the effect of the Pueblo's involvement in political action upon its own attitudes.[21]

The meeting was significant not only because it inspired the Indians to once again take political action, but also because it seems to mark Bernal's return to the idea of seeking trust title. For, at a later meeting when the subject came up and Martinez vehemently objected (he had not been present at the first), Locker reports that he and Bernal had a "vigorous discussion." Bernal "lectured Severino [sic] on the threat of recreational developments," and then instructed Locker to write the letters of invitation to the candidates, since the Tribal Council had already approved the idea.

The whole matter is also noteworthy insofar as it reveals Locker's attitude toward the Tribe at this time to have been maternalistic, almost patronizing. She had decided that they ought to seek trust title, and took it upon herself to stimulate them into action. She deliberately sought to steer them away from their desired course of action (protecting their rights under the permit) and towards her own of obtaining title. Since soon after she charged Schifter and AAIA officials with ignoring the Indians' wishes and urging their own agenda, it is well to remark here on her own similar behavior.

In any event, Locker's strategy worked and, reawakened to the possibilities promised by political action, Taos Pueblo became deeply involved in the planning and implementation of the forum. As a result, Locker could report with satisfaction to Schifter that "the Indians are beginning to stir, and I hope it will lead to a more realistic involvement in the Blue Lake struggle."[22]

In addition to the revival of the Tribe's political consciousness, 1964 and 1965 brought other developments which contributed directly to brightening prospects for a new title quest.

For one thing, Bernal began quietly working to increase local sympathy for the Indians' problems in the Blue Lake area. Although in early December of 1963 he "still sounded depressed," and remarked "that things were not the same as they used to be and not good,"[23] he nonetheless discussed with a few local politicians, old acquaintances of his, the need for the Tribe to gain greater control of the watershed. He was quite gratified when they accepted his point of view, since they had previously signed petitions against the title quest. Locker regarded the

> action as an important step for the Indians towards responsible involvement
> and away from complete reliance on outside guidance.[24]

In January of 1964, Locker told Mitchell that there were "many indications of a softer attitude toward the Indians' claim on Blue Lake."[25] She attributed this to Proctor's "overly vigorous" insistence on the Forest Service's point of view, and the "comparatively mild but firm" response by the Pueblo. She felt that the Tribe's restraint had won it friends and greater respect. Bernal agreed "that a change for the better has come in the attitude of local businessmen and a number of residents who have no connection with the Forest Service."[26]

To encourage better town-Tribe relations, the Pueblo in July granted the Acequia Madre del Rio Lucero Ditch Association permission to enter Indian land to make major improvements on their ditch. In addition to local good will, "the Indians obtained from the farmers a verbal commitment not to oppose the Blue Lake claim."[27] The following year the Tribe granted permission to another ditch association, the Acequia Madre del Prado, to enter Indian land to concrete-line their ditch. This, too, created better relations, and the Tribe received a letter from the association praising "the fine spirit of cooperation and friendship existing between the people of the Taos Pueblo and those of El Prado."[28]

Another opportunity to better the Tribe's community standing was offered when local politicians approached them about getting permission to construct a flood control project on Indian land. Immediately aware of the proposal's potential strategic value, the Tribe decided to withhold action on it "as a means of ensuring that those people do not oppose the Blue Lake legislation."[29] In December of 1964, the Tribe signed an agreement giving the town permission to conduct a preconstruction assessment of the Las Cruces Arroyo, the site chosen for the flood dam. All concerned were very appreciative, but the Tribe still withheld approval of actual construction not only because they wanted to first see the blueprints but also because they planned to later make political use of their granting of final approval. The project progressed further when, in the fall of 1965, the Tribe met with the mayor and Taos Town Council and received assur ance of support for the Pueblo's title quest in exchange for an easement to construct the Las Cruces Arroyo dam.

Beneficial also to the title quest was George Proctor's transfer to Arizona in the spring of 1964. He had consistently opposed the Tribe, and had done a great deal to stir up local anti-Indian sentiment. The Pueblo and its advisors felt that anyone who replaced him could not be more inimical.

Things took a turn for the better at the *Taos News*, too. Edited for years by Jim Colgrove, another bitter opponent of the title quest, the *Taos News* had lost no opportunity to oppose the Indians. Mitchell suggested to his friend Marcus Johnson, governor of Nambe Pueblo, that he approach Robert McKinney, publisher of the *Taos News*, to complain about Colgrove and the paper's anti-Indian line. Governor Johnson reported to Mitchell that McKinney's sympathies were with the Tribe, and that "he did not know why his editor would do what he had done and that he did not like it either; that the editor would probably not be there very much longer."[30] McKinney made good his word, transferring Colgrove to Santa Fe and replacing him with Keith Green, who at least was not overtly anti-Indian. In early 1965, a friend of the Tribe could optimistically report to Locker that

> the worst Taos enemies of the Indians have left; the anti-Blue Lake uproar years ago was organized by Jim Colgrove, now editing the Santa Fe *New Mexican* and much repressed, I hear, and George Proctor, transferred by the Forest Service to Arizona. The trouble is that they galvanized the rabid right faction in Taos into a real fervor.[31]

With their "worst enemies" gone, the Tribe had a much easier time encouraging local good will.

Two additional personnel changes proved highly beneficial. One was the hiring of Walter Olson as the new BIA superintendent at the United Pueblos Agency, the office which had responsibility for Taos. Olson was an experienced, dedicated public servant sincerely committed to improving the lot of the Indians. Over the coming years, he proved an intelligent and resourceful supporter of the Blue Lake cause.

Even more important was the retention of Albuquerque attorney Rufus Poole as AAIA southwest associate legal counsel. Born in South Dakota, he was the senior partner in the law firm of Poole & Poole of Albuquerque, where he had lived since 1957. He had served as assistant solicitor in the Interior Department from 1933 to 1937, during the time Collier was commissioner of Indian Affairs. Poole also worked as assistant solicitor in the Labor Department, and became their principal draftsman and administrative spokesman for significant federal legislation. Here he gained skills which he put to good use in the Blue Lake fight. In addition, Poole had for many years served as secretary of AAIA, and in that capacity worked with La Farge on behalf of the tribes. After not having been involved in Indian problems for several years, he was excited about his new posi-

William Byler, Executive Director of AAIA, who saw clearly that the Tribe's only hope for victory lay in stressing religious freedom as the heart of their claim. C. 1966, photo by Dan Budnik.

tion as AAIA counsel. His hiring by AAIA resulted from recruiting efforts by Locker. Poole's widow Suzie recalls:

> I know he came home one day and said, 'I'm sick unto death of corporate law. This isn't why I became a lawyer. I want to do something in the public sector. . . ' This was just a few weeks before you [speaking to Locker] came into his office to ask him to help.[32]

The Pueblo was extremely fortunate that Poole wanted out of corporate law. His legal knowledge, legislative experience, and understanding of America's native peoples contributed greatly to the success of the Blue Lake battle.

With things looking more and more favorable, the Tribal Council decided that the time had come to think once again about reviving the title quest. The council met in September of 1964, with Locker and AAIA executive director William Byler as special guests. Thinking that the ICC would soon hand down their decision, Byler agreed with the Tribe that it was time to start planning a campaign to "get" Blue Lake. He felt the key to the success of the campaign was to enlist the support of groups both within and without New Mexico. Two groups he saw as especially important:

One group consists of the churches, because of the religious significance of Blue Lake. Most congressmen do not understand about the religious meaning. If their own religious leaders support Taos Pueblo, then the congressmen are more likely to listen. The second group are the organizations interested in conservation, and in national and state forests.[33]

The council authorized AAIA to begin making contact with these groups, and quietly soliciting support for the renewed title quest.

Byler also suggested that the Pueblo begin thinking about producing a small pamphlet setting forth their claim to the sacred area. To this the Tribe agreed also. It was decided to withhold publication of the pamphlet until a new title bill had actually been introduced, since Collier pointed out that only then would people actually be able to do something. Nevertheless, the Tribe retained Phillip Reno to develop the brochure, asking him to stress the issues of the legality of the Tribe's claim, continued protection of the watershed, and religious need. Beautifully written and illustrated, the first of the "expensive-looking" brochures came off the press late in 1965.

With regard to soliciting the support of church groups, just before he went to New Mexico to meet the council Byler contacted Russell Carter, the executive secretary of the Board of Home Missions at the National Council of Churches, to find out if they would favor helping the Tribe. He told Locker that "the prospect looks good, including perhaps National Council testimony at hearings on the Blue Lake legislation."[34] Byler had now set in motion a force that was to prove crucial in the coming conflict.

In 1964 and 1965, while these positive developments were unfolding, some new problems arose as well. Perhaps the most serious was a growing estrangement between Locker and the various attorneys working on behalf of the Tribe. During this period of time, eight different attorneys counseled the Pueblo. Dudley Cornell and Mark Clayburgh were the Tribe's general counsel, and Darwin Kingsley and Frank Karelsen were in charge of the ICC case. They, in turn, hired Taos attorney Steven Mitchell as local community liaison. Richard Schifter and Alan Wurzel were attorneys on retainer to AAIA who worked on various legal matters pertaining to its involvements. Schifter was also consulting attorney for the Joint Efforts Group and in that capacity, as well as in his advisory role to AAIA, provided counsel on the ICC claim. Finally, Rufus Poole served AAIA as their legal consultant for matters related to the Southwest.

When La Farge was alive, he had functioned as the attorneys' nexus, keeping all of them informed as to what the others were doing. With his death, the conduction of information deteriorated, bringing with it problems in communication that were to plague the title quest. In addition, Locker had a serious personality conflict with Mitchell, and Bernal, too, disliked the Taos attorney. Matters came to a head when Locker discovered that Mitchell was trying to put together a deal to construct expensive houses on Indian land under ninety-nine-year leases. Saying she did not like the deal "one sleazy bit," Locker said of Mitchell,

"The man continues to be obnoxious, interested only in asserting his views and obtaining his ends."[35] She also complained that Mitchell worked only with Schifter and Kingsley, failing to keep AAIA informed of his activities. The Locker-Bernal-Mitchell conflict took its toll on the overall legislative battle.

Schifter, too, came in for Locker's disapprobation. She was becoming increasingly uneasy about his advice, and it was increasing problems with the claims attorneys that had occasioned her recruiting visit to Poole's office. Late in 1964, she accused Schifter of placing his own interests above those of AAIA and its clients. His stock with Locker further declined when she learned that he had been consulting with Mitchell on the land-lease deal. From that time forward, Locker became more and more suspicious of and hostile toward Schifter. That attitude later triggered an explosive confrontation which resulted in the total disruption of the Blue Lake campaign.

Another serious difficulty obstructing the title quest was the issue of Indian voting. It had been a factor in causing the Tribe to abandon the title quest in 1963, and it continued to be a divisive problem over the next two years, when Martinez and Bernal once again locked horns over the issue.

Bernal favored the position of La Farge and Schifter, that the Indians needed to vote in order for the Blue Lake legislation to be taken seriously. Martinez feared voting and saw it as unnecessary. His son remembers why:

> His rationale was, how in the heck are we going to pay taxes when we don't have a money economy. . . .Why do you want to be like the white man. Right now, nobody is tearing your piece of bread, whatever you have, in half. When you become involved in the white man's game, that's what's going to happen. They're going to tax you . . . .That was his major reason for not wanting the people to vote.[36]

The conflict between Bernal and Martinez became so serious that for a time in 1963 it caused a "complete break"[37] between them. It also divided the Tribal Council into pro-Martinez and pro-Bernal factions. In early 1964, while it appeared that the pro-vote Bernal faction was gaining ground, the issue remained unresolved. Further, the very existence of the controversy weakened the title initiative.

Problems also were posed during this time by the continuing conflicts with the Forest Service. The most critical of these centered on the old issue of visitor permits. In 1964, the Tribe again declined to sign visitor permits. In January of 1965, Taos district ranger A.L. Foster wrote the Pueblo governor to complain that, "many people, knowing that they could not get a permit, went anyway."[38] The situation got out of control, and Foster wanted to avoid a recurrence of the problem by establishing a system of issuing permits.

In early February, Foster met with the Tribal Council and told them he wanted to revise the permit policy. He proposed issuing permits only for visitors going to Blue Lake itself, but not for those who would be in other sections of the special-use area. He also wanted to issue permits for trail riders entering from Red

River. In addition, Foster, ignorant of the conflict in the early sixties over the request that the Tribe have a valid reason for not signing a permit, suggested that "the new application would require that a reason be stated for not issuing a permit."[39] He further affronted the Tribe by informing them that he planned to send applications to the war chief and, if they were not returned signed in five days, he would issue a permit without tribal concurrence.

Schifter advised the Tribe that these proposals departed significantly from the protections afforded them by the 1940 use-permit, and the Tribe politely but firmly then told Foster his proposals were unacceptable. This firm stance taken by the Tribe left permitting procedures unchanged.

Another problem arose when rangers in the Blue Lake area observed tribal members fishing. Since the lake had been closed to all fishing at the request of the Tribe, the Forest Service legitimately felt that the Indians ought to be the first to comply. Unfortunately for Tribe-Forest Service relations, Foster made his protest in rude and dictatorial language, writing the Tribe a condescending letter which threatened to reinstitute fishing privileges for visitors if Indian fishing continued.

In their temperate reply, the Tribe said that if violations were in fact occurring, "it does not follow that the regulation should be changed but that steps should be taken to correct the violations."[40] The Tribe thanked Foster for bringing this "serious matter" to their attention, and promised to take action to prevent its recurrence. Nevertheless, further damage had been done to Tribe-Forest Service relations by the tone of Foster's letters.

In the long run, Foster's arrogant, insensitive approach strengthened the title quest. It made the Tribe realize the validity of what Schifter had told them in 1963: that their rights under the 1940 permit were by the "grace" of the government, subject, at best, to bureaucratic interpretation, and, at worst, to complete revocation. The only effective means of protecting their rights was through trust title. As the Tribe told Superintendent Olson:

> Until our title to the Blue Lake Area has been confirmed by the United States Congress there will never be a satisfactory working condition between the Forest Service and the Taos Pueblo; the Pueblo considers this Area as its own sacred land.[41]

Their resolve was further firmed when, in early 1965, both John Collier and Seferino Martinez dropped opposition to the title quest. Now united in their desire to get trust title, the Pueblo and its advisors were prepared to launch a full-scale legislative campaign. The only obstacle now was the ICC. The Tribe, its attorneys, and AAIA all agreed that the campaign's chances for success would be vastly increased if the ICC decided for the Tribe.

Filed in the summer of 1951, the Pueblo's ICC claim had now been under adjudication for fourteen years. The interminable delay was due partly to the fact that the Taos claim had been one of the last of the Indian claims filed, and there-

The Tribe's sacred mountains, in all their winter grandeur, overlook the village and the Rio Pueblo, which flows serenely between the North and South Houses. Photo by Dan Budnik, c. 1970.

fore was given a low priority. Other factors were the complexities of Indian law, the confusing nature of the case, and the usual dilatoriness of government.

Prior to 1946, an Indian tribe could sue the government over land it felt had been illegally or wrongfully taken only if the government consented to such a suit. The wealthier tribes, able to afford litigation, filed such suits and had their day in court, but the poorer tribes lacked the money necessary to initiate legal action. Congress passed the Indian Claims Commission act in 1946 to remedy this situation. To lay to rest centuries of Indian grievances, the ICC Act waived the statute of limitations from 1946 to 1951, during this period according tribes the right to "file claims based on Government misdeeds ever since the beginning of the Republic."[42]

Many tribes, including Taos, did so file. The act of 1946 had established the Indian Claims Commission as a special judicial tribunal to hear their cases. The function of the ICC was to hear the tribes' claims for land lost, determine government liability, and then fix the amount of damages to be paid. Reparations were exclusively monetary; returning the land in dispute was not considered. One of the major difficulties posed by the Taos case, as we have seen, was their refusal to accept money for the sacred watershed. Dollars, they emphatically maintained, could never compensate them for the loss of the sacred area. They insisted on its reconveyance.

By 1965, the Taos claim had passed through several stages. The Claims Commission held hearings on the Taos case in each of the years from 1953 to 1956. The central aim of the Tribe's attorneys in these hearings was to establish "original Indian title"; that is, to prove that the Taos people had continually used and occupied the area they claimed even though they did not have a "paper" title. Such use, in the Taos case, had to be shown as far back as 1848, the date of the signing of the Treaty of Guadalupe Hidalgo by which the Mexican government ceded to the United States the New Mexico Territory.

To make their case, the Pueblo called to the witness stand the oldest members of the Tribe. Tribal elders such as John Concha, Seferino Martinez, Julian Lujan, Antonio Mirabal, Hilario Reyna, Manuel Cordova, and Cesario Romero testified to their own continual usage of the area claimed throughout their lifetimes. They also testified that this was true of their fathers and grandfathers, as well. The government commissioners dutifully recorded this information, and then returned to Washington to obtain from the Department of Justice its defense against the Taos action. However, Justice, beleaguered with several other cases filed before that of Taos, did nothing. The Taos claim lay dormant.

During the latter years of the Eisenhower administration, the Pueblo's attorneys tried to move the case along by initiating settlement discussions with Justice. They sought to work out a deal similar to the Tribe's old offer to the Pueblo Lands Board. The Pueblo proposed waiving all potential monetary compensation due it in exchange for the return of the sacred watershed. The Attorney General's Office had little sympathy for the idea of returning land to Indians, and refused to cooperate. When Kennedy became president, the claims attorneys approached Assistant Attorney General Ramsey Clark with the same offer, but were unable to get his cooperation either.

Frustrated in their dealings with Justice, the claims counsel pressed the ICC for a trial date, which finally was scheduled for November of 1961. In preparing for the trial, the attorneys still focused on proving continual use and occupancy. To corroborate the evidence provided by the tribal elders at the hearings in the mid-fifties, the attorneys decided that they needed a highly qualified "expert witness," either an anthropologist or an ethnologist familiar with southwestern Indian culture. The expert's job would be to relate the testimony of the tribal elders as to the land use from 1890 to 1920 "to the occupancy of the land in 1848, the crucial year, in which the United States assumed responsibility for the Indians of New Mexico."[43] They also needed to put the elders' testimony into proper anthropological form.

The claims attorneys had been given the name of Florence Hawley Ellis, a distinguished anthropologist from the University of New Mexico, and they consulted La Farge. He replied that

> Dr. Ellis has been actively engaged in the study of the Pueblos for many years, she is most sympathetic to them, and knows as much about them as anyone in the field, if not more.[44]

The anthropologist Florence Hawley Ellis, whose testimony before the Indian Claims Commission was instrumental in convincing them of the authenticity of the Tribe's claim to aboriginal title. 1989 photo courtesy of the author.

When La Farge approached Ellis about helping, he discovered that she already knew a great deal about the case, having been present at the Santa Fe courthouse to hear the ICC testimony of the Taos elders.[45] She unhesitatingly agreed to assist the Tribe and set about putting the existing testimony in order. In addition, she met with the Tribal Council and the elders present confirmed and clarified for her the testimony taken in the fifties. She also proposed proving the antiquity of the Tribe's land-use by doing a limited excavation of a midden, or ash-pile, near the Pueblo.

Her proposal led to an archaeological dig that has become famous in professional circles. The Taos elders, wary of anthropologists and archaeologists, had never before given permission for any sort of excavation on their land. Now, realizing the potential value of such work to their claim, they reluctantly agreed to allow Ellis to do a dig in their oldest midden, or refuse pile. However, they made one condition: she was granted only one day, from sunrise to sunset. Those who supported her work worried that tribal members who were opposed would disturb her dig at night. They advised her to "be very careful, go out there first thing in the morning that you can see any light and dig until it's dark . . . ."[46]

The actual labor was done by Ellis' confederate, J.J. Brody. Ellis recounts how he became involved:

> I was called to Washington and couldn't be in Taos on the appointed day. I was at my wit's end about how we were going to do this. Brody had the

New Mexico State Historian Myra Ellen Jenkins, an influential expert witness before the Indian Claims Commission and in the Senate Subcommittee Hearings. 1989 photo courtesy of the author.

> semester off, and he had been working on some Taos early sites . . . . He was staying up there in the Taos area and I called him that night and asked if he would go ahead and do this and I would do the classification of the pottery. . . . Brody said he would drop his other work and do the work on that and would be there at dawn until moonlight . . . .[47]

As promised, Brody arrived long before daybreak and worked feverishly, without pause, until the light waned. Relying on the artifactual evidence gathered by Brody, Ellis was able to show that the Indians had occupied the site since at least A.D. 1300.

In addition to Ellis, Dr. Myra Ellen Jenkins, head of the records division at the New Mexico State Archives, provided expert testimony. Professionally trained as a historian, Dr. Jenkins specialized in the study of New Mexico. Fluent in Spanish, she strengthened the Pueblo's case by casting light on the land policies of the Spanish colonial government. She also provided important information relative to land-use patterns during Spanish and Mexican sovereignty, and their effect on the indigenous population.

Unfortunately, other commitments made it impossible for Ellis to testify in November, and the trial was postponed until 1962. At that time, the Tribe's attorneys, expert witnesses, and the Department of Justice presented their cases to the members of the Indian Claims Commission. The next step was for both sides to file formal briefs. This the Pueblo did in November of 1963, and the government shortly thereafter. The last stage of the tortuous legal battle took place on June 29, 1964, when both parties to the suit presented oral arguments. After thirteen years of delay and legal wrangling, the fate of the Blue Lake area was now in the hands of the commission. Fifteen months of deliberation ensued. Finally, on September 8, 1965, the ICC handed down their long-awaited decision.

To understand the ICC decision, it is important to grasp the nature of the Pueblo's claim as presented by Kingsley and Schifter in the "Petitioner's Findings of Fact and Brief." A complex ninety-two-page document, the "Findings of Fact" set forth in detail the basis of the Tribe's claim. It covered two distinct land areas.

One section of the brief concerned land lost by the Tribe in the town of Taos, land which was part of the area patented to them in the nineteenth century and for which they held recognized title. It was to this area that the Tribe had waived its claim in exchange for the return of Blue Lake in the Pueblo Lands Board double-cross. It was this area that the Senate investigating committee of the early thirties determined was worth $297,000 and for which, under the "Pueblo Relief Bill" of 1933, the Tribe received the fifty-year use-permit instead of money.

The other section of the brief covered some 300,000 acres which the Tribe claimed on the basis of aboriginal use and occupancy. It included the 50,000 acres of the sacred watershed. A prior ICC decision in the Cochiti Pueblo case whittled down the area eligible for adjudication to 130,000 acres. All of this area had been included in the executive order which brought Blue Lake into the Carson National Forest in 1906.

The Pueblo's brief embodied two approaches. One was a presentation of relevant government documents that in any way recognized the Tribe's continued exclusive use of the area "since time immemorial." These documents were drawn from the periods of Spanish and Mexican control, as well as from the time of United States sovereignty. Concerning them, the Pueblo's brief said:

> Perhaps the most convincing evidence supporting the Pueblo's claim is the documentary material taken from Government files. Here we find repeated statements of Government officials that the Pueblo of Taos has used the claimed lands since time immemorial. . . .What these documents prove is that the Pueblo Indians had been left undisturbed in their use of their aboriginal hunting, grazing and gathering lands until the first decade of this century.[48]

The second approach centered on the testimony of tribal elders as to their historic and continuing use of the area. It provided evidence that the Tribe had used the claimed area for many purposes, including hunting, fishing, food and medicine gathering, woodcutting, and grazing.

Evidence of these more mundane uses was important in demonstrating the Pueblo's claim. Even more important, however, was the elders' testimony that the Tribe used sites throughout the area for ceremonial purposes, and had a deep and abiding religious attachment to the land. As the brief said:

> The native religion of Taos is to this day very much involved with the daily life of the people. This religion does now and has for centuries tied them closely to the land . . . .This attachment to the land . . .is symbolized by

shrines at which the Taos people worship. These shrines are visited almost daily. . . .Where the location of a shrine has passed into non-Indian owner-ship, Taos men still visit it for ceremonial purposes.[49]

The brief went on to stress that in the Taos religion specific ceremonials must be performed at specific sites at specific times. These practices had been carried on for hundreds of years, and neither the ritual nor its site could be changed. The claims counsel introduced into evidence a detailed listing and map of these sacred sites, along with a description of their roles in the Pueblo religion. These included shrines at various lakes, hunting shrines, food gathering shrines, shrines at springs, and shrines associated with keeping the solar calendar. Blue Lake was identified as the holiest of these native shrines and the focal point of tribal worship.

The brief concluded that government records and the testimony provided by Drs. Ellis and Jenkins, as well as that of the tribal elders, proved beyond doubt that the Taos Indians had enjoyed undisputed and uninterrupted possession of the claimed area down to 1906; and were therefore entitled to it under the prin-ciple of aboriginal use and occupancy. In conclusion, the brief made clear to the ICC that the Tribe did not want a cash award in case of a favorable judgment. They wanted the land itself.

> The Pueblo of Taos is aware that under the Indian Claims Commission Act this Commission can render only money judgments in favor of petitioners. However, the Pueblo does not wish to obtain a money judgment on claimed lands which are now contained in the Carson National Forest and which include the sacred Blue Lake. It is the Pueblo's hope that on the basis of the Commission's interlocutory decision on the issue of Indian title, Congress will convey the land to the Pueblo.[50]

The government attorneys contending against the Pueblo's claim on behalf of the United States used two main arguments. The first was a matter of law. They maintained that when the Tribe received from the Spanish its one square league of land, it lost thereby any right to claim acreage which they were using but which lay outside of the league's boundaries. The second was a matter of fact. Relying on information provided chiefly by Dr. Harold H. Dunham, a profes-sional historian with expertise in the area of Spanish and Mexican land policies, the defense attorneys tried by various methods to prove that the area claimed by the Indians had not been used by them exclusively. When the claims commis-sioners handed down their decision, it was clear that they had completely rejected these arguments and found wholly in favor of the Tribe. Schifter and Kingsley had won a "sweeping victory."

With regard to that part of the claim which concerned the land in the town of Taos, the commission determined that the use-permit granted the Tribe in 1933 was not equal in value to the $297,000 owed the Tribe for the land taken. To rectify this imbalance, the commissioners awarded the Pueblo $297,000 minus the value of the use-permit.

With regard to the 130,000-acre claim, the commission held that the Tribe successfully established Indian title through three sorts of evidence. The first, of course, was the testimony of the tribal elders. The commission was impressed with the fact that the exact boundaries of the claimed area were quite clearly defined in the minds of "the elderly Indians," and that each one agreed that the area

> was in the possession of and used exclusively during his lifetime for beneficial purposes by the Taos Indians, and that it was a tribal tradition that the area had been so used by his ancestors from time immemorial.[51]

Crucial to the ICC's acceptance of the testimony by the tribal elders was Florence Hawley Ellis' explanation of the difference between Pueblo culture and the culture of nomadic Indians. She distinguished between the Taos Indians' relation to their land, similar to that of a modern agricultural society, and that of nomadic Indians who had no fixed place of residence. She demonstrated that, while the 7,000-foot elevation of Taos made it necessary for the Tribe to rely more than the southern Pueblos on hunting and gathering than on agriculture, nonetheless Taos conformed to the typical Pueblo pattern, with a central village surrounded by well-tended agricultural plots. The ICC ruling agreed that as a sedentary, agricultural people

> the attitude of the Indians toward the land they considered their own would undoubtedly be very similar to that of the white settlers toward their villages, homes and supporting farm lands.[52]

The commissioners felt that land traditions in such a community would have a "higher probative value" than would those of nomadic Indians, and cited this as one of the reasons they ruled in favor of Taos, when in many other cases they found "informant testimony" unpersuasive. Because the testimony of the Taos elders was rooted in "well founded traditions," the commissioners held "that considerable weight should be given to the Indian witnesses."[53]

The second kind of evidence the commissioners found compelling was that provided by Ellis and Jenkins, the Tribe's expert witnesses. Dunham, the witness for the government, vigorously asserted that by 1848 the Spanish outnumbered the Indians six to one in the Taos area. He reasoned that this numerical imbalance made it impossible for the Tribe to have had exclusive use of the area claimed.

Thoroughly familiar with New Mexico land-use patterns, both Ellis and Jenkins pointed out that while the Indians did use their low-lying agricultural lands, they relied heavily on the extensive adjacent mountainous areas for subsistence, too. By contrast, the Spanish confined themselves to bottom land, leaving the mountains to the Indians. The commission threw out Dunham's "population ratio" argument on the grounds that

Corinne Locker and Paul Bernal at the Museum of Natural History in New York, 1966. Many others gave of their time and effort in the Blue Lake fight. Locker and Bernal dedicated their lives. Photo by Dan Budnik.

comparative population figures can suggest the relative rights in land only if the groups compared have similar modes of living and thus similar patterns of land use.[54]

Since the Spanish and Indians had very different living/subsistence patterns, the commissioners held that "no sound conclusions can be derived from population figures alone."[55]

Dunham also tried to discredit the testimony provided by Ellis concerning the antiquity of the Indians' habitation of Taos. The commissioners, however, felt that Ellis's testimony was extremely valuable in questions of Indian title and that it should be given

> considerable weight because of her archaeological work in the field which furnished strong evidence of the presence of Taos Indian villages and activities in the claimed area, continuously or for a long time prior to and including 1848 when United States sovereignty came into being in the area.[56]

Noting that Jenkins's testimony wholly supported Ellis's, the commissioners found the Pueblo's expert witnesses entirely persuasive; and dismissed Dunham's arguments, saying that his work dealt with matters previously ruled on or irrelevant to the question of Indian title.

Also persuasive to the commissioners was the third kind of evidence provided by Taos, government documentation. They held that in this documentation

> we find repeated statements of Government officials that the Pueblo of Taos has used the claimed land since time immemorial. These statements were made by men who were in the area and who were thoroughly familiar with the facts.[57]

The commissioners concluded that the government documents demonstrated that the Taos Indians had exclusive use of the land claimed until 1906, when the forest reserves were created.

The Taos victory was complete. Dismissing the government's arguments, the commissioners ruled that the Tribe had conclusively made their case through testimony of the elders, through expert witnesses, and through evidence drawn from government documentation. The Tribe now finally had the favorable interlocutory judgment they had long been seeking. Flush with this vindication, they prepared once again to approach the New Mexico delegation to develop a bill which would convey to them trust title to the 50,000 acres of the sacred watershed.

By late 1965, the Tribe not only had the ICC victory to show for their efforts. They had also matured politically in the process. At the time of La Farge's death, Locker had little faith in the Tribe's political ability. She felt they had a "complete reliance on outside guidance," that they lacked confidence and were dependent on the "reassurance of personal consultation" with outsiders. She was concerned about their ability to develop political self-reliance, but she was to revise this opinion.

John J. Reyna (left) and Paul Bernal. By the time of the ICC decision, Bernal had become the Tribe's powerful leader in the fight to reclaim Blue Lake. 1970. Photo by Dan Budnik.

During the two years between the death of La Farge and the ICC decision, Locker and Bernal formed a strong bond and developed a good working relationship. It became obvious to her that Bernal had matured into a true leader, the kind of man who could effectively guide the Tribe in a difficult political fight. Not only did he work well with non-Indians, but he also had the requisite political influence within the Tribe. As the Tribal Council secretary and interpreter, he guided the flow of council meetings, and this position gave him a great deal of control over the direction of tribal politics. In 1963, Locker had hoped that the Indians would "take action themselves." In 1965, with Bernal now firmly in command of the tribal quest, Locker felt the Indians were really prepared to do so.

5

The First Hearing

SOON AFTER THE ICC DECISION, Schifter, Karelsen, Byler, and Locker traveled to Taos to confer with the Tribal council about plans for the Blue Lake legislative campaign. At the meeting, the council and its advisors decided that the Pueblo would focus its efforts on developing local support for the Blue Lake bill among business, religious, and civic leaders; that AAIA would concentrate on building a reserve of support among national religious and conservation groups; and that the attorneys would work to further the legislative campaign in Washington. All concerned breathed a sigh of relief when December 8, 1965 passed without challenge to the ICC decision: it was the last day on which the government could do so. The Pueblo's victory before the ICC was now official. The campaign to regain possession of the sacred watershed could begin in earnest.

The Tribe and its attorneys immediately set to work developing a bill for the next legislative session. The most significant problem they had to face was the issue of watershed conservation. Since it had a direct impact on the many non-Indians downstream, it had the potential to generate disruptive political opposition. Who would be given responsibility for this important function?

Soon after the ICC decision, Don Seaman, the local Carson National Forest supervisor, stated publicly that, in his judgment, the Indians were incapable of handling conservation of the land, and that it should remain under the jurisdiction of his office. He made it clear that the Forest Service would vigorously oppose any move to reduce its authority in this area.

While the Forest Service was unequivocal, the question sharply divided the Pueblo's advisors. Schifter, Karelsen, and Mitchell favored a conservation clause

During the 1950s and early 1960s, the Tribe's plea for return of their sacred land was little understood by a culture which seemed to worship the dollar. Public sympathy began to increase after 1965. Drawing by Chuck Asay. Courtesy of Tony Reyna.

which gave virtually complete control to the Forest Service. They believed that getting the bill passed would be difficult to achieve, and that leaving conservation authority with the Forest Service would reduce the force of their opposition. Locker and Poole, however, agreeing with the Pueblo that the Forest Service would oppose the bill in any case, saw no reason to compromise on the issue. They doubted that the Tribe and the Forest Service could develop a satisfactory working relationship, and were concerned that the Schifter-Karelsen-Mitchell clause would allow the Forest Service to ignore the Indians and do exactly as they pleased. As Poole put it:

> Based on my experience while in the government, I think it would be unwise to give the National Forest Service responsibility for "the protection, conservation and utilization of the watershed, forestry and grazing resources" of this land. It was generally conceded that the Forest Service had the most uncompromising and bureaucratic minded staffs in the government. Their attitude over national forests is more possessive than that of a private property owner.[1]

Poole and Locker, therefore, argued for a conservation clause which would say simply that the Forest Service would "assist" the Tribe with conservation.

This dissension was important not only because of the substantive issue involved, but also because it deepened the rift between Schifter, Karelsen, and Mitchell on the one hand, and Poole and Locker on the other. Locker was especially incensed at the way Karelsen handled the matter at a Tribal Council meeting in early 1966. She accused him, for his own selfish reasons, of giving the council the impression that she and AAIA backed the Forest Service conservation clause.

> It was a slimy business, since he knew that I felt we should try for the additional wording, but that I could not very well raise the issue at that point without upsetting and confusing the Council.
>
> It seems apparent that one of the reasons the attorneys do not want to go all hog is the danger of delaying Anderson's approval in the process of convincing him of the merits of any changes in the original draft, because the claims contract runs out in August and they want to avoid renegotiation. At least this will give them reason to push as hard as possible for the bill's passage, but Ugh![2]

While Schifter and Karelsen did finally concede, and drafted language acceptable to the Tribe, the fact that they both served not only as claims counsel for the Pueblo but also as directors of AAIA further complicated a touchy situation. The disagreement left Locker with a growing suspicion that there was a conflict of interest between the Washington attorneys' dual role as AAIA directors and the Pueblo's claims counsel.[3] For the time being, however, the Tribe's advisors set aside their differences and agreed on a conservation clause which gave the Pueblo "exclusive use and benefit" of the watershed, while providing that "the secretary of Agriculture shall supervise the establishment and maintenance of conservation measures for these lands."[4]

With the conservation matter settled, the Tribal Council unanimously approved the draft of the trust-title bill. Mitchell then sent it to Anderson on February 1, 1966 with a request that he review it, and, if he found it acceptable, introduce the bill in the Senate. In his transmission letter, Mitchell told Anderson,

> I advised the Governor and members of the Council of the Taos Pueblo of your receptive attitude and cooperation on the Blue Lake matter. They are deeply appreciative as I am.[5]

These words of Mitchell clearly show that both he and the Tribe considered Anderson friendly to the bill and interested in finding "a solution of this delicate matter which has troubled so many people for so many years."[6] As requested, on March 15, 1966, Anderson introduced the Pueblo's bill as S. 3085.

In the meantime, there were other favorable developments for the Tribe's cause. One of the most important locally was the changed tone of the *Taos News* under the new editorship of Keith Green. Convinced by the ICC decision of the validity of the Tribe's claim, he believed it would be simple decency on the part of the government to honor its promises. In an early January editorial reviewing the events of 1965, he identified the Pueblo's success before the ICC as one of the "plus marks" for the previous year, and praised the Tribe for making "a new and conscious move toward cooperation with the Town of Taos and other government agencies."[7]

A good example of the results of this cooperation was the further progress now achieved on the matter of the Las Cruces Arroyo flood dam. In February, the Tribal Council voted to approve the flood dam easement, but to withhold their signature on the agreement until the Taos Town Council endorsed the Blue Lake bill. Two months later the Town Council did so, and the *Taos News* observed that the endorsement "demonstrated to the Indian community the willingness of a new mayor and council to cooperate with the Indians for the benefit of all the people of Taos Valley."[8]

Another manifestation of the new climate of cooperation was the Tribe's friendly relations with the Acequia Madre del Prado ditch association. The previous year the Tribe had given them permission to enter Indian land to concrete-line their ditch. The association now returned the favor, sending Anderson a telegram in April asking him to support S. 3085. At about the same time, the Acequia Madre del Rio Lucero ditch association did likewise. They too had recently been given permission to do ditch work on Indian land, and now repaid the Tribe by sending Anderson a resolution endorsing S. 3085, although qualified by a clause that baldly made their support contingent upon Pueblo approval of the flood-dam easement.

The Tribe got further local backing when the five supervisors of the Taos Soil Conservation District not only voted unanimously to support the Indians' title bid, but also elected Taos Pueblo governor John Reyna as a public member of their board. Since the supervisors' district had overall responsibility for the Carson National Forest, including Blue Lake, this endorsement was especially significant in view of the opposition to the bill raised by others on conservation grounds. Because of these positive local developments, Mitchell could write to Congressman Tom Morris that,

> Friendly and effective working arrangements between the Pueblo and the remainder of the Taos community are producing good results and the sharp rivalries and criticisms of the past have been reduced considerably.[9]

Other Indians sympathetic to Taos Pueblo's cause also backed S. 3085, stressing religious freedom as the primary issue at stake. The New Mexico Commission on Indian Affairs passed a resolution which supported S. 3085 on the grounds that Taos Pueblo had used the area for purposes of sustenance and religion since "time immemorial," and had had their rights confirmed by the ICC. In addition, the National Congress of American Indians, the most powerful pan-Indian organization in the country, strongly endorsed the Blue Lake bill. Citing the Pueblo's "immemorial" usage of the land and its unjust approbation by the federal government, NCAI, by unanimous resolution, called upon Congress to pass S. 3085 and restore to the Taos Indians their constitutional right to freedom of worship.

With the ICC decision in its favor, the Tribe commenced the campaign for trust title in earnest. In Washington lobbying Congressman Tom Morris for the Blue Lake Bill are (left to right) Geronimo Trujillo, Seferino Martinez, Morris, and Paul Bernal, 1966. Courtesy of Tony F. Martinez.

At this time when the Tribe was receiving positive endorsements, there was opposition, too, the Taos County Commission's being especially vigorous. They denied the validity of the Pueblo's claim, saying that "only recent records, less than 100 years old bear any proof that the Indians used Blue Lake for spirit consultation"[10], and passed a resolution blasting the trust-title bill. The resolution condemned S. 3085 on the grounds that the Indians would be unable properly to conserve the watershed and that their possession would therefore threaten the water rights of downstream users. The commissioners also opposed the bill because, with its passage, Taos stood to lose one-sixth of the tax revenue currently being paid the county by the Forest Service. The strength of the commissioners' opposition increased when they received the support of the local chapter of the Veterans of Foreign Wars.

The cattlemen, too, were up in arms. They felt threatened by the bill's provisions which allowed the Tribe to purchase existing grazing rights in the watershed. They also were concerned about the conservation issue, the tax issue, and the Indians obtaining exclusive use of what had until then been public lands. As Roberto Martinez, secretary of the Capulin Livestock Association, wrote to Anderson:

> If the Indians get it everyone else would be out. I thought we were trying to integrate and get along with each other—no matter what race or color. This looks like segregation to me.[11]

Nor was opposition confined to local opinion. A number of non-Indians throughout New Mexico also objected to the trust-title bill. State Senate majority leader Bill Gallagher spoke for many when he complained that, under the bill, the Indians would be granted privileged use of a part of the public domain. He especially objected in view of the fact that while all state and federal forests were open to Indians, non-Indians did not have the reciprocal right to use Indian land. He insisted that if the watershed were given to the Indians they should at least, like other citizens, pay taxes on the land.

Also damaging to the Pueblo cause was a widely publicized visit paid by their old nemesis, Elliott Barker, to Lt. Gov. Mack Easley. Now secretary of the New Mexico Wildlife and Conservation Association, Barker told Easley that he did not "consider the picture as clear cut as the Indians painted it."[12] Noting that the Tribe already had exclusive use of 30,000 acres, he dismissed the threat posed to Indian religion by outside visitors.

In May 1966, two important endorsements for S. 3085 balanced the opposition of Gallagher and Barker. The first came from Bruce Rolstad, chair of the Christian Social Action Department of the New Mexico Council of Churches. Throughout the spring, the Tribe had been in contact with the NMCC to try to get their support. While the NMCC took no action as a group, Rolstad spoke for many churchmen when he wrote the following to Sen. Henry Jackson, chair of the Senate Committee on Interior and Insular Affairs:

> May I express my concern that Senate Bill 3085 be passed . . . .This bill

restores to the Taos Pueblo their right of ownership to the Blue Lake area, which is, in fact, their church. The heart of the issue is the simple right of the Taos Indians to the same principles of religious freedom as are guaranteed to all Americans.[13]

Even more important support, in the light of New Mexico's overwhelmingly Catholic population, came from James P. Davis, the archbishop of Santa Fe. In an open letter he wrote:

> I am happy and honored to be able to lend my support to the Taos Indian Pueblo and their struggle to regain possession of the Blue Lake area . . . . It is difficult to conceive any argument that can take precedence over the sacred convictions of a people. It is impossible to interpret the American principles of justice and equality in any way that fails to pay due respect to religious convictions. I heartily endorse, support and encourage passage of legislation aimed at returning the Blue Lake area to its rightful owners who in their faith have it in trust from God.[14]

Luis D. Jaramillo, vice-chancellor of the Santa Fe Archdiocese and chaplain of the New Mexico House of Representatives, further strengthened the Pueblo's religious claim:

> As a Christian and an American citizen, I strongly hold that the Federal government has no alternative but to return ownership of the Blue Lake area to the Taos Pueblo. Whatever arguments may be proposed in opposition are in violation of a people's religion.[15]

It is clear that the Pueblo's plea for religious freedom had struck a deeply responsive chord. A torrent of favorable articles would appear nationally when, under a cover letter from Byler, the Tribe gave wide distribution to the publicity booklet they had prepared and printed in 1965.

For strategic reasons, the Tribe had withheld circulation of the booklet until they actually had a bill before Congress. A week after Anderson introduced S. 3085, the Tribe mailed the booklet and a letter from Byler to 100 editors of leading newspapers throughout the country.

Byler's letter was a stroke of publicity genius. It opened, "Can you imagine the public outcry if the Federal Government seized consecrated church ground and turned it into camping sites?,"[16] and continued with a summary of the Tribe's claim to Blue Lake and the ways in which S. 3085 addressed it.

Byler's point about turning shrines into campsites proved editorially irresistible and newspapers across the country used it as a focus in their supporting articles. For example, in one of Bob Considine's "On the Line" columns, syndicated in more than 100 newspapers, he wrote:

> How loud would be the public hue and cry if the Federal Government seized, let's say, the great Protestant Cathedral in Washington, or Temple Emanuel in New York, or one of the California missions of Junipero Serra and turned same into camping sites? Well, we did it to the Taos Pueblo Indians of New Mexico. Fifty thousand acres of their religious sanctuary,

including their sacred Blue Lake, were taken from them in 1906 . . . and we built campsites around the lake.[17]

Considine went on to praise S. 3085, saying it was sixty years overdue and that its passage by Congress would enable Americans to say, without qualification, "that we really do believe in guaranteeing religious freedom to all Americans. Even to the original ones."[18]

Similar "shrines into campsites" pieces appeared in scores of newspapers from New York to Los Angeles. The quest for Blue Lake had become a national issue, and it is evident that it did so because of public response to the plea for religious freedom. Credit for developing this highly successful approach must go largely to Martinez and Byler. It was they who had insisted that the Pueblo's most effective strategy for obtaining trust title would be to focus on religious freedom in their publicity appeal.

In this regard, the booklet prepared by the Tribe also proved crucial. While Byler's letter gave editors a punchy image, the booklet treated the matter in depth and helped the reader to gain a real understanding of the problem. It was remarkably persuasive, and handsomely repaid its printing costs with favorable column inches.

Late in March, the *Taos News* made a most effective use of the booklet. Headlining his editorial "An Opportunity," Green summarized for his readers the contents of the Pueblo's "beautifully designed and printed appeal." While he touched on the booklet's statements regarding water rights, other interests, conservation, the ICC, and legal history, he devoted his attention principally to the question of religious freedom.

> As long as the Federal Government holds title to the area, the right of these American citizens to practice their religion depends upon the sufferance of the government. The fundamental sanctity of their altars is subject to the changing policies of changing administrations. Federal ownership of the Blue Lake area endangers the principles of religious freedom for all Americans. . . . It has been well established that the government, even in the framework of its own findings, has not dealt justly with the Taos Indians. Now the opportunity is at hand to rectify the matter.[19]

The Tribe could not have hoped for stronger support, and there is no question but that their appeal booklet and its summary presentation in the *Taos News* did much to sway local opinion.

As for national impact, even the august *New York Times* took notice. On Sunday, April 24th, 1966, the lead editorial in the *Times* sympathetically reviewed the Tribe's plight and concluded that S. 3085 "deserves prompt enactment."[20]

The Tribe's booklet evidently had impressed the editors of one of the country's most prestigious newspapers. The following day, having earlier sent a reporter to Taos to cover the story, the *Times* published an extensive article headlined "Tribe Fights to Regain Church," centering on the issue of religious liberty. It opened:

With freedom of religion long assured to most citizens, a remote tribe of the nation's first Americans is now urging Congress to apply the full force of the First Amendment to them . . . .The story they told was a familiar one of the white man's seizure of Indian property in violation of solemn treaty. But here in the six-century-old Taos pueblo there was a difference. The white man left the pueblo and its fertile pasture but took away the Indians' "church."[21]

The article quoted an eloquent statement of Pueblo governor John C. Reyna to illuminate the spiritual identity felt by the Tribe with the sacred watershed.

The lake is as blue as turquoise. It is surrounded by evergreens. In the summer there are millions of wild flowers. Springs are all around. We have no buildings there, no steeples. There is nothing the human hand has made. The lake is our church. The mountain is our tabernacle. The evergreen trees are our living saints. They are with us perpetually. We pray to the water, the sun, the clouds, the sky, the deer. Without them we could not exist. They give us food, drink, physical power, knowledge.[22]

Drawing on information in the Pueblo's booklet, the article summarized the Tribe's legal claim to the area as established by the ICC, and emphasized their refusal to accept money for the sacred watershed. Again they quoted Governor Reyna: "Without energy provided by God, we are helpless. We will never accept money for our place of worship."[23]

The feature concluded by stressing the Indians' conviction "that their only assurance of freedom of religion lay in reestablishing title to the land of their shrines,"[24] and explained how S. 3085 would restore to the Pueblo title to the Blue Lake watershed. This and other emotionally provocative and factually balanced articles inspired strong public sympathy for the Pueblo's cause. All that was now needed was to translate sympathy into political pressure.

Tribal officials took an important step in this direction when, in early May of 1966, they visited New York to address the annual meeting of the Association on American Indian Affairs. Governor Reyna, Seferino Martinez, and Bernal represented the Pueblo. Natural objects of media attention because of their braids and colorful native dress, their visibility increased dramatically when Sen. Robert Kennedy greeted them upon their arrival. Dan Budnik, a young photographer, had drawn Kennedy's attention to the Blue Lake quest. Just before the delegation left for New York, Budnik informed Locker that

Senator Robert Kennedy is most interested, not only in Blue Lake, but the numerous other Indian problems that plague the country. I had a long talk with him recently and he is anxious to visit places and talk to people. I gave him the Blue Lake booklet you had given me and asked him to do his best.[25]

Kennedy's support meant a great deal to the Tribe, and they subsequently told him in a letter that his "very strong encouragement and help gives us more hope for success then [sic] we have ever had before."[26]

At the AAIA annual meeting, the tribal representatives delivered an impassioned plea for the return of the sacred watershed. Again, the focus of their

In Pennsylvania Station, New York City, television reporter listens to Senator Robert Kennedy's procla-
mation of support for the return of Blue Lake to the Taos Indians. Left to right, television reporter, Paul
Bernal, Governor Reyna, Mary Lou Payne, Seferino Martinez, Senator Kennedy, behind Kennedy, Bill
Byler. 1966. Photo by Dan Budnik.

argument was religious liberty. They emphasized that "without energy provided by God, we are helpless. Religion is the most important thing in our life." They went on to explain the purpose of their visit.

> We came here to New York City to tell you that the government wants to pay us for the Blue Lake, but we don't want to accept the mighty dollars. We want the land itself, and we would like to go over there and do our worship freely. This is the reason we came here to New York to ask your support. Freedom of worship is the same thing for all, it is for everybody, in all walks of life. You are the people that we are appealing to to give us support. You are the people who are going to contact the Congressmen, and the Senators in Washington to urge them to support this bill—S. 3085.[27]

The impact of the appeal spread far beyond the meeting room when it was carried on the three major television networks and on radio. As a result, thousands of people expressed their sympathy for the Tribe's cause by sending letters of support to their congressional representatives.

One of the most important individuals to hear the Tribe's plea was Interior secretary Stewart Udall. As a guest speaker at the AAIA meeting, he had shared the dais with the Pueblo representatives. AAIA president Alden Stevens had met

Secretary of the Interior Stuart Udall pledges to do all that he can to help the Blue Lake cause. From left, Paul Bernal, Governor Reyna, Udall, and Seferino Martinez. 1966. Photo by Dan Budnik.

with Udall the previous fall in a get-acquainted session which resulted in the invitation to Udall. At that time Stevens had briefly mentioned the Blue Lake quest, and Udall had agreed to meet with the Taos Indians to learn first-hand of its significance for them.

Udall conferred with a tribal delegation in Santa Fe in early April of 1966, just a month before he saw them again in New York. Listening to them describe their yearning for Blue Lake, he was at once sympathetic. By the end of the AAIA meeting, he was an avid supporter of S. 3085. He even agreed to testify personally on behalf of the Tribe when the Senate held hearings on the bill, and his backing was of inestimable value in the coming conflict with the Forest Service and the Department of Agriculture.

While in New York for the AAIA meeting, the tribal delegation received word that the Senate Subcommittee on Indian Affairs had set the hearings on S. 3085 for May 18th, less than two weeks away. During the course of their preparations to testify, they learned from Udall that opponents of S. 3085 were planning to smear it as an economically motivated land grab cloaked in religious garb.

Udall suggested a means of deflecting this argument: amending S. 3085 to bring the 50,000-acre watershed under the protection of the Wilderness Act, which had been passed largely through his efforts two years previously. The Tribe conferred with Schifter who approved the idea. Just before the hearings, he informed the legal branch of the Interior Department of the developing amendment:

> As you may know, Secretary Udall has suggested to the Taos delegation that they consider supporting an amendment which would constitute the acreage covered by the bill a wilderness area. The delegation considered the matter and agreed. . .as long as the present uses of the area by the Pueblo would not be interfered with.[28]

Udall then set to work with his legal staff at Interior to perfect the amendment, which they finished just two days prior to the hearings.

The Tribe had now done all it could to create a climate of opinion favorable to its bill. They had persuaded Clinton P. Anderson, one of the most powerful men in the Senate, to sponsor and introduce S. 3085. The nationwide distribution of their appeal booklet had generated favorable coverage in newspapers from the *Taos News* to the *New York Times*. They had been diligent in building local support, as endorsements from the Town Council, ditch associations, and the supervisors of the Soil Conservation District attested. They had secured the backing of Indian organizations, both in New Mexico and nationally. Prominent clergymen, both Catholic and Protestant, had written impassioned pleas on their behalf. They had the advantage of AAIA's support in furthering their cause. Stewart Udall, a popular and well-known Interior secretary, was taking a personal interest in their quest. Sen. Robert Kennedy, heir to the Kennedy mystique, had publicly advocated passage of S. 3085. Finally, and most importantly, the Tribe had successfully made the return of Blue Lake a national issue by presenting S. 3085 as the only means of putting an end to the ongoing violations of their First Amendment right to freedom of worship.

That point was underscored by an editorial which appeared in the *Washington Post* on the eve of the Senate subcommittee hearings. Titled "Restoring a Shrine," the editorial began by explaining to readers that favorable ICC judgments procedurally resulted in monetary payments being made to the tribes for their land.

> In this case, however, the people of Taos have indignantly refused to accept money for the land and the lake which are essential elements in their worship. The wrong can be set right only by returning the green mountains and blue waters from which these children of nature obtain their religious inspiration.[29]

Noting that only Congress was empowered to return to Taos their "religious preserve," the editorial concluded, "We think Senator Anderson's bill should be passed in deference to the principle of religious freedom."[30] With their case for religious liberty now widely accepted by the public, the Tribe was finally to have their hearing before the all-important Senate Subcommittee on Indian Affairs.

The subcommittee was chaired by Sen. Lee Metcalf of Montana. The subcommittee members present at the hearing included Anderson, Quentin Burdick of North Dakota, Milward Simpson of Wyoming, and Paul Fannin of Arizona. Metcalf began the hearing by noting that the committee members had received "a substantial amount of mail" supporting S. 3085. He then called on Udall, accom-

The Tribal delegation and its allies arrive in Washington for the hearing before the Senate Subcommittee On Indian Affairs. From left, Bill Byler, Governor Reyna, Seferino Martinez, Corinne Locker, and Paul Bernal. 1966. Photo by Dan Budnik.

panied by the newly appointed commissioner of Indian Affairs, Robert Bennett, who, as Udall said, was present to emphasize "the importance we attach to this legislation," to develop the opening testimony.

Udall began by establishing that the Taos Indians were a deeply spiritual people with a profoundly religious attachment to their land. He then praised Gifford Pinchot and Teddy Roosevelt for organizing the national forest system, but said that for the Taos Indians their action had been a "tragedy and disaster." He outlined the history of problems between the Tribe and the Forest Service, and gave two reasons for the Pueblo's desire to acquire trust title. The first was that their "freedom to practice their religion depends on their being able to conduct their sacred ceremonies in private."[31] The second was that their possession of the land under the act of 1933 was insecure, since Congress had the power to repeal the act and take their land from them. Trust title as conveyed by S. 3085, he asserted, would solve both problems.

Udall identified three main arguments against the bill. The first addressed the danger of precedent: that if Taos were to receive land instead of money, other tribes would try to do the same. While accepting the objection as "serious and important," Udall said he did not consider it apposite, since the Taos case was unique. "The religious significance of this land to the Taos Pueblo Indians warrants favorable action as an exception to the general rule."[32] If other tribes were to make such a claim, they would have to demonstrate "similar unique circumstances," and he said he thought few would be able to do so.

The second argument concerned non-Indian permits and leases. S. 3085 gave the Tribe the right to buy existing permits in the watershed. To pay for such a permit, so the argument ran, seemed to establish it as a "vested interest" rather than a privilege. Udall simply dismissed the concern, saying he saw little possibility that passage of S. 3085 would establish grazing privileges as vested interests.

The third argument was that the Tribe's real motivation for acquiring title to the watershed was to profit from exploiting its timber resources. Udall said that when he had explained the seriousness of this charge to the Indians, and suggested making the watershed a wilderness area, they readily agreed. Udall then read into the record the "Wilderness Amendment," stressing that as a "gesture of compromise" it provided for continued Forest Service responsibility for conservation measures. This amendment, Udall said, should lay to rest once and for all the charge of commercial designs on the part of the Indians, since it mandated that the land remain "forever wild." He pointed out that, in fact, "the religious values which the Indians attach to the land require the preservation of the land in its natural state."[33] He concluded his testimony by emphasizing the symbolic importance S. 3085 had assumed for tribes around the country, and the positive psychological effect its passage would have on all of them.

In his highly effective presentation, Udall had set forth the key arguments on which the Tribe would base its case in all of the coming debates. Each of them led back in some way to the issue of religious freedom. Given their importance, it will be useful to examine them in greater detail.

The primary argument centered on the question of privacy. The Tribe required complete privacy in the practice of their faith because the presence of outsiders made the celebrants ritually impure and their devotions, therefore, ineffective. Fear of covert observation was a constant concern. As one tribal member, Richard Romero, recalls:

> I remember our people and my father and grandfather talking about people spying on them during our ceremonials, during the sacred times when people were up there. There was always this kind of an ominous feeling that someone was around looking to see what we were doing at that time, during those specific times of the year when that area is used.[34]

To eliminate this anxiety and to protect the purity of the rituals, absolute prohibition of all outside visitors was essential. The sole way to guarantee this was to give the Pueblo trust title.

If their religious liberty required the exclusion of outside visitors, it required freedom from the presence of the Forest Service, too. As things stood, the Pueblo's religious privacy was uncertain and intermittent. Since the Forest Service regarded its permissions for religious activities as privileges granted to the Indians rather than as rights, there was always the chance that a change of supervisors might mean new and prohibitive policies. As Keith Green had said, "The fundamental sanctity of their altars is subject to the changing policies of changing administrations." The Pueblo's freedom of religious practice was at present contingent upon permissions unpredictably granted or refused, an intolerable situation which trust title would abolish. This uncertainty was exacerbated by the Indians' awareness that the act of 1933 could be rescinded and the permit of 1940 revoked at any time. The granting of trust title would lay to rest this substantial fear.

Control of the watershed by the Forest Service had made the Indians feel like strangers in their own land. Intensifying this discomfort was the fact that the tribal religion required the taking of certain forms of game at times of the year prohibited by the white man's hunting laws. Religious observance required breaking these laws, with the attendant uncomfortable necessity of eluding the Forest Service patrols. To quote Romero:

> One of the major things that I became aware of was when people would go up there for their hunts, to go up and take what they needed, there was always, always, forever that fear that they were going to get prosecuted, or caught, or seen. I remember as a young boy, when I would go up there with my dad and my grandfather, it was always hiding. You never were free just to go out there and enjoy, whether it would be for religious or whatever purpose you were up there for. There was always that, like, you know, that you were trespassing on someone's property.[35]

As long as the Forest Service patrolled and administered the sacred watershed, the Tribe could never feel that the land was unquestionably theirs, to use as custom and tradition required. The only solution was to put an end to Forest Service control.

The final argument for trust title was based on the need to insure protection of the plants and animals in their natural state. The Tribe had a sacred duty to do this, and was particularly incensed at continual Forest Service threats to log the watershed. The destruction of the La Junta Canyon remained a poignant warning, and the Tribe never felt it could trust the Forest Service to leave the timber undisturbed. Once again, the solution was to remove the watershed from the threat of Forest Service "multiple use" by placing it under the authority of the Tribe through trust title.

Udall did an excellent job of making these points, and his effectiveness was increased by the obvious esteem in which the members of the committee held

him. His idea of making the area a wilderness preserve was an especially impor-
tant contribution, since not only was it coincident with the wishes of the
Indians, but it also undercut one of the strongest arguments of their opponents.
In Udall, the Tribe had a true and tenacious proponent and friend.

The star witness for the opposition was Arthur W. Greeley, associate chief of
the Forest Service. In opposing S. 3085, Greeley advanced the following seven
basic arguments:

1. The Blue Lake watershed is one of the most productive in all of New
    Mexico. If the Tribe should assume control and mismanage conserva-
    tion measures in the area, the water supply of downstream users
    would be threatened.

2. There are 230 million board feet of "over-mature" trees in the area that
    ought to be harvested lest the timber go to waste. Tribal control would
    preclude such harvesting.

3. Under the provisions of the Wilderness Act, areas set aside must com-
    prise a minimum of 5,000 acres. If S. 3085 passes, 2,000 acres will be
    lost from the Wheeler Wilderness, reducing the acreage to 3,000, well
    below the statutory minimum.

4. While the Indians complain about infringements upon their religious
    freedom, in fact the Forest Service understands their needs well and
    has done everything possible to accommodate them, including prevent-
    ing camping and fishing at Blue Lake itself. All visitors are required to
    obtain a permit signed by the Tribe, and the entire watershed is closed
    to outside visitors during the August Blue Lake ceremonial. Further,
    recreational use of the area by outsiders is in fact quite light, and hardly
    poses a threat to Indian religion.

5. Under the procedures set by Congress when it established the Indian
    Claims Commission, tribes were to be paid cash settlements for land
    lost. If S. 3085 passes, it will set a dangerous precedent which will
    encourage other tribes to do likewise. Millions of acres will be
    threatened.

6. As presently written, S. 3085 would transfer trust title for the water-
    shed to the Department of the Interior on behalf of Taos Pueblo, while
    leaving the Forest Service in charge of and responsible for conservation
    and administration. To create such an arrangment will prove cumber-
    some at best and, very likely, unworkable. As things stand now, the area
    has available the resouces of the Forest Service for fire protection,
    insect abatement, and timber management—all of which would be lost
    if it were withdrawn from the National Forest. Moreover, if the land is
    the Tribe's in trust under jurisdiction of Interior, while at the same time
    under the administrative authority of Agriculture, who has the final
    say and what would supervision really mean in such a case?

7. S. 3085 would allow the Tribe to buy grazing permits now in force in
    the area. To buy and sell such permits appears to give them the charac-
    ter of "vested interest" rather than privilege, and it is unwise to estab-
    lish such a principle.

While Greeley made these points in measured tones and without evident animosity, it is clear that he was in deadly earnest. He believed that S. 3085 threatened Forest Service control not only in the Blue Lake area but in many other forests that might potentially be claimed by Indians. His seven points of opposition were, therefore, in the nature of a policy statement applicable not only to the present issue but to any situations of a similar nature which might arise in the future. On these points the Forest Service henceforward undeviatingly took its stand.

In the combined testimonies of Udall and Greeley, virtually all of the arguments for and against a Blue Lake trust-title bill had been articulated. Their basic lineaments remained unchanged during the four succeeding tumultous years. Testimony provided by others merely stressed or restated these basic arguments. A quick review of the testimony at the 1966 hearings makes this readily apparent.

Gov. John Reyna, Martinez and Bernal represented the Tribe. Martinez opened by making the point that the Tribe has occupied the area from the beginning of time, that all of it is sacred, and that they use it primarily for religious purposes, purposes threatened by the presence of the Forest Service in the area. Governor Reyna followed, stressing the desecration of the area because of recreational use and the Tribe's desire to preserve the watershed in its natural state. Bernal, in conclusion, emphasized that it is not only Blue Lake that is sacred to the Tribe, but that the entire watershed contains shrines whose sanctity is continually threatened by visitors and Forest Service personnel. Therefore, he testified, tribal possession of the entire "Bowl" was essential to their enjoyment of true freedom of religion.

To buttress their argument for religious liberty, the Tribe called upon three friendly witnesses: Theodore Hetzel of the American Friends Service Committee and the Indian Rights Association; Serge Hummon, chair of the Committee on Indian Work of the National Council of Churches; and William Byler, executive director of the AAIA.

Hetzel, testifying first, identified religious freedom as the central issue. "This is a matter of the freedom of American citizens to worship God in their traditional way."[36] He said he had visited Taos six times to talk with members of the Tribal Council, and they had convinced him that, as long as others controlled the area, their rituals were at peril. He concluded, "Our forebears crossed the ocean to achieve religious freedom; let us not deny it to those who were already here."[37]

Hummon, too, focused on religious liberty, stressing its importance to the National Council of Churches as an issue about which they were ever vigilant. Noting that, while the Tribe's claim to property rights as validated by the ICC was important, it did not in and of itself justify returning the land. That justification stemmed from the fact "that the lake is essential to the religious life of the tribe, and has been the sacred site of its ceremonials and devotional pilgrimages continuously up to the present."[38] While the ICC decision established the Tribe's property rights,

> the force of the plea of religious liberty is directed to the Indians' insistence that money or "equivalent" acreage elsewhere will not take the place of Blue Lake in their religious life. It is unique and irreplaceable for religious reasons.[39]

Hummon then made the point that the consideration of specific sites as sacred is well known in religious history, adducing the Kaaba in Mecca and the Holy Sepulcher in Jerusalem as familiar examples. Just as it would be blasphemous to offer money to Moslems and Christians in exchange for these sites, so was it blasphemous to expect the Taos Indians to take money for Blue Lake. Citing the primacy of religious faith in our society, Hummon insisted that it should take precedence over considerations about timber, sport, and fishery. He supported passage of S. 3085, he said, "so that the petitioners need no longer worry that their sanctuary will be taken from them by distant and capricious forces."[40] He movingly concluded:

> It is rare enough in our rushed and harried society that a group of people treasures an isolated area for religious reasons. When it is a remote and elevated area such as this—for which there is little or no competing demand—and when the property right itself is not in question—what reason can there be not to grant the modest and reasonable plea of the Indians of Pueblo de Taos? It is certainly the least that a great nation can do for the religious freedom of a neglected people.[41]

Byler then opened his remarks by emphasizing the Indians' immemorial usage of the area and its "profound religious and cultural significance" to them. He made much of the relationship between the welfare of the Taos people and the undisturbed continuity of their observance of their traditional religion. Enactment of S. 3085, he said, would "assure to the people of Taos the spiritual security which is indispensable to their well-being . . . ."[42]; give the Tribe pride; underscore the importance of harmonious relations with their neighbors; and perhaps even help the economy of the area. He concluded,

> S.3085 presents Congress with a rare and historic opportunity—the chance to right a past wrong without impinging upon any adverse interests and without cost to the United States.[43]

Just as Hetzel, Hummon and Byler helped the Tribe establish its arguments for religious freedom, so a supporting statement by William Zimmerman, on behalf of the Sierra Club, helped the Tribe weather opposition from other conservation groups. The Tribe needed all of the support it could get, since that opposition was formidable indeed.

The most forceful came from Louis S. Clapper, representing the National Wildlife Federation. Clapper's organization "adamantly" opposed S. 3085 on several counts: because of the precedent it would set for other tribes; because they disapproved of public land being transferred to the exclusive use of a closed group; and because they considered the Forest Service the only entity that could be relied on to protect and conserve the area properly. Praising the management of the area by the Forest Service, Clapper insisted that the Pueblo could not be trusted to take care of it, and that giving it to them would have long-term negative consequences not only for the general public but also for the Indians themselves. Regarding the issue of religious freedom, the NWF's position was that the Indians had all of the religious protection they needed under the use-permit, and that the current light levels of usage by non-Indians did not justify a wholesale giveaway of public land to Taos Pueblo. In addition, they were opposed to the withdrawing of 2,000 acres from the recently established Wheeler Peak Wilderness Area. Clapper concluded by introducing into the record a personal statement from Elliott Barker, as well as a resolution passed by Barker's New Mexico Wildlife Conservation Association (the local affiliate of Clapper's NWF) unequivocally opposing S. 3085.

Stewart Brandborg, executive director of the Wilderness Society, was the next opposition speaker. His group opposed S. 3085 primarily on the grounds that land once given wilderness status should not later be withdrawn for any reason. While they hoped that a plan could be worked out which would give the Tribe the necessary religious access to the 2,000 acres, they did not want it separated from the Wheeler Wilderness. Brandborg qualified his opposition only to the extent that he said he would like to study Udall's wilderness amendment before his group made a final judgment.

Two years earlier, Byler had predicted that strategic to the success of the Blue Lake campaign was securing the support of religious and conservation groups. Certainly, the hearings in 1966 proved him right, for most of the discussion and testimony at those hearings centered on important issues in these two areas of interest. Subsequent hearings would simply tread ground already covered. The one startling revelation of the later hearings concerns Anderson's changing position.

Since his introduction of S. 3085 in March, the Indians considered Anderson a true friend. None of his statements in the May hearings gave them reason to think otherwise. Further, the proceedings were basically irenic because the Agriculture Department and the Forest Service checked their opposition. While they certainly made their points, they did so in restrained and gentlemanly fashion. After all, Anderson was a former secretary of Agriculture, was now a very powerful senator, and S. 3085 was his own bill dealing with an issue from his home state. Everyone naturally assumed that Anderson supported the Indians and wanted to see the bill pass. Consequently, the opposition from Agriculture and the Forest Service deferred to him at the hearings, pulling their punches. Their treatment of the Indians was in every way respectful, the questions politely inquisitorial.

The hearings so pleased the Tribe that, upon their return to New Mexico, they wrote to Anderson, "The Taos Pueblo delegation left Washington with profound feelings of gratitude for your help in presenting your bill S. 3085 to the Senate Subcommittee on Indian Affairs."[44] The Tribe would not have felt nearly so grateful if they had paid closer attention to what Anderson actually had said at the hearings, and to the possible consequences of the questions he had asked.

It is of considerable significance that Anderson introduced S. 3085 "by request," a sign to other senators that he did not really favor the bill, having introduced it only because asked to do so by constituents. He explained his position at the hearings:

> I admit that I believe 50,000 acres is a lot of territory. Someone may ask why I introduced a bill for that. It is because the Taos Indians asked me to, to have a day in court here as well as before the Indian Claims Commission. But I would like to understand what that land might mean as we go along, and yet not jeopardize good conservation practices or jeopardize the possibility of timbering that land in an intelligent fashion on a sustained-yield basis. That is a very fine piece of ground. It should be protected.[45]

In these remarks, Anderson revealed a number of reservations. He introduced the bill, he says, only because asked and he thinks 50,000 acres is "a lot of territory." He does not want to jeopardize conservation measures (the implication being that they should remain in the hands of the Forest Service), and he does not want to jeopardize the timbering of the land on a sustained yield basis. All of these views accorded with the testimony of Greeley.

Other questions put by Anderson also subtly revealed a pro-Forest Service stand. He asked about the Tribe's position on insecticide spraying to halt a serious infestation of budworms. The Forest Service volunteered that the Tribe opposed spraying because this practice had previously resulted in the destruction of wildlife. Bernal replied that the Tribe as yet had no definite position on spraying. While nothing further came of the exchange, it demonstrated that Anderson favored this long-standing Forest Service practice. He expressed concern that, if the area were designated a wilderness, further spraying would not be possible.

Two other lines of his inquiry reveal Anderson's real thinking. The first concerns the amount of "territory" to be given the Pueblo in trust title. At one point, saying to Greeley that "some of us would like to see Blue Lake restored to the Taos Indians," he then asked, "Is it possible to split Blue Lake off from the rest of the 50,000-acre area and some surrounding area around it?"[46] Anderson then inquired if the Forest Service had made a study of how much land this would entail. Greeley said that they had not, but that it could be done. Metcalf, as chairman, then instructed Greeley to provide the subcommittee with the information. This was an ominous turn, given Metcalf's ill concealed doubts about the Tribe's need of 50,000 acres for its "church."

The second line of Anderson's inquiries centered on timbering. He asked Greeley if the timber in the watershed was ripe for harvesting, and Greeley replied that, if anything, it was "over-mature." Anderson commented, "My impression was that this is timber that should be harvested now."[47] Anderson noted that there was a privately-owned ranch to the east of the permit boundary, and if it could be acquired "you could timber this whole area."[48]

At a later point in Greeley's testimony, Anderson again raised the issue of timbering, asking Greeley if there were buyers interested in Taos timber. When Greeley answered in the affirmative, Anderson commented, "I think it is important to save this timber and not to destroy the timber on other lands."[49] Since his comment followed from the discussion on spraying, it seems fair to infer that he meant that the timber should be sprayed to halt the spread of the infestation so that it could then be cut down and sold.

At a still later point in the testimony, Anderson inquired of Bernal what the Tribe thought of the idea of wilderness status. Bernal replied,

> I think this program is very, very good because we believe in nature and because we believe not in any way to desecrate the living trees or the living shrines in this area.[50]

Anderson agreed that the wilderness area was a "fine suggestion," but then continued,

> I do question this timber area that I pointed to a while ago, which is very heavily timbered now, and which needs to be harvested if it isn't going to be destroyed entirely.[51]

Anderson's questions and comments are particularly revealing when studied in the light of correspondence he was carrying on with a Moreno Valley lumberman, Robert Le Sage. A month prior to the May hearings, Le Sage wrote to Anderson concerning a deal he was trying to put together with the Forest Service. This would allow him to exchange 19,000 acres of land he had clear-cut for the rights to timber on the "Indian land that joins our Colfax County land on the West."[52] He complained to Anderson that the land he wanted to timber was "included in the gift to the Indians," and that if S. 3085 passed it "would no doubt eliminate any chance of our making this exchange, as there is not enough other timber in that vicinity to equal the value of this land."[53] He reminded Anderson that they had tried to make this exchange "a few years ago," but the deal had fallen through. Now, however, the Forest Service was eager to proceed, because they wanted his 19,000 acres "for recreation facilities." He informed Anderson that he had built a sawmill on the prospect of making the exchange, and that it would have to be shut down if the deal again failed, since there would not then be enough timber available to him to make the mill pay. Pointing out that the mill supported the economy by employing 200 locals, he said he hoped to discuss the matter with Anderson come Easter.

Anderson replied by letter immediately, addressing Le Sage as "Bob." He told him that he was just leaving for Albuquerque, taking the maps of the area with him, and would try to find out how the situation stood. In closing, he gave Le Sage his home phone number where he could be reached in his absence from Washington.

The day after he wrote to Le Sage, Anderson received a letter from the Taos regional forester concerning the proposed exchange. The forester explained that the exchange had been held up because they had not as yet been able to agree on the relative values of the timber on Indian land and the 19,000 acres offered by Le Sage. However, they were working on the problem and wanted to see the deal go through, because they felt the land offered by Le Sage should be in "public ownership." Regarding S. 3085, the forester said, "We feel that the transfer of the lands to the Taos Indians could have an adverse effect on the exchange proposed by Mr. Le Sage."[54]

It is evident that while Anderson appeared to be supporting S. 3085, he was, in fact, involved in working out a deal which would give Le Sage all of the timber on 20,000 acres of the sacred watershed. After the hearings, Bernal wrote to Anderson:

> I want to express my personal feelings to you about the warm friendship that I have gained with you during my short visit in Washington. I have felt like I am more close to you now than I have ever been before, for the fact that openly you and I have expressed thoughts about the Blue Lake trust bill . . . .dear friend, the Governor, the Council and the people of Taos Pueblo join in with me [in] wishing you the best of everything."[55]

Bernal and his allies were soon to discover that their "dear friend" had no intention of giving the Taos Indians trust title to 50,000 choice acres that contained "over-mature" timber which badly "needed cutting," whether or not this land had been sacred to their use since before recorded time.

6

Things Turn Sour

T HE TRIBE'S POST-HEARING OPTIMISM got a boost when, ten days after the close of the Senate hearings of 1966, Florida congressman James A. Haley, chair of the House Subcommittee on Indian Affairs, introduced H.R. 15184 as a companion bill to S. 3085. A Taos Pueblo member, John Rainer, had asked Helen Peterson, a Sioux in close contact with Haley, to discuss with him the merits of the Pueblo's cause.[1] After she had done so, a tribal delegation visited Haley, who became a stalwart champion of the Blue Lake quest. He lost no time in introducing H.R. 15184, so that there might be a chance that his sub-committee could soon hold hearings on the bill, approve it, and send it on to the Committee on Interior and Insular Affairs, chaired by Colorado congressman Wayne Aspinall, for its approval and introduction before the full House of Representatives. Haley hoped for action on the bill before the close of the legislative session.

Beginning in June of 1966, the Tribe could take encouragement from the resolution of some old problems and some positive new developments. They agreed to participate in the spraying program when the Forest Service promised to use malathion in reduced concentrations, instead of the DDT that had been used before. There was the decision by the Wilderness Society to back S.3085, provided that the 2,000 acres were not taken from the Wheeler Reserve, and the land conveyed to the Tribe was given wilderness status. This was followed by the final signing of the Las Cruces Arroyo Flood Dam Easement. Then ABC television proposed to do a film on the Blue Lake issue. Russell Carter of the National Council of Churches, who informed the Tribe of this possibility, thought it "would be a good vehicle by which the true story could be portrayed for all

This contemporary Taos Indian, wearing a modern parka and tennis shoes rather than the blanket and moccasins of his ancestors, takes water from the Rio Pueblo in the same way tribal members have for centuries. c. 1970. Photo by Dan Budnik.

America to see."[2] Filmed in August and aired in mid-November, "The Sacred Lake of Taos" brought the story of the Tribe's plight to countless viewers.

In addition, the Tribe picked up support from the American Civil Liberties Union. The director, Lawrence Speiser, wrote to Rep. Wayne Aspinall that, "Consistent with the high esteem which this nation has always had for the religious liberty of all groups, the ACLU believes that Congress should enact this legislation."[3] Support came, too, from other Indians, including the New Mexico All-Indian Pueblo Council, the Jicarilla Apaches, the Southern Utes, the Mountain Utes, and the Miccosukees. The Tribe even received the backing of the New Mexico Democratic party, which made support for S.3085 one of its planks at the state platform convention.

Just when everything seemed to be going the Pueblo's way, serious problems surfaced. Rep. Aspinall, chair of the House Committee on Interior and Insular Affairs, informed Henry Forbes of the AAIA Executive Committee that it was doubtful that action would soon be taken on H.R. 15184 because of the "heavy schedule" of bills pending before Aspinall's committee, many of them introduced long before the Taos bill. Aspinall said that there would be no more consideration of Indian bills for this congressional session, and that it would be especially difficult to get approval for one as "highly controversial" as H.R. 15184.

Hard on the heels of this disappointing news came Albuquerque resident Preston Gunther's charge on a radio talk show that the Pueblo had already been paid $180,000 for the Blue Lake area in 1926. He made the same accusation before a group representing the Albuquerque Council of Churches, which then came to the brink of opposing S. 3085.

Shortly thereafter, the newspapers published a story on the San Juan Indians' land claim to "vast acreage" in the vicinity of Espanola, New Mexico. The publicity about this claim was most inopportune, since it appeared to substantiate the "precedent" objection: that if Taos sought land, other tribes would soon do so, too.

As to Gunther's charge, the commissioner of Indian Affairs, Robert Bennett, promptly refuted it, pointing out that the payment cited by Gunther was for the land in the town of Taos, not for the Blue Lake area. The Pueblo itself rebutted the "precedent" objection, arguing that the San Juan claim only underscored the "uniqueness" of that of Taos. In a June press release, the Tribe made clear that San Juan had not established a legal claim to the land they sought, and had not filed for it within the period of time set by the ICC. The release further stated that San Juan had economic reasons for seeking the land, and would dispossess the present owners if successful. By contrast, Taos had asserted ownership continuously since 1906, had filed for the land with the ICC in a timely fashion, and had won their ICC case on the grounds of their land's "intense religious meaning and use which continue to this day."[4] Further, they would be dispossessing no one, since the Tribe had maintained exclusive use of the area since time immemorial. Despite these rebuttals, both the Gunther charge and the San Juan claim adversely affected the public perception of the justness of the Pueblo's quest. Then, in mid-July, Anderson dropped a bombshell.

The real battle for Blue Lake began with the opening salvo fired by Anderson, covered in an article printed in the *Albuquerque Journal* on July 12, 1966. He revealed that he had developed a new bill which would give the Tribe trust title only to Blue Lake and its immediate surround, some 3,100 acres. An additional 27,000 acres would be placed under the Wilderness Protection Act, while the 2,000 acres in the Wheeler Wilderness would remain with that parcel. About the 18,000 acres remaining, Anderson said nothing. The article quoted Anderson as saying he knew that the substance of his new bill differed from what the Indians had wanted, but that he felt that it was "reasonable." He planned to propose it to them at a meeting scheduled two days later.

At that meeting, Anderson bluntly told the Tribe that, respecting S. 3085, the "principal obstacles are rights to ten million dollars worth of timber in approximately 18,000 acres and 2,000 acres of Wheeler Peak Wild Area."[5] A week later, through covert channels, the Tribe obtained information relative to the Le Sage exchange. Alarmed that the long-feared timbering in the watershed was about to become reality, the Tribe asked Schifter to make Anderson a counterproposal. Udall, also concerned, made a similar request to him. This touched off six weeks of confusing negotiation, as the claims attorneys, Poole, the Tribe, and Anderson tried to work out a mutually acceptable bill.

Schifter, supported by Karelsen and Mitchell, developed a draft which eliminated the 2,000 acres in the Wheeler area, put Blue Lake and its surrounding 3,100 acres in trust title, and gave the Pueblo a use-permit "in perpetuity" for the remaining 45,000 acres. While his draft precluded timbering by making the entire area wilderness, it allowed non-Indian visitation with Pueblo consent.

Locker and the Tribe thought that Schifter's proposal was "over-generous," and in early August wrote Anderson to insist on restoration of the full 50,000 acres. At the same time, they authorized Poole to meet with Anderson and try to work out a compromise. Anderson and Poole conferred, and tentatively agreed on a bill that would eliminate both the 2,000 acres in the Wheeler and 8,000 acres on the east side. It also considerably strengthened the conservation authority of the Forest Service.

The new proposal would leave the Tribe with only 40,000 acres in trust. They now had a hard decision before them. If both they and Anderson accepted this proposal, then the Tribe would have to abandon their claim to twenty percent of the watershed. If they did not accept it, they might get no bill at all.

Negotiations with Anderson continued throughout August and September. When he remained adamant against conceding trust title to the 8,000 acres on the east side (where his friend, Le Sage, wanted to timber), the Tribe finally concluded that they, too, could not compromise. While they were willing to give up their claim to the 2,000 acres in the Wheeler, since it would remain wilderness, they felt they could not in good conscience abandon 8,000 acres to the depradations of Le Sage. Their resolve was stiffened by the fact that he had just trespassed into the Bonito Park area, illegally cutting timber for which he had no permit. The Tribe decided to insist on a minimum of 48,000 acres in trust title, and informed Anderson that they were "prepared to wait for years if necessary to obtain satisfactory legislation."[6]

With both sides intransigent, there was no chance for passage of a bill in 1966. Anderson, bitterly angry with the Indians, said "I have wasted a good many years of my life trying to get a decision that could be implemented by legislation."[7] The Indians, in turn, felt they had been deceived and sold out by Anderson. The Departments of Agriculture and Interior were deadlocked, with the Bureau of the Budget equivocating between their two positions. S. 3085 died in the crossfire of this conflict. As Locker told AAIA president Alden Stevens, "The going has been extremely rough, and Rufus Poole fears that we may yet have to resume an all-out public campaign."[8]

The issue also brought Locker and the claims attorneys into critical conflict. During the tense summer negotiations, she felt that the attorneys pressured the Tribe to go along with Anderson. While, in October, the BIA had extended to 1976 the attorneys' contract with the Pueblo, Locker now wanted to exclude them entirely from all involvement in the quest for Blue Lake. Bernal agreed, and when the AAIA director, Al Josephy, came to Taos in the fall of 1966, Bernal used the "opportunity to develop support for the Pueblo's position as against the claims attorneys."[9]

Locker expressed her bitterness toward the claims counsel in a thirty-five-page diatribe titled "The Association and the Taos Blue Lake," which she sent to Byler in mid-November. In it she pointed out that Schifter was playing a dual role, serving both as claims counsel for the Pueblo and legal advisor to AAIA. Karelsen, too, served in a double capacity, as principal claims attorney and, since 1965, as a member of the AAIA Executive Committee. She also charged Mitchell with a series of offenses that began almost as soon as the claims attorneys retained him as local liaison.

After detailing at length the malefactions of Schifter, Karelsen, and Mitchell, she identified their most serious offense as their behavior during the negotiations with Anderson. It was then that the consequences of their "dual roles" became most apparent, she said. They had tried to dissuade the Pueblo from opposing Anderson, "finally and shockingly on the grounds that this method of approach would prolong settlement of the case and further delay payment of the claims attorneys' fees."[10] Referring to the interest in the Pueblo's cause throughout the country, she concluded:

> In short, we are operating in a fishbowl. The fact that two of the attorneys who have a financial interest in the claim are otherwise connected with the Association in positions of major importance makes our advisory role automatically suspect, should anyone care to question it.[11]

In conclusion, Locker sharpened the focus of her "conflict of interest" charge against Kingsley, Karelsen, and Schifter, who held important positions in AAIA while acting as the Pueblo's claims counsel. Regarding Karelsen's membership on the AAIA executive committee, Locker said that "the representations he has made in behalf of his private practice while holding this position, cannot help but weaken the Association from within and denigrate it from without."[12] As for Kingsley, Locker noted that he had recently been inactive and had not "injected himself into the Blue Lake activities," but he nonetheless retained a financial interest in the Taos case and controlled a major AAIA fund, a situation which carried "with it an unavoidable implication of potential influence."[13]

Of Schifter, Locker complained that he had of late been unavailable to field personnel like herself because he had become the campaign manager for the incumbent Maryland governor. Even when he offered advice it was suspect, because he preferred to work through accommodation and compromise. AAIA and the Indians needed someone who would do whatever was necessary for their clients' interests. In addition, because he worked both for AAIA and the Tribe. "Mr. Schifter has been in the position of serving two clients with different interests in the same matter."[14] She charged him with consistently putting the interests of AAIA last, and said the Taos situation had been saved only through the efforts of Rufus Poole.

While Locker objected to the conduct of the attorneys, Bill Byler and the attorneys objected to hers, centering on her shift from tribal liaison to policymaker. It is clear that as Bernal assumed control of the fight within the Tribe, and as he and Locker drew closer together, they increasingly were making decisions without consulting with the claims attorneys and AAIA. This tendency accelerated with the hiring of Poole, on whom Locker and Bernal leaned ever more heavily for legal advice.

By August of 1966, Locker's behavior verged upon insubordination, as she strenuously opposed the claims attorneys' approach to the negotiations with Anderson. Byler felt compelled to rein her in. Protesting that she had shifted from liaison to policymaker "in opposition to me," he insisted that she limit her activities "to that of liaison and to those specific actions which are clearly in accordance with my directives and what you know are my intentions."[15] She was conscientiously to transmit all information to the appropriate interested parties, and to keep her disagreements respecting policy to herself.

> Although you may privately disagree with me, I must insist that in your dealings with representatives of the Pueblo you uphold the position of the Association. . . . .I trust that you will either accept the terms of this letter or withdraw from the Blue Lake case and concentrate on other matters.[16]

On the basis of this letter, Locker concluded that Byler did not really understand the "genuine danger" posed by the claims attorneys, and it provoked her lengthy indictment of them. Byler passed Locker's criticisms along to the claims attorneys to get their side of the story, and Schifter composed a detailed reply.

Regarding the charge that he pressured the Tribe into compromising with Anderson in order to get his fee, Schifter pointed out that as counsel to the Joint Efforts Group, he was entitled to .65 percent of the Taos ICC judgment. If the ICC awarded the Tribe six hundred thousand dollars (in his view an inflated expectation) he would receive a total of thirty-two dollars. Further, he made it clear that he was not the claims counsel in the ICC case, but simply advised Karelsen and Kingsley on a fee-for-service basis. Since he was paid by the hour, dragging out the case would be in his financial interest.

Nor did Kingsley and Karelsen stand to reap a windfall, he said. The Pueblo's cases were in fact "loss leaders" for the firm; and, given the time they had spent over sixteen years, they did not stand to make much money from them at all.

He also explained that it was in their interest for the Tribe to get the land in trust title rather than either a perpetual easement or a cash settlement. If the Tribe got the land, the fee would be computed on the basis of the value of the land at the time of the award. If the Tribe got cash, the fee would be computed on the basis of the value of the land in 1906. Since the former was obviously higher than the latter, it was in the financial interest of the claims attorneys to press for the actual return of the watershed. The same held true for a perpetual easement: its value would be far less than that of the land returned in trust title. The very fact that the attorneys had urged the Tribe to adopt this course of action proved that their commitment was to protecting the Pueblo, not increasing their fees.

Turning to the negotiations with Anderson, Schifter explained that his "perpetual use-permit" approach gave the Tribe the same rights as they would have with title, but cast in a different form: "instead of identifying this bundle of rights as trust title subject to limitations, it would have identified them as a perpetual easement."[17] While all the attorneys involved understood this, Locker did not. As a result she persuaded the Tribal Council to oppose his draft, Schifter said, accusing him of selling out into the bargain.

Schifter concluded that Locker's failure to understand the relevant legal issues had led her to adopt a totally unrealistic position. In his view, the Pueblo's only hope for any kind of bill lay in the goodwill of Congress which, at that point in time, meant the goodwill of Clinton P. Anderson. Given the political realities in Washington, anyone who thought the Tribe could achieve its ends by fighting Anderson was "doing the Pueblo a grave disservice."[18]

While events were to prove Schifter wrong on that score, it does seem that to a great extent Locker's charges unfairly maligned the claims counsel. Her most serious accusation, that the claims attorneys gave the Pueblo bad advice because they wanted their fees, was effectively refuted by Schifter's carefully reasoned arguments. While it is undoubtedly true that the claims attorneys wanted to see the matter settled, it seems highly unlikely that they were acting from self-interest. The most absolving fact for the claims counsel is that in 1963, when they had no reason to assume that Anderson was a bitter opponent of trust title (he had made known his reservations on this score only to La Farge), they repeatedly told the Tribe that their rights were insufficiently protected by the use-permit, and strongly urged them to seek trust title. By the summer of 1966, however, Anderson had made abundantly clear his determined opposition to the title initiative; and, given the political realities in Washington, the claims counsel then judged it impossible for the Tribe to succeed in their quest for trust title. Accordingly, Schifter developed the perpetual easement proposal intended to protect the Pueblo's rights while avoiding a provocation of Anderson's opposition.

Schifter and the claims attorneys simply wished to pursue a strategy that they felt had a realistic chance of success. They were pragmatists who wanted the problem solved. They pressed for what they thought could actually be achieved and felt that Locker's failure to understand the legal issues involved had led to the adoption of an "unrealistic" position. Locker, instead of just accepting that she and the attorneys had conflicting strategies, felt compelled to accuse them of acting out of self-interest.

The upshot of this conflict was the total disruption of the title quest. Initially, AAIA president Alden Stevens sought to end the conflict by summoning Locker to New York, where he proceeded to deal out some very "straight talk." Locker remained unconvinced and uncooperative. In February of 1967, she insisted that what progress had been made in the negotiations was due entirely to herself, Bernal, and Poole, "free for the first time of intervention and conflicting directives from the East."[19] She told Stevens that her dispute with Byler was "irreconcilable," and accused him of ignoring both the wishes of the Pueblo and the Board of AAIA.

Stevens had had enough, and sent Locker a telegram of dismissal.

> FOR MANY MONTHS WE PERSISTED IN THE HOPE THAT YOU WOULD ATTEMPT TO REESTABLISH AN EFFECTIVE WORKING RELATIONSHIP WITH THE CENTRAL OFFICE. RATHER THAN IMPROVING, THIS RELATIONSHIP HAS DETERIORATED. IT IS NO LONGER POSSIBLE TO CONTINUE IN THIS SITUATION. AFTER LONG THOUGHT AND WITH SINCERE REGRETS, WE MUST ASK YOU TO SUBMIT YOUR RESIGNATION EFFECTIVE UPON RECEIPT OF THIS TELEGRAM.[20]

He followed up with a letter which said that the events of the past six weeks had made it painfully clear that she was unable to work with Byler, and charged her with disobeying instructions from the central office. He explained that an organization cannot have its field people acting independently, as she repeatedly had done, and criticized her for trying to be a policymaker, a role that was unacceptable for a subordinate to assume. Further, Byler, Schifter, and Karelsen had made it quite clear that all of them would quit if Locker weren't fired.

When the Tribe learned of Locker's dismissal, they wrote AAIA to request that it be rescinded, and asked to meet with the AAIA Executive Committee to discuss the situation. A tribal delegation met with the executive committee in New York on February 16th.

As a result of the Tribe's protests, the executive committee reinstated Locker, placing her under the supervision of AAIA board member Roger Ernst instead of Byler. At about the same time, in an effort to placate Schifter and Karelsen, the executive committee passed a resolution expressing complete confidence in the attorneys. It seemed that the conflict was over and that they all could get on with the trust-title initiative.

Unfortunately, the uneasy peace disintegrated all too soon when, in late April, Anderson again introduced legislation conveying to the Tribe only 3,100 acres. In an inflammatory telegram to members of the Board, Locker blamed this on AAIA's "weakness."

> NEW BLUE LAKE LEGISLATION INTRODUCED THIS WEEK. CLEARLY INTENDED TO UNDERMINE POOLE BEFORE ANNUAL MEETING IN HOPE BOARD WILL ABANDON INDIAN TO EQUIVOCATION AND THE COMPROMISE. THIS DEVELOPMENT IS DIRECT CONSEQUENCE OF ASSOCIATION'S WEAKNESS OF WHICH I WARNED AS RESULT OF UNHOLY ALLIANCE BETWEEN BYLER, KARELSEN, AND STEVENS. TAOS PUEBLO REMAINS FIRM IN SUPPORT OF POOLE. ONLY STRONG AND UNEQUIVOCABLE [sic] ACTION BY BOARD CAN RESTORE HONOR OF ASSOCIATION AND CONFIDENCE OF INDIANS.[21]

The "unholy alliance" dig proved too much even for the forbearing members of the AAIA Board. The telegram enraged Roger Ernst, Locker's supervisor and the board member primarily responsible for her reinstatement. He immediately wrote to her, expressing his bafflement at her "continued attacks on Byler, Karelsen, and Stevens." After reading the thousands of words written by her and by Schifter, he said he had difficulty understanding "what you have been doing which is so right or what they have been doing which is so wrong." He went on with no holds barred:

> Your continued attacks upon all who might differ with you seem to be doing more damage to the Association than anything else I can think of. You have succeeded in splitting the Executive Committee and, I assume, in turn, the Board. You have succeeded in pitting old friends against each other. Rather than attempting to set forth an unemotional, practical program as a good employee should, you seem to enjoy making continued accusations and cry the Association is being destroyed. Believe me, I am unable to pinpoint anyone in the Association who seems to be working harder at bringing about disunity than you are. . . . I hoped your staggering experience in February would prompt you to busy yourself with more routine tasks while the delicate issue of Blue Lake awaited full Board consideration. . . . The atmosphere of hysteria which you have created makes it most difficult to give businesslike direction or advice.[22]

Ernst then ordered her to cease all activity in the Blue Lake matter until she heard from the board.

A week later, when the AAIA Board of Directors met, they took up the matter of Locker. President Stevens reviewed the history of her firing, her reinstatement under Ernst's supervision, and then read her "unholy alliance" telegram. Ernst commented:

> This telegram includes statements that are untrue and it is insulting to peo-
> ple connected with the Association. I have written her a stiff letter. I see no
> excuse for the wire and I think it is grounds for dismissal.[23]

The board agreed, passing three resolutions: the first two affirming confidence
in Stevens and Byler, and a third dismissing Locker as the Southwest field secretary.

Aware of the reaction this decision would provoke at Taos Pueblo, the board
dispatched Hildegard Forbes to Taos to meet with the Tribal Council. Accompanied by Rufus Poole, Forbes assured the council of AAIA's continuing support
for their cause, and they in turn assured her that they wished to maintain
friendly relations. It was clear, however, that there had been a definitive change.
The Tribe now determined to assume complete control of strategies in the Blue
Lake quest, without consulting further with AAIA. Praising her as a woman of
peace, the Council thanked Forbes for coming. As she left, "every Indian smiled
at me as he shook my hand."[24]

Driving back to Albuquerque, Poole told Forbes that it now seemed best that
he withdraw as the AAIA attorney on all matters concerning Blue Lake. He
would now work directly with the Pueblo, without connection to AAIA and
without pay. Locker had already resolved to do the same. With the official withdrawal of Poole, the long-standing AAIA-Taos alliance had been irrevocably
severed.

The departure of Poole also marked the end of the claims attorneys' direct
involvement in the Blue Lake matter. They essentially withdrew from negotiations for the sacred area, leaving these to Poole, the Tribe, and Locker. Eventually, the Tribe's ICC case would be treated as two matters: the disposition of the
48,000 acre watershed; and that of the remainder of the claim. While the claims
attorneys continued to work toward securing a cash settlement for the balance
of the ICC claim—the 80,000 acres and the land in the town of Taos—they left all
matters pertaining to the sacred 48,000 acres in the hands of the Tribe and its
chosen allies. While these arrangements were not finalized until early in 1970, it
is clear that the claims attorneys lost heart for the Blue Lake fight at the termination of AAIA's relationship with Taos Pueblo in the summer of 1967.

Ironically, it was Byler who had earlier made contact with the group that was
now to supplant AAIA as the Pueblo's main outside champion, the National
Council of Churches. At the time that AAIA and the Pueblo parted ways, this
appeared to be a serious setback. AAIA had played a crucial policymaking role in
the struggle up to that time; and it is certain that the many letters of support
written by its members had had a pronounced effect on the subcommitte's senators. Loss of AAIA support appeared to be a devastating reversal.

Subsequent events, however, revealed this development in a different light. It
had forced the Indians to seek organizational help elsewhere, help which the
NCC now began to supply. The advocacy of the National Council of Churches
went right to the heart of the matter, since the Tribe's fight was being waged on

At this all-important meeting, leaders of the National Council of Churches agreed to make common cause with the Indians. From left, Russell Carter, John J. Reyna, Seferino Martinez, Paul Bernal, and Dean Kelley. 1966. Photo by Dan Budnik.

religious grounds. There was no organization more influential and credible to support them on these grounds than the NCC.

When contacted by Byler in the fall of 1964, Russell Carter of the NCC immediately pledged their assistance. He urged Byler to confer with their director of the Commission on Religious Liberties, Rev. Dean Kelley. Byler relayed the suggestion to Bernal, who contacted Kelley during a visit to New York. Kelley agreed to help, and he and Carter "got a resolution through the governing board which formed the policy basis for our taking action."[25] It was the first Indian religious claim handled by the NCC. They saw it, Kelley remembers, as "an important issue of religious liberty, and we had not previous to that time done much with respect to Native American religious liberty interests."[26] The NCC then proceeded to assist in a multitude of ways: with duplicating, mailing, public relations, provision of access to religious and general press outlets, contacts with people in Washington, receiving of mail and calls in New York, and with fund raising, serving as a tax-exempt conduit for contributions.

The NCC also agreed to cooperate with the Tribe in presenting its case. In this regard, Kelley helped draft the testimony prepared by the NCC for the subcommittee hearings. While he did not himself present the testimony, he attended the hearings and assisted in drafting the NCC press release issued the day after. It placed great emphasis on the religious freedom aspect of the Tribe's quest, and received wide national circulation, especially in periodicals of a religious nature.

Kelley's attendance at the hearings proved crucial. As he listened to the Tribe attempt to convey to the senators the idea that the whole watershed was their church, he realized that they were not reaching their audience. He recalls that the Indians

> tried to get their point across as best they could and I think they had tried to find an analogy that would speak to the non-Indian mind. To some degree they had succeeded by comparing it with the European idea of a church, but that got them into the European idea of holy ground as being rather specifically located in an artificial setting, a building that you build and then that's the sacred precinct, and outside of it is not sacred. And that lent itself to being used by Anderson and others in saying, "Well, just tell us where this particular precinct is and we'll let you have that."[27]

In other words, the Indians' use of the church analogy was partly responsible for Anderson's restricting his bill to the 3,000 acres immediately surrounding Blue Lake, which he took to be the identifiable "sacred precinct."

The hearings convinced Kelley that an objective outsider might be helpful to the Tribe in translating their wishes into language the subcommittee could understand. When he went to Taos, where he met with the Tribal Council for several hours, he came to understand

> that it was not a matter of spatially identified little shrines in the area but that they felt akin [sic] to the whole watershed. My understanding was helped by driving my rental car on the other side of the ridge just outside the watershed, where the Forest Service had just finished allowing somebody to do the clear-cutting of the timber there. You know what that looks like; it was devastating. I could see why the Indians didn't particularly relish having that done in their sacred watershed. And so that reinforced my already strong empathy for their cause.[28]

As a result of his visit to Taos, Kelley wrote a short article that effectively explained to outsiders the sanctity of the entire watershed. Published in the *Journal of Church and State*, the article proved critical in the debate over the religious need of the Tribe for all of "the Bowl." In his piece, Kelley eloquently explained:

> The members of the tribe feel an ancient identity, not only with Blue Lake—the headwaters of their life-sustaining stream—but with the entire

watershed, its plants and animals. Anything which mutilates the valley hurts the tribe. If the trees are cut, the tribe bleeds. If the springs or lakes or streams are polluted, the lifestream of the tribe is infected. The mining of ore would inflict wounds upon the land and upon the people who revere it . . . . The spiritual kinship which the tribe feels for the sources of their life and livelihood clearly cannot be localized in any one spot or a few, but extends to the whole region. The aura of sanctity, which has its source in the water-courses where the Creator's life-sustaining water flows out to the inhabitants of a semi-arid land, is indivisible from the related lands and the living things that they produce.[29]

Published in the spring of 1967, Kelley's moving arguments played a central role in the hearings and debates that followed. The advocacy of Kelley and the NCC proved to be a crucial factor in the battle with Senator Anderson.

While the Locker affair was unfolding, Poole and the Tribe were still able to carry on halting negotiations with Anderson. Although in the fall of 1966 Anderson and the Tribe seemed to be caught in an unbreakable deadlock, both sides made a genuine attempt at compromise when Seferino Martinez became governor in January of 1967. During a surprisingly cordial meeting, Anderson explained "that all he wanted really was to allow Le Sage to harvest the timber in the 8,000 acres on the east side."[30] He asked the Indians if they would consider allowing Le Sage to harvest the timber in this area for the next twenty years, at the end of which time the Tribe would be given trust title. He offered to assist them in securing immediate title to the rest of the watershed, excluding the 2,000 acres in the Wheeler Wilderness.

Martinez replied that the Tribe would consider the offer only if they were given title to the entire 48,000 acres immediately, with the government retaining twenty-year timbering rights to the 8,000 acres desired by Le Sage. Neither side made a commitment, but Anderson promised to confer with Poole further about the compromise soon after he returned to Washington from New Mexico, where the meeting was held.

Ten days after this meeting, Anderson's office called Poole and asked him to prepare land descriptions for both the 40,000 acre and 8,000 acre sections. Poole immediately did so, and also drafted the language of the compromise bill. There now appeared to be an excellent chance that concession of the timber on the 8,000 acres would win the support of Anderson for conveyance of the entire "Bowl," excluding the 2,000 acres in the Wheeler Wilderness. For sentimental reasons, Locker hoped that this would come to pass. As she wrote to Poole,

> Severino Martinez is an old man, he and others have spent many years of their lives seeking the return of the Blue Lake Area, and they long to see that the whole area is in the inalienable possession of their people before they die.[31]

The chances that reconveyance would come to pass improved when Haley reintroduced, as H.R. 3306, the identical bill he had submitted the previous summer.

Given the apparent thaw in the climate of negotiations and the real possibility of achieving a compromise, the Tribe read with concern an article in the Santa Fe *New Mexican* of January 22. The article quoted Anderson as saying that a "new proposal" to deed the Taos Indians 3,150 acres surrounding Blue Lake was under discussion. The Tribe immediately issued a press release which called the article an obvious "misunderstanding." Explaining that the Pueblo had months ago rejected this proposal as "unjust and unreasonable," the release continued:

> Senator Anderson has been working hard since then in the interest of jus-
> tice to get a good bill ready for this session of Congress. From an exchange
> of ideas during a recent conference with the Senator, we feel sure that satis-
> factory legislation will be worked out.[32]

When the *Taos News* contacted Anderson about the "misunderstanding," how-ever, he said nothing about the recent compromise proposal, mentioning only the already-rejected 3,150-acre plan.

The Pueblo's fear that something was amiss increased when Anderson repeat-edly frustrated Poole's efforts to meet with him to finalize the compromise bill. Anderson confirmed their worst suspicions on the 26th of April, simultaneously introducing S. 1624, which gave the Tribe outright ownership only of the 3,150 acres around Blue Lake, and S. 1625, which put the same acreage in trust title. While Anderson publicly said his bills represented "fair treatment" for the Indians and the "best offer" that he was going to make, the Tribe, in "unanimous opposition," dismissed them as "not deserving of serious consideration." Poole then met with Anderson and made clear that his bills were "absolutely unac-ceptable," that the Indians insisted on the full 48,000 acres. Anderson retorted that "we might close our books if they. . .persist in that . . . ."[33] As the once-promising compromise deteriorated into countercharges in the newspapers, the *Taos News* commented that "the Blue Lake situation stands unresolved, unchanged, and indescribably fouled- up."[34]

Shortly thereafter, the *Taos News* published a lengthy article by Anderson in which he explained his position. He did not want to give the Indians the entire acreage both because he doubted that they could properly manage its conserva-tion and because there was valuable timber on much of the area that ought to be harvested. He concluded by saying that the Tribe's rejection of his 3,150-acre proposal

> makes me wonder whether the claim is true that the Taos Indians want this
> land only to use as their church. If they refuse to take a 3,150-acre tract and
> maintain it as sacred, we are bound to have some doubts of their religious
> sentiments.[35]

Behind Anderson's "doubts" about the Indians "religious sentiments" was a long-standing conviction that the Tribe's real motive for obtaining the watershed was a desire to profit from the timber. This suspicion had been expressed as early as 1965 in a meeting between Schifter and Claude Wood, one of Anderson's chief aides. When Schifter told Wood that the uniqueness of the Taos claim lay in the Pueblo's "deep religious identification with the Blue Lake area," Wood said "he just didn't believe that this was so . . . ." He revealed that both he and Anderson "believed the entire religious argument was advanced in recent years to justify an essentially economic interest in the land."[36]

Since Anderson's objective was to help his friend (and campaign contributor) Le Sage profit from timbering the watershed, he found it comfortable to conclude that the Pueblo harbored the same ulterior motive. Restricting them to 3,150 acres was an effective means, as Anderson saw it, of blocking an economically motivated land grab. Dismissing the entire watershed-as-sacred argument, Anderson said that the Tribe's refusal to accept the 3,150 acres proved that their motivation was economic.

He said as much to Preston Walker, editor of the *Daily Sentinel* in Grand Junction, Colorado, Aspinall's congressional district:

> I think we all agree that there is a difference in purpose behind the claims to the Blue Lake religious area and the claims to the general Blue Lake area. Religious motives undoubtedly underlie the claims to the Blue Lake religious area. However, the claims to the general Blue Lake area encompassing 50,000 acres of timber and minerals go beyond religious motivations.[37]

Speaking to Stewart Udall, Anderson dismissed the effort to have the entire 50,000 acres restored as nothing more than "a grab to benefit the claims attorneys."[38] Both charges reveal that Anderson believed that cupidity, not religion, motivated the pursuit of trust title.

Anderson's suspicions were supported by two academics, Dr. George L. Tragar, professor of anthropology at Southern Methodist University, and Dr. M.E. Smith, assistant professor of anthropology at Florida State University. Tragar had been visiting Taos for thirty years and was thought to know the Tribe well. Much of Smith's M.A. and Ph.D. work dealt with Taos Pueblo.

The professors told Harry Summers of the New Mexico Council of Churches that the annual Blue Lake pilgrimage had become popular only recently, "when it seemed that pilgrimages would help them establish a right to the acquisition of the territory."[39] The clear implication was that the Tribe had promoted the religious pilgrimage among its people simply to make more credible their economically motivated claim to the watershed. Summers reported,

> Both Dr. Tragar and Dr. Smith feel that Gov. Seferino Martinez and his political organization was interested in obtaining the land in order to exploit it for its commercial value.[40]

He said that they further charged that "most Taos Indians don't care about Blue Lake."[41]

The grounds for rebutting this accusation lie in the issue of wilderness status and the Tribe's attitude respecting it. When Udall first proposed wilderness status, just before the 1966 hearings, the Tribe readily accepted the proposal and Bernal so testified. They assumed that Anderson favored the idea, too. After all, he had supported the basic concept of wilderness reserves since 1919 when

Aldo Leopold first discussed the idea with him, and had been a major supporter of the Wilderness Act.

At the hearings, and during the summer following, however, when Anderson himself spoke against wilderness status, the Tribe accordingly dropped the idea. Clearly Anderson now opposed it because he and Le Sage were hoping to timber the watershed. The Tribe, despite their willingness to accommodate Anderson, had until then supported Udall's proposal because they had no designs on the timber. Wilderness status was entirely compatible with their desire to protect the land for exclusively religious purposes. When Anderson accused the Tribe of economic motives, they promptly renewed their support for wilderness status, and made sure that provisions respecting it were incorporated into all subsequent legislation, thus refuting Anderson's accusations.

As to the charge that the Tribe was promoting participation in the Blue Lake ceremonies only to make credible an economically motivated desire for the watershed, this increasing participation was more a function of the times than of economics. Referring to the 1960s, tribal member Richard Romero remembers:

> Across the nation you had a movement start that was geared towards taking care of the earth, and taking care of nature, and more observance of back to earth kind of things. And I think that made a lot of our young people realize—it gave them the feeling that, hey, we have something, there is something here that is a lot better than what we've been told . . . . So I think that what happened was all of a sudden there was a kind of a reawakening in the sixties and it grew stronger.[42]

While the facts make evident that the Indians had no plans commercially to exploit the sacred area, Anderson's belief that they did redoubled his resistance to giving up the entire watershed. When he told Poole that "he would not even consider" acreage beyond his offer of 3,150, the Tribe felt it had no choice but to reopen its appeal for public political support. Accordingly, late in June of 1967, the Tribe prepared and gave wide distribution to their "Statement by the Taos Pueblo Council on the Blue Lake Legislation."

Reaffirming that the entire watershed was the "religious sanctuary" of Taos Pueblo, the statement made clear that the existing use-permit was not satisfactory because it was

> subject to different interpretations by changing administrations. It violates basic American principles by making religious freedom and justice depend upon the sufferance of the Government and the whim of bureaucratic officials.[43]

The statement objected to Anderson's most recent bills because they would give the Tribe only a tiny island of land without access, and would take away the Tribe's exclusive use of 29,000 acres in the present permit area. It would also grant the Forest Service "new powers to dictate and control Indian and non-Indian uses alike"[44]; and would open the way to increased recreational use while

WELCOME TO TAOS PUEBLO

Our people have lived in this same village and on these lands since 1300 A.D. We hope you enjoy yourself while you are here learning of our Indian ways.

WE NEED YOUR HELP

The people of Taos Pueblo have been engaged in a struggle for 60 years to regain possession of their sacred Blue Lake Area, which lies in the mountains that you see to the east. This Blue Lake Area has always been and is today the religious sanctuary and the source of sustenance and water to our people. Here in the Pueblo you can see the stream, the *Río Pueblo de Taos*, that flows down from the Blue Lake.

These holy lands were confiscated from the Pueblo by the Federal Government in 1906 and placed in the National Forests.

Legislation to correct this injustice has been pending in the United States Senate since June, after unanimous passage by the House of Representatives. This bill, H. R. 3306, would end forever the desecration of our sacred shrines by placing the Blue Lake Area in trust for the Pueblo and protecting its sanctity as a wilderness. Unless the Senate acts soon, however, the bill will die.

You can help our people to obtain justice by sending a letter or wire urging the United States Senators listed below to support passage of H. R. 3306 before Congress adjourns (a special rate for wires to Congress is available):

    Hon. George McGovern, Chairman, Subcommittee on Indian Affairs,
        United States Senate, Washington, D. C.,
    Hon. Clinton P. Anderson (senior member of Indian Affairs Subcommittee),
        United States Senate, Washington, D. C., and
    Your own Senators, c/o United States Senate, Washington, D. C.

We appeal to you to add your voice to this historical struggle for justice and religious freedom.

                        The Governor and Council of Taos Pueblo

---

I heartily endorse, support and encourage passage of legislation aimed at returning the Blue Lake area to its rightful owners who in their faith have it in trust from God.
                        — Most Rev. James P. Davis
                          Archbishop of Santa Fe

The Indian Claims Commission ruled last year that the land did properly belong to Taos Pueblo, but special legislation is needed to carry out the decision.... It deserves prompt enactment.

                        — Editorial, New York Times

It's 60 years overdue, but when it passes the Congress we will be able to say, without qualification, that we really do believe in guaranteeing religious freedom to all Americans. Even to the original ones.

                        — Bob Considine

...the least that a great nation can do for the religious freedom of a neglected people.

                        — National Council of Churches

This 1967 handbill, distributed at Taos Pueblo, urged the support of visitors in the Tribe's fight for title to preserve the sanctity of the watershed lands. Courtesy of Taos Pueblo War Chief's Office.

stripping the Tribe of its right to approve visitor permits unless they applied for that right every year. The statement affirmed agreement with Udall's wilderness proposal, and denounced those who wanted to despoil the area for commercial profit. In conclusion, it asked for public support for Haley's H.R. 3306.

In addition to distributing this statement, which the *Taos News* printed in full, the Tribe sent letters to all of its known supporters presenting the facts of the current situation, and asking once again for their help with H.R. 3306. At the Pueblo itself, visitors were given a small flyer which presented a brief history both of the area and the quest for Blue Lake, asking the reader to send letters to their own congressional representatives as well as to Haley.

The NCC participated fully in the new public appeal, issuing a news release in early July of 1967 which gave a brief history of the conflict; pointed out that "the lake and some 20 natural 'shrines' in the territory have been vital to the religious life of the Taos tribe for nearly seven centuries"; and blasted Anderson's designs on the timber as "white man's greed."[45]

In addition, Kelley suggested that the Tribe form a national committee of prestigious people in support of the return of Blue Lake. The Pueblo seized upon this idea at once, and asked La Farge's widow, Consuelo, to serve as chair. She consented, and with her help, the Tribe then developed a list of other people who might be willing to join the committee. They hoped to have the membership set and the committee in full operation by the end of the year.

Kelley also recommended that the Tribe contact Lee Hobert, president of the New Mexico Council of Churches, to try to get their endorsement, since their backing would greatly influence the rest of the New Mexico congressional delegation. During the summer and fall of 1967, the Tribe worked hard to get NMCC approval. Hobert, Harry Summers, and Bruce Rolstad, the chair of the Christian Social Action Committee who had written in support of the Tribe at the 1966 hearings, took the lead in marshaling votes for the Pueblo. Archbishop Davis, too, continued to be an unwavering advocate.

The Tribe enhanced its chances with the NMCC by taking Hobert and Rolstad on a trip to Blue Lake. The opportunity arose in conjunction with the filming of a television special on the Blue Lake quest by Joe Phipps of WFIL-TV in Philadelphia. With the television crew and the NMCC representatives in tow, Bernal led a horseback party into the sacred wilderness. He was careful to include a visit to areas which Le Sage had already clear-cut. Just as it had with Kelley, the desecration done by Le Sage had an enormous impact on Rolstad. He remembers that his visit

> convinced me of the passion, how important it was and what was happening to the land. I think if anything, it was seeing what the Forest Service had allowed to happen with the timber industry there. Blue Lake is absolutely beautiful, it is a beautiful church, that was important, but anticipating, thinking of what happens if they don't get it back and the encroachment of the timber industry, that had actually clear-cutted [*sic*] the land . . . that convinced me right then.[46]

Hobert and Rolstad returned from Blue Lake determined to see justice done.

After thoroughly studying the facts on both sides, the NMCC members heatedly debated the issue at their annual meeting in late October. Rolstad recalls that the debate "really got down to first amendment rights and the support of the Roman Catholic and mainline Protestant bodies of [the Indians] ability to regain the title of their church."[47] The pro-Pueblo forces carried the day, and the NMCC passed a resolution upholding the Taos claim on the grounds that "it is impossible to interpret the American principles of justice and equality in any way that fails to protect the rights and religious convictions of a people."[48] The NMCC endorsement received wide coverage in the newspapers and convinced many who had been undecided of the validity of the Indians' claim.

Gearing up for a long battle, the Tribe also took steps, through applications to several charitable foundations, to raise money to finance the campaign. In addition, they began to meet privately with New Mexico Governor David Cargo, whose help Udall asked in working out a compromise with Anderson. While at that time Cargo felt "it would be politically unwise for him to express his support publicly,"[49] he nonetheless backed the Haley bill and worked behind the scenes on behalf of the Pueblo.

As a result of the Tribe's lobbying and publicity efforts, Anderson began to feel the political pressure. He was now faced with the condemnation of both the NMCC and the NCC, as well as Indians from New Mexico and throughout the country. In addition, the Tribe was getting extremely favorable press which resulted in other organizational endorsements as well as letters of support from voters everywhere. To back the Tribe was to oppose Anderson, and he became more and more obsessive about the issue as he was increasingly cast as the villain in the drama. Rolstad well says that for Anderson the Blue Lake battle

> was a real threat for him, to his ability to manage and to govern and to represent what he considered the whole of New Mexico. It just really gnawed. Because the Indians had persistently, for all these years, kept after it. I mean it didn't go away. It was not a winter time soldier situation. They were there all the time. And the digging at the research as to who contributed to his campaign, where the contracts were made, clear-cutting, violation of Forest Service regulations in themselves as to how they cut. It crossed not just the issue of church and state and religious liberty but it crossed environmental, social, cultural, all these issues. And so it was more than just the one thing. And so he was constantly being bombarded with these questions.[50]

Anderson considered Corinne Locker the person most responsible for his increasing political torment. Mistakenly believing that she worked for the NCC, Anderson told the director of the NCC Washington office that "You have a representative in the New Mexico area who butchers me day by day for a bill in which I tried to help the Taos Indians."[51] One of Anderson's staffers agreed, reporting that "The Indians were completely satisfied with your proposal until Mrs. Corinne Locker, a secretary to the late Oliver La Farge, got into the act. It was she who convinced the Indians to demand more . . . ."[52]

Anderson was fully aware of the crucial and praiseworthy role played by Locker at this time. Schifter had said that anyone who advised the Tribe to fight Anderson was doing the Tribe a "grave disservice." As the pressure on Anderson mounted, however, it became clear that hers could be the winning strategy.

Perhaps Locker's greatest contribution to the Blue Lake quest stemmed from her genius for publicity. She was a brilliant writer of quotable prose that was highly informative, esthetically pleasing, and, without being sentimental, provided an emotional appeal that inspired readers to action. The numerous press releases she wrote during this time were so effective that they often appeared in newspapers almost verbatim.

In addition, Locker shouldered the enormous burden of correspondence the struggle required. She made the Tribe aware of the importance of following up on all contacts, and saw to it that every inquiry, however apparently insignificant, received a reply. She also kept those working with the Tribe fully informed, maintaining a steady stream of memoranda and letters to key supporters like Kelley and Udall, as well as to representatives from conservation groups. Further, Locker worked very well with Poole, and was discerning about the subtle nuances of legal language. She, therefore, was able to provide the Tribe with sound advice concerning bills and their formulation.

Locker was also a master tactician. It was she, in the early sixties, who had inspired the Tribe to again take up the title quest, and who had recruited Poole to provide the necessary legal advice. She correctly discerned that the claims attorneys were too easily influenced by developments in the Washington political scene, and blocked their attempts to compromise with Anderson by giving up on the quest for trust title. From the outset she was suspicious of Mitchell, who in fact turned out to be a fifth columnist in Anderson's camp.

Perhaps most important, it was Locker who emphatically had insisted that the quest remain under the absolute control of the Tribe, resisting all efforts by AAIA and the claims attorneys to impose their will on the Indians. This required considerable courage on her part, as exemplified by her sending the "unholy alliance" telegram, which she undoubtedly knew would result in her firing.

Indeed, she acknowledged that in the matter of the claims attorneys she had "exceeded her authority," but that she had done so simply because she felt she had no choice. With the fate of Blue Lake hanging in the balance, she had done what she had to do, as she saw it, to insure that nothing would jeopardize the Tribe's struggle for "inalienable possession" of the watershed.

As a result of her unswerving dedication, Locker had the absolute confidence and support of the Indians, who were, after all, in the best position to judge who their real friends were. When AAIA initially fired Locker, the Tribe sent them an impassioned letter in her defense, signed by sixty councilmen. They then sent a delegation to New York which made an "eloquent and moving request" on her behalf. When Hildegard Forbes met with the Tribal Council after Locker's second firing, the Indians made it clear that "Mrs. Locker was their chosen guide, protector and friend . . . ."[53]

Indeed, the key to the Blue Lake battle from the summer of 1966 forward was the close cooperation between Locker, Bernal, and Poole. The three of them would devise their strategy, Bernal would explain it to the Tribal Council and get approval, and Locker would then write the document necessary to implement the strategy—whether letters, resolutions, press releases, memoranda, pamphlets, or statements. While Anderson's charge late in 1967 "that the Pueblo is being controlled by a woman"[54] is undoubtedly an exaggeration, it nonetheless underscores the importance of the role that Locker played in the battle for Blue Lake.

The importance of that role increased after the spring of 1967, as Poole became seriously ill. By the end of 1967, he was unable to work, and he asked an Albuquerque attorney, William Schaab, to take his place. He had known Schaab for some time through casual social contact, and was convinced that he was the man for the job. Poole told his wife Suzie that Schaab was a man "with a hunger for public service and he'll do a beautiful job."[55]

While Schaab had no previous experience in Indian affairs, Poole felt he had the requisite toughness and tenacity to take on Clinton Anderson. Schaab gives us the background on his selection by Poole:

> It grew out of a case I had involving the mandatory mark-up law on liquor. We had acquired an interest in a saloon and we couldn't make any money running the saloon so I said, what the hell, let's file suit to have the mandatory mark-up law invalidated. And so we did. And three years later we won in the Supreme Court. And Rufus was so impressed that we could take on the wholesale liquor industry in New Mexico and beat the bastards that he though that I was probably up to Clinton Anderson.[56]

Poole's intuition about Schaab proved correct when he became an important contributor to the successful conclusion of the Blue Lake fight.

The Tribe was now getting very close to finding out, as Consuelo La Farge put it,

> whether white men will be permitted to steal and exploit the last unspoiled sanctuary of a living Indian tradition remaining out of this nation's rapacious past.[57]

Schaab was to do brilliant legal work in defense of Mrs. La Farge's conviction that Blue Lake

> is not simply a matter of historically mistreated Indians versus petty greed; it is an opportunity to preserve an American heritage while protecting the most fundamental rights of fellow citizens to justice and religious freedom.[58]

7

The Tide Begins to Turn

T HE GLOOM OF THE PREVIOUS TWO YEARS began to dissipate in January of 1968, when Schaab signed on as special counsel to the Pueblo in the Blue Lake fight. While the Tribe had to borrow the $7,500 to pay his retainer, they were convinced that he was worth it. As Locker said, she and the Tribe believed Schaab would bring to the battle "the sort of meticulous approach—a la Ralph Nader or the well-known attorney, Louis Nizer—that we have badly needed and that is fundamental to success in an effort of this kind."[1]

Also grounds for optimism was the formation of the National Committee for Restoration of the Blue Lake Lands to the Taos Indians. Its purposes were to raise money to be sent to a special tax-exempt fund at the NCC, and to stimulate letters to Haley. In the process of formation since the summer of 1967, the committee was established in January of 1968, as the Tribe's press release announced. The NCC also distributed the release, "with a strengthened religious angle," both to "the daily newspaper press and a heavy list of religious periodicals." Newspapers everywhere picked up the release, and the Blue Lake fight received considerable new publicity.

With Consuelo La Farge as chair, the committee boasted a prestigious membership that included merchandiser John Wanamaker, political cartoonist Bill Mauldin, conservationist and photographer Eliot Porter, and the faithful John Collier.

Perhaps even more important than these notables were the religious members of the committee. Headed by Russell Carter and Dean Kelley from the NCC, they also included James Davis, the archbishop of Santa Fe, Lee Hobert, the president of the NMCC, and Howard Squadron, chair of the Commission on Law and Social Action of the American Jewish Congress. Squadron's participation was especially significant because it made the fight for Blue Lake now a truly ecumenical effort. As Locker said in her telegram to news editors announcing the committee's formation, it "INAUGURATES CAMPAIGN REMARKABLE IN AMERICAN HISTORY FOR ECUMENICAL SPIRIT INVOLVING LEADING CHURCH AUTHORITIES IN SUPPORT OF ABORIGINAL INDIAN RELIGION."[2]

Soon after this flurry of favorable press, with coverage by hundreds of publications, Schaab traveled east to research the Tribe's claim and to make contact with those who would have some influence in deciding the fate of Blue Lake. He succeeded in both objectives, turning up a good deal of valuable information as well as meeting with the commissioner of Indian Affairs, Robert Bennett; Udall's legislative assistant, Robert McConnell, who was to be an important contact; the claims attorneys, New Mexico congressmen Johnny Walker and Tom Morris; and representatives from the Departments of Justice, Interior, Agriculture, and the Bureau of the Budget.

More importantly, Schaab met with the two men most directly connected with the legislative fate of Blue Lake—Anderson and Haley. Anderson admitted that he was disturbed by his unfavorable publicity, but remained adamant about returning no more than 3,000 acres. Further, he said that he was now unwilling to give the Tribe trust title even to that limited acreage. Anxious about the precedent involved, he said that he would discuss only a long-term permit. Anderson's concern about precedent was a new development. At the Senate subcommittee hearings in 1966, he had stated that, in his judgment, it did not present a problem.

Haley seemed rather nonchalant, and told Schaab that he planned to hold Washington hearings later in the spring. He advised him not to worry about the bill's eventual passage, that "he had never lost an Indian bill since he had become chairman of the subcommittee, and he expressed confidence that he could have the Blue Lake bill passed despite Anderson's opposition."[3]

Schaab's eastern foray convinced him that a hard-hitting memorandum setting forth the legal history of the Tribe's claim would arouse Congress and get the House subcommittee to act on H.R. 3306. Based on information gathered in Washington, Schaab set to work developing the memorandum, which he completed in early March. It was sent, along with a plea for support of H.R. 3306, to key members of Congress as well as to many other interested parties. A masterpiece of legal drafting, the memorandum ("the result of about one month's solid work") for the first time set forth in detail the complete history of the Pueblo's claim. It became a significant piece of evidence in all of the coming legislative battles.

By mid-March of 1968, Haley, ready to hold hearings on H.R. 3306, was reluctant actually to do so until the Bureau of the Budget and the Departments of Agriculture and Interior released their comments on the bill. They had been in disagreement since the spring of 1967. Schaab asked Udall's help in resolving the interdepartmental conflict. Through his intercession, the reports finally appeared in April. Predictably, Interior supported H.R. 3306, if amended to put all of the land returned to the Tribe under the protection of the Wilderness Act. Just as predictably, Agriculture opposed H.R. 3306, supporting instead Anderson's 3,000-acre bill of the previous year, now watered down to give the Tribe only a long-term permit for exclusive use. They argued that "outright conveyance, regardless of the acreage involved, would be a far-reaching, undesirable precedent."[4] The Bureau of the Budget, representing the opinion of Pres. Lyndon Johnson, tipped the balance, siding with Agriculture and their recommended permit.

As both sides prepared for the impending House hearing, Schaab and Kelley fine-tuned the Tribe's religious arguments. Schaab favored stressing the Tribe's need for secrecy to practice their religion, because without this emphasis "there appeared to be no satisfactory way of explaining why the entire Blue Lake area is religiously important to the Pueblo."[5] While Kelley appreciated that not many could accept the Pueblo's need for a 50,000-acre "church," and while he saw the relevance of the secrecy argument to establishing that fact, he nonetheless opposed, on purely practical grounds, the emphasizing of this argument.

> I have tried to avoid highlighting that aspect of the claim of religious freedom because I have found that it tends to rub people the wrong way. . . .It may be cogent; it is largely true, but it does not tend to elicit cooperation.[6]

Schaab took the matter up with the Tribal Council and "established that secrecy is indeed at the base of the Pueblo's objection to intrusions into the area."[7] He now had his confirmation for the decision to give weight to this point in his testimony.

With the arguments on their behalf set, the Tribe determinedly prepared for the hearings, which Haley had called for early May. Lacking funds to send their delegation to Washington, they dispatched an urgent plea to the Field Foundation for an emergency ten thousand dollar grant: "Pueblo's funds drained and situation desperate."[8] They were also several thousand dollars in debt to Schaab, and unable to pay his mounting bills.

Throughout the spring the Tribe had been preoccupied with raising money, projecting a three-year campaign that would require about $150,000. Locker unsuccessfully attempted to retain a professional fund-raiser and also prepared grant applications that were submitted to several foundations. None of these proved fruitful, however, since the foundations were concerned about contributing money to a cause that involved lobbying Congress. Unable to find money from outside sources, the Tribe finally tapped their own reserve firefighting fund to finance the trip to Washington.

On the morning of May 9, Haley opened the hearing by noting that if the bill were amended as Agriculture wished, "there would be no occasion for this bill because you would absolutely kill the intent of this bill."[9] He then called Udall and Robert Bennett, commissioner of Indian Affairs, as the first witnesses. Udall essentially repeated his testimony of 1966, stressing the religious significance of the land for the Indians and reiterating his earlier arguments against the three main objections to title reconveyance: precedent, grazing permits as vested interests, and commercial designs on the part of the Tribe.

Representatives Aspinall of Colorado, Berry of South Dakota, Edmondson of Oklahoma, McClure of Idaho, and Steiger of Arizona then questioned Udall. His replies established the religious significance of the Indians' claim, as well as their commitment to exclusively noncommercial uses of the watershed. The congressmen's questions, especially Steiger's, showed them to be friendly to H.R. 3306. Steiger confronted the precedent issue by noting that no governmental department was more "zealous" than the Forest Service in holding on to land in its trusteeship. He went on to say that he hoped that H.R. 3306 would set a precedent, that its passage

> would imply that Forest Service lands are not inviolate as they have been in the past with regard to exchange or disposal or removal from the trusteeship of the Forest Service.[10]

Haley then called on Edward P. Cliff, chief of the Forest Service, to present the next testimony. Cliff opened by telling the committee that his agency found it difficult to reconcile their policy of multiple-use with the Indian desire for exclusive use of the area. He argued that, while Schaab's memorandum contended that the act of 1933 and the permit of 1940 gave the Tribe exclusive use, his department believed that they granted the Tribe only special rights in an area still reserved for multiple uses.

Cliff was of the firm opinion that the permit of 1940 gave the Indians all the religious protection they needed. The Forest Service was nonetheless willing to increase the protection afforded them by granting a permit for exclusive use of the Blue Lake area itself. However, he opposed giving them title because of the adverse precedent involved. He also raised the grazing permit issue, and the problem of unduly reducing the size of the Wheeler Wilderness if 2,000 acres were given to the Indians. He concluded that the taking of the Pueblo's land into the forest reserves was no different from the appropriation of millions of other acres by Teddy Roosevelt. This was a position apparently supported by President Johnson, since the Bureau of the Budget favored Agriculture and the Forest Service.

Representative Edmondson of Oklahoma pointed out that the ICC thought the appropriation of the Taos land was different from other acquisitions under the Forest Reserve Act, and Haley was quick to agree. "These lands, in my humble opinion, belong to the Indians and, therefore, you are not giving them anything. You took something away from them and I hope that we can rectify that."[11] Edmondson also noted that the Taos Indians' refusal to take money for their land was unique, and proved their religious attachment. After further discussion of such matters as grazing permits, water production, and timbering, proceedings recessed for the day.

Schaab began the next day's testimony, introducing into the record the complete text of his memorandum with 104 supporting exhibits. He summarized its contents, presenting the relevant facts from the ICC decision and moving on to the history of the Tribe's struggle for the watershed. Next, he discussed with emphasis the sacredness to the Indians of the entire watershed, and their need for ceremonial secrecy, explaining that the private and secret nature of the ceremonies made it impossible for the Indians to talk about them in detail. "However," he continued,

> it is quite clear that if that land were opened to the public or if commercial timber operations were allowed to occur within the watershed, the land would be desecrated in their eyes, and they would refuse to practice their religion.[12]

Schaab asserted that there were two essential arguments opposing H.R. 3306: the precedent issue, and the denial that the Indians' religious practices require the entire 50,000-acre "Bowl." Regarding the precedent issue, Schaab said that the Forest Service had no supporting evidence of any comparable claims and were only hypothesizing that some might be made. The truth was that there were no similar cases, proving that "the Taos case is thus unique on the facts and that there is no dangerous precedent created."[13]

With respect to the religious need of the Tribe for the whole watershed, Schaab maintained that this was a matter of Indian belief which they were entitled to hold, and that they had demonstrated their good faith through sixty-five years of persistent struggle to regain the land. To the charge that the Tribe hoped to profit economically from the land, he countered that making money "is completely inconsistent with their traditional religious practices and that it is the religion which is truly the grounds for their claim."[14]

To the question of whether or not the cash settlement proposed by the ICC as compensation for the land was adequate, Schaab answered emphatically: "No, because of the unique character of this land in the life of the Pueblo Indian." He explained,

> It is religious land, and they are deeply attached to it. The religion is the essence of their lives. It is the foundation for their social and political structure.[15]

He concluded that to open the land to outsiders or to commercial activity

> would make it completely impossible for them to practice their religion. The destruction of their religion will destroy the basic institutions of their lives; it will finally destroy their culture. This is why this bill is so terribly important to them.[16]

With the legal arguments well made in his effective testimony, Schaab introduced the tribal delegation: Gov. Querino Romero, Seferino Martinez, Louis Castellano, and Paul Bernal. Each of them made religious freedom the focus of their remarks. Martinez explained that they had come to Washington "because our freedom of religion has been violated by the United States Government."[17]

Noting that the Tribe had used the area for religious purposes "since the beginning of time," Martinez pleaded for its return to insure their survival as a people. Romero and Castellano made essentially the same point, that the advent of the white man infringed upon their right to freedom of religion, and that they required trust title to protect that freedom.

Bernal took a more combative stance. He said that while the Indians had not resisted the appropriation of their land in 1906 because they were uneducated and could not effectively express their objections, they now knew better and were prepared to fight until they got it back. He denied that their case set a precedent, and then launched into an attack on Forest Service management of the area, complaining about the old issues of recreational use, fish stocking, dynamiting of sacred lakes, and invasion of religious privacy. As evidence of the Tribe's sincerity, he told the subcommittee that they had spent nearly all of the money in the tribal treasury to get to Washington, and were prepared to make any sacrifice to reclaim the sacred watershed.

Lee Hobert, representing the NMCC and Archbishop Davis, then testified on behalf of the Tribe. He said that his group had thoroughly researched the issue before deciding to back the Pueblo, and had concluded that the Indians required the entire watershed for the safe and effective practice of their religion. He concluded by reading Archbishop Davis's strong statement of support.

Final testimony was given by John Stillman, representing the Blue Lake National Committee. He reviewed the widespread sympathy for the Pueblo's cause and the importance of religion in the life of the Taos people, maintaining that return of the watershed to the Tribe was "the highest form of conservation. It is conservation of spiritual and moral values, conservation of a religious heritage."[18] With the introduction of a statement supporting H.R. 3306 by the ACLU and one opposing it by the National Wildlife Federation, the hearings drew to a close. Kelley, on a field trip for the NCC for much of May, was not present to testify.

The subcommittee then proceeded to mark up the bill. First, they deleted the claim to the 2,000 acres in the Wheeler Wilderness, in order to remove any possible conflict between the Tribe and the Forest Service over this area. Second, they amended the bill to make it clear that non-Indians would be permitted entry into the watershed only with tribal consent. Third, to protect the land against multi-purpose usage, they assigned wilderness status to the entire watershed, placing it under the administrative authority of the Department of the Interior. The subcommittee then voted unanimously for passage of H.R. 3306 in this amended form. Locker reported that: "The effect of the news of this initial success upon the people of the Pueblo was electrifying. The response throughout the community has been one of renewed pride and hope."[19]

While jubilant about the outcome of the vote, the tribal leaders were disheartened by their near insolvency. They estimated that they now needed between twenty-five thousand dollars and forty thousand dollars to carry the fight through the House and Senate. Up to this point, they had raised only about two thousand dollars, and were ten thousand dollars in debt, with six thousand dollars owed to Schaab and past due for nearly three months. Indeed, Schaab was able to get to the Washington hearings only by charging the expense on his personal credit card. A week after the hearings, he wrote the Tribe requesting payment of the six thousand dollars due him, gently reminding them that his contract gave him the right to terminate services for non-payment. To meet their financial obligations, the Tribe withdrew the remainder of the money from the firefighting fund, leaving them without further resources.

Further tempering the Tribe's optimism was unexpected opposition to H.R. 3306, due for House consideration in early June under suspension of the rules. The opposition came from the House Agriculture Committee, which blocked action on the bill. Undaunted, Haley quietly withdrew H.R. 3306 from the House calendar and took it to the Rules Committee, which granted a rule on the bill and scheduled it for floor action on June 18. The full House of Representatives was now to vote on the fate of Blue Lake.

Crucial to the success of H.R. 3306 was the position taken by Colorado Congressman Wayne Aspinall, chair of the House Committee on Interior and Insular Affairs. Since his committee had oversight responsibility for Haley's Subcommittee on Indian Affairs, the assembled congressmen looked to Aspinall as a bellwether.

Aspinall opened the House debate on H.R. 3306 with a long presentation of the history of the Taos claim and of the problems between the Tribe and the Forest Service. He recognized that sixty years of conflict had been occasioned by the Indians' need for privacy to practice their religion and the Forest Service's insistence upon promoting recreational uses of the watershed. To him, the resolution of the issue hinged upon which party's need for the land was greater and he had concluded that "the question of equity is on the side of the Indian in this matter."[20] They needed the land in order to preserve their culture, while the Forest Service had identified no federal need that would be threatened by enactment of H.R. 3306.

Aspinall confronted the main argument against the bill—that land once put in the forest reserves ought never to be taken out, and that to give the watershed to the Indians was to set a dangerous precedent for doing so. Aspinall dismissed the precedent argument, saying that the Taos case was unique and that passage of H.R. 3306 would be a recognition of the special needs of this one Tribe. "But more importantly," he declared,

> no program should be regarded as immune from change, and if the United States unjustly took land from the Indians, it should not say that it will keep its ill-gotten gains solely because the lands are now in a national forest.[21]

The Tribe could not have hoped for a more favorable presentation of their cause. Aspinall's strong support dramatically improved the chances for passage of H.R. 3306.

John Saylor of Pennsylvania, the ranking minority member of the Interior Committee, spoke next. He, too, proved a tribal supporter, calling passage of H.R. 3306 a "matter of simple justice."[22] He emphasized a point already made by Aspinall, that the conflict lay in promotion of multiple use by the Forest Service versus the Indian need for exclusive use to protect the privacy of their rituals. He saw the conflict as "a case where bureaucratic desires have been allowed to interfere with equitable values," and was of the decided opinion that,

> If the bureaucratic issue is removed, the equities are all on the side of the Indians. A limitation on recreational use of the area by 90 non-Indians [in] a year is a small price to pay for the protection of the religious life of an entire Pueblo Indian community.[23]

He urged "that this bill be enacted to preserve the religious needs of a small minority group whose rights have been so violently violated."[24]

Now it was Haley's turn, and he did not disappoint. After reviewing the history of the Pueblo, he put religious privacy at the heart of the argument:

> The Taos Indians are a closely knit group, and religion permeates their communal life. The Blue Lake area is the most holy symbol of their ancient religion, and the symbolism attaches to the entire watershed. The watershed is the source of their life. Although the nature of their religion is secret, it is clear that if the area were extensively used for recreation by the public, it would be desecrated in the eyes of the Indians.[25]

Haley made a point of stressing the wilderness provisions of H.R. 3306 as amended by his subcommittee, and their compatibility with the Indians' veneration of the watershed. Noting that the Indians had suffered religious interference since the inclusion of their land into the forest reserves sixty years ago, he thundered:

> The Indians did not agree to the taking, they were not paid for the land, and they want their land back. It is only fair that they get it. Restoration of the land to the Indians will right a wrong in the only manner that is acceptable to the Indians . . . I urge that the bill be enacted.[26]

Astonishingly, no one rose in opposition to the bill, and the Speaker called the question. H.R. 3306 passed by unanimous consent, without a single dissenting vote. The Indians were overjoyed and wired Haley: "Your success today House passage H.R. 3306 brings joy and happiness to hearts of people of Taos Pueblo. Profoundly grateful for your unswerving support and friendship."[27]

Four days later, the Tribe held a "Justice Day" celebration in Haley's honor. There were dances and feasting, and hundreds, including several Indian dignitaries from other tribes, participated in the fete. Archbishop Davis delivered the invocation from a platform in the Pueblo plaza across which stretched a huge banner reading "THANK YOU CONGRESSMAN HALEY". Raymond Nakai, chairman of the powerful Navajo Tribe, delivered the keynote address, calling the passage of H.R. 3306 a victory for all Indians and a demonstration that the people of

Taos were doing their part to preserve the culture and religion of the American Indian. "Without this," said Nakai, "we are but census numbers in a file cabinet in Washington, D.C., waiting like sheep to be absorbed into the dominant society."[28] He concluded:

> Blue Lake signifies a new day for all our Indian brethren. Let us hope that it may signify a new day of respect and honor for Indian culture and Indian religion.[29]

The Tribe's sweeping victory in the House redoubled the pressure on Anderson, especially in his home state. An editorial in the Santa Fe *New Mexican* reviewed the Pueblo's claim, urging that "the Senate act quickly and wisely . . . . we trust that recent celebrations and dances at the Taos pueblo will not have been indulged in for naught."[30] The *Taos News* said that the House action shattered any objection to Blue Lake's return for all "but the most myopic," and found great significance in the fact "that nobody in the House spoke against the bill on final passage."[31] The *Albuquerque Journal* hoped that the Indians' sixty-year effort to reclaim their land would be successful, and called on Anderson to drop his bill and back H.R. 3306: "The Blue Lake area rightfully belongs to the Taos Indians; it is the center of their religious life . . . ."[32]

The finger of public opinion now pointed critically at Anderson as the chief adversary to the cause of Indian religious freedom, and the media increasingly portrayed him as an unfeeling curmudgeon. The temper of the times magnified the unacceptability of his position. In the spring of 1968, 221 political and social demonstrations were held on more than 100 campuses. Martin Luther King was assassinated in April, and Bobby Kennedy just two weeks before the Tribe's dramatic vote in the House. In that same month, the massive Poor People's March descended upon Washington, and as the congressmen voted on Blue Lake, demonstrators were planning the disruptions that plagued the Democratic convention in Chicago later that summer. Eldridge Cleaver's *Soul on Ice* made the bestseller list, and minority rights and cultural pluralism became burning issues.

A sympathetic climate of opinion was created for Blue Lake by the surging counterculture. The first great "Be-In" in San Francisco's Golden Gate Park was called "The Gathering of the Tribes." The Caucasian identification with Indians mounted as thousands took up communal existence, often living in tipis while sporting braids, beads, and feathers. While few of them voted or wrote to their congressmen, nonetheless they were expressing an appreciation of and respect for Indian values. All of this made Anderson's stance look that much more reprehensible.

Also significant was the fact that the Tribe's plea for religious freedom was joined to and based upon a reverence for their land. For the Taos Indians, freedom of religion entailed the right to worship and protect the land in the same way as had their ancestors for centuries past. The Indians worshiped the land itself. As Tribal councilman Tony Reyna said:

The Indians have something. They've got a base. You people don't have any-thing really. Your descendants came from Europe looking for freedom of religion. And yet when they got here they imposed their ideas on the Indians. The best religion is Indian—Nature. We don't push fancy dresses, we don't have no collection, spiritual is spiritual. . . .The same Man that gave us the mountain, the water, the air, the health is the same Man that you guys are trying to glorify by singing, making collection and big donation and tax deduction. We don't do that. We pray for everyone and give thanks for everything.[33]

The Tribe's veneration of nature was perfectly in tune with the spirit of the times. As Charles Reich said, in his influential *The Greening of America*:

There is a revolution coming . . . .It is now spreading with amazing rapidity, and already our laws, institutions and social structure are changing in con-sequence. It promises a higher reason, a more human community and a new and liberated individual. Its ultimate creation will be a new and endur-ing wholeness and beauty—a renewed relationship of man to himself, to other men, to society, to nature and to the land.[34]

Those who were seeking a renewed relationship to the land and who were concerned with ecology naturally rallied to the cause of an Indian tribe with a centuries-old tradition of worshiping nature, and who also were fighting to pro-tect their wilderness from the depradations of timbering and poisonous sprays.

In short, the Tribe's quest resonated with some important themes of the later sixties— cultural pluralism, minority rights, and the back- to-nature movement. Their quest for religious freedom to protect their culture and their sacred land was favored by the temper of the times. In spite of Clinton P. Anderson, the prospects for passage of a Blue Lake bill grew stronger.

Pumped up by these cultural developments, the pressure on Anderson mounted steadily. The Tribe now had the endorsement not only of the local *Taos News*, but of the other two leading papers in New Mexico as well. The unani-mous vote in the House underscored the national sympathy for the Tribe, a sym-pathy made manifest by a mid-July editorial in the *New York Times*. Titled "The Indians Need Blue Lake," the editorial reviewed the history of the Tribe's claim, giving emphasis to the "prominent spiritual significance" of the watershed for the Indians "for centuries." It concluded that H.R. 3306 "gives the Senate a clear opportunity to correct one of the multitude of tragic mistakes of the past in the abuse of the American Indian."[35] The National Congress of American Indians agreed, passing a resolution which said that H.R. 3306, "by recognizing the reli-gious rights and freedom of the Taos Pueblo Indians, is vitally important to all Indian tribes as well as to all American citizens."[36] The NCC's support also was critical. Through their efforts, countless letters and telegrams of support inun-dated Anderson's office and those of other members of Congress.

With the tide of public opinion running in their favor, a tribal delegation visited Washington to appeal directly to Anderson for support of H.R. 3306.

While initially discouraging, Anderson later discussed with the delegation the possibility of amending the bill to make it acceptable to both parties.

Faced with mounting public indignation, Anderson retreated from his position on returning a maximum of 3,000 acres. He now offered to give the Tribe 48,000 acres in trust status, with exclusive possessory rights subject only to provision of the necessary conservation measures by the Forest Service. Under this proposal, the Tribe's rights to the area would continue as long as they complied with various purposes to be set forth in the bill itself. To these provisions the Tribe agreed. However, the Tribe refused when Anderson insisted that the 8,000 acres on the east side be timbered, and negotiations broke down. Anderson angrily vowed to keep the bill bottled up in committee, and the Tribe retorted that he could expect to see them coming back until they were granted all 48,000 acres under trust title.

Shortly thereafter, the *Washington Post*, learning of the failed compromise, published a July editorial attacking Anderson. It began, "An old injustice inflicted on the Taos Indians of New Mexico should be set right before Congress adjourns." Taking direct aim at Anderson, it continued:

> But a Senate Subcommittee continues to ignore the bill, allegedly at the behest of Sen. Clinton P. Anderson. If the Senator has any legitimate objection to righting a wrong done more than 60 years ago, he ought to lay his cards on the table. It seems inexcusable to suppress a bill of this kind, involving the national integrity, in the face of the action by the Claims Commission and the House.[37]

When the oracle of Washington accused him of compromising "national integrity" with "inexcusable" behavior, it hit Anderson hard. George McGovern, who chaired the Senate Interior Committee's Subcommittee on Indian Affairs where action on the Blue Lake bill was blocked, promptly conferred with Anderson and issued a press release which called for Senate hearings on the Blue Lake bill:

> It appeared earlier this week that we had reached agreement on a measure which could be recommended to the Senate and sent to conference with the House.
>
> However, since questions continue to be raised in the press about the matter, and Congress will return in September, a public hearing seems necessary and desirable.[38]

McGovern's call for hearings was welcome news to the Tribe, but they were still beset by financial problems. With the firefighting fund depleted, the Tribe was reduced to financing the operation of the campaign with the fees collected from visitors to the historic Pueblo. The tribal delegation had been able to go to Washington to meet with Anderson in late July only "with the help of emergency contributions from several individuals."[39] In the past year alone, the Tribe had spent nearly nineteen thousand dollars, much of the disbursements paid out of the now exhausted fire-fighting fund.

Of the twenty-seven hundred dollars collected by the National Committee for

Restoration of the Blue Lake Lands to the Taos Indians, twenty-three hundred dollars had already been spent. The Tribe now owed Schaab an additional eleven thousand dollars, and he sent them another dunning letter. Saying that his firm "feels that we should not have to finance the Pueblo's Blue Lake campaign at our risk,"[40] he reminded them again that the contract could be terminated for non-payment.

Locker was doing all she could to help, and in late August prepared a lengthy "Appeal for Emergency Funds." Fearing the "collapse of their historic campaign," she emphasized its importance for the preservation of the religion and culture of all Indians, and its unique ecumenical backing.

> This is the first time in American history that the major, organized religions, both local and national, have joined to recognize and support the equal rights of an aboriginal Indian religion . . . . this ecumenical development has major implications for the history of Indian affairs.[41]

Her appeal estimated expenses for the upcoming Senate hearings at thirteen thousand dollars, and concluded that, "Unless the present emergency is met, the Pueblo's position will be seriously, and perhaps irremediably, damaged."[42] The appeal, sent to several foundations, met with universal rejection, again chiefly because the Blue Lake fight involved lobbying Congress.

Compounding the bleakness of the financial picture was a letter sent to the tribal war chief in early September of 1968 by Duane R. Freeman, district ranger for the Carson National Forest. Freeman informed the Tribe that he had just returned from Blue Lake and found that

> the area had been left in somewhat of a mess after the cerimonials [sic] in August. Cans and bottles were strewn about as were cigarette and gum wrappers, etc. Tee Pee [sic] poles were scattered also and had not been replaced in the area provided.
>
> I realize it has been Forest Service policy in the past for the Forest Service to cleanup [sic] the area after cerimonials [sic]. However, with the significance that you people place on Blue Lake I would think you would be somewhat embarrassed to have someone else cleanup [sic] a mess in an area which you claim as a shrine.[43]

Freeman's was a serious charge indeed, and it was not the first time that the Indians had been accused of leaving their sacred shrine "a mess." As early as 1961, the chief of the Forest Service told one of the AAIA attorneys that "the Indians did not come with clean hands and that a substantial part of the rubbish of the Blue Lake area is attributable to them."[44] When La Farge learned of this, he wrote Schifter to say he would soon see the Pueblo governor about the matter.

> I have never before taken up with him the oft-repeated charge that the Taos Indians themselves are responsible for a substantial part of the rubbish in the Blue Lake area. I think it time now that this was brought out into the open and I shall take it up with him as a possibly troublesome factor in our campaign. I can imagine the Governor making a very moving presentation

of the sacred nature of the Blue Lake area before a congressional committee and then being followed by a forest ranger who would testify that the Indians threw as many tin cans around there as anybody else did, with the effect of pretty well destroying the emotional value of the Governor's presentation.[45]

Developments at the Senate hearings confirmed La Farge's presentiments.

The mood of the Senate hearings of September 19 and 20, 1968 was very different from that of the first Senate hearings in 1966. At the earlier hearings, Anderson himself had introduced the Blue Lake bill, and represented himself as favoring the return of the watershed. Those testifying against his bill tempered their remarks out of deference to Anderson. By 1968, however, Anderson's bitter opposition was well known, and he was in fact orchestrating the upcoming testimony of those who agreed with him—primarily sportsmen's groups as well as the Forest Service and its parent Department of Agriculture. The gloves were off, and those opposing the Pueblo were prepared to deliver their heaviest blows. Opening in an atmosphere of suspicion and distrust, the hearings grew increasingly acrimonious.

The purpose of the hearings was to gather information relative to the two "3,000-acre" bills Anderson had introduced in the summer of 1966 (S. 1624 and S. 1625) as well as H.R. 3306, the Haley bill passed recently by the House. Lee Metcalf, acting chairman of the Senate Subcommittee on Indian Affairs, called Stewart Udall as the Tribe's first friendly witness. The other senators present were Henry Jackson, Anderson, Paul Fannin, Clifford Hansen, and Mark Hatfield.

While Udall's testimony repeated much that he had said at previous hearings, he contributed important new insights, too. He pointed out that all three bills, by conveying acreage to the Tribe, recognized that a wrong had been done. The bills differed only in the amount of land to be returned to rectify that wrong. He also observed that acreage desired by most other tribes could not be restored to them because it was now being used by others ("you can't unscramble those eggs"). In the Taos case, however, return would be a relatively simple matter because the Tribe had maintained exclusive use.

Senator Hatfield, concerned about the precedent issue, asked Udall about the cases of two other New Mexico tribes which seemed similar to that of Taos. Would he favor returning land to them, too? Udall agreed that the precedent issue was the crucial policy question at stake, and asserted that if other tribes could prove religious grounds as Taos had done, their land, too, should be restored. Saying that he was concerned more with justice than precedent, Udall stated that "if other Indian groups have a similar case . . .I would like to see them get justice if that is justice in the view of the Congress."[46]

Metcalf then asked questions which brought out his three main objections to H.R. 3306. The first was to give the Tribe land instead of money. He insisted that every time the Senate had done that "we have gotten into trouble."[47] His second objection involved precedent. He asserted that there are Indian tribes all over America just waiting at the barrier to have bills introduced to get thousands of acres of land that they can justifiably claim has a spiritual relationship to their tribe.[48]

When Udall replied that all three bills established the same precedent and differed only in the amount of land to be conveyed, Metcalf raised his third point. He said he could approve granting a small area of land of special religious significance but found the idea of a 48,000-acre sanctuary difficult to accept. "To say a whole valley is of spiritual and natural and religious significance is something we have never recognized."[49]

Anderson's queries also stressed the precedent issue. He later cited a magazine article which claimed that Indians regarded the 477 million acres in public ownership as their "promised land." Another of his expressed concerns related to the transfer of land from the Department of Agriculture to Interior, especially since it involved a wilderness tract in a crucial water-production area that required sophisticated conservation measures.

Arthur W. Greeley, associate chief of the Forest Service, testified after Udall. His remarks centered on the exclusive-use multiple-use controversy. He argued that neither the act of 1933 nor the permit of 1940 gave the Indians exclusive use of the area (the central contention of Schaab's lengthy memorandum), and cited language from both which specifically mentioned uses by others.

At this point, Anderson interrupted with another concern: that the Tribe's religious usage of the land might in future decline. "Should this occur the Indians, a sparsely-populated group, will own a large area of choice land."[50] He also asserted that there was evidence "that not all Pueblo residents give the same importance to. . .traditional beliefs and practices," and that some of them would undoubtedly "prefer a monetary judgment to receipt of land title."[51] Further, he said that the Tribe had not made a case for their charge of religious interference, and that, in his view, the issue had been trumped up to justify a specious land claim.

Witnesses friendly to the Tribe followed Greeley. The first was Lee Hobert, who replied to doubts about the sanctity of the entire watershed with an effective metaphor: "If the Blue Lake is thought to be the altar, then certainly the region surrounding it becomes the sanctuary."[52] He also stressed the Indians' worship of nature, arguing that their faith should be protected because there is much that it can teach us about "nature's eternal worth that may turn the value systems of our land right side up again."[53]

Joe Phipps came next, testifying on behalf of the Blue Lake National Committee. He supplied a list of the committee members and read a moving statement on behalf of H.R. 3306 from Rufus Poole's wife Suzie. John Belindo, executive director of the National Congress of American Indians followed, introducing resolutions supporting H.R. 3306 approved by the general membership and the executive committee of NCAI. Both resolutions stressed the issue of religious liberty and the importance of H.R. 3306 as a symbol of America's commitment to preserving native culture. The first day's hearings then recessed.

Schaab opened testimony on the 20th. He introduced into the record his memorandum, and followed with a discussion of the Taos Pueblo religion. He likened Blue Lake and its river to the symbols of Christianity, and described the role played by these sites in the Taos rituals. He then emphasized the centrality of religion in the life of the Tribe, going on to explain that the practice of the Indian religion demanded secrecy, and that to open the watershed to outsiders was to make observance of the rituals impossible.

Schaab also stressed the sacredness to the Indians of the entire watershed, making it clear that Indian religion was practiced all year in places throughout the watershed. To restrict the Indians to only 3,000 acres would be like telling a devout Christian, "From now on you can only go to church on Easter."[54] While certain rituals were performed at specific sites, in fact, "The essence of the religion is identification with the total natural environment and then the watershed."[55]

To counter Greeley's argument that both the act of 1933 and the permit of 1940 specifically mandated usage of the watershed by others, Schaab introduced several documents which demonstrated the contrary, with special emphasis on Collier's affidavit of 1962.

Schaab delineated the differences between the act of 1933 and the permit of 1940. While the former gave the Indians exclusive use of the area, the latter contained provisions which opened the way to multiple use. Schaab identified this policy as the chief source of problems between the Tribe and the Forest Service. Arguing that the letter of the 1940 permit departed from the spirit of the 1933 act, Schaab asked the senators to honor the intentions of 1933 and convey the entire "Bowl" to the Tribe in trust title.

Schaab closed with remarks on the Tribe's refusal to take money for the sacred watershed. While financial compensation could be a suitable remedy for land that was not sacred, he said that it could not compensate for land that was. He testified that this was why the Pueblo felt justified in asking for "a return of the land itself, to prevent the destruction of the religion and the culture of these Indians."[56] Metcalf rejoined that if they established a policy of giving land instead of money, "we are going to destroy our whole public land system." He warned Schaab that "you will have to have a great deal of justification and present a case for a very unique situation before I would concur in that."[57]

After an acrimonious exchange with Anderson and Metcalf over the issue of visitor permits, Schaab introduced the tribal delegation. Seferino Martinez led with a stinging critique of Forest Service management. He emphasized the devastation caused by clear-cutting in the La Junta Canyon, and the timbering trespass committed by Le Sage on the east side, blaming the Forest Service for not preventing both. He also complained about the Forest Service cabins and corrals at Blue Lake, which he argued were not only desecrating the area but polluting the Tribe's water source. His concluding remarks stressed the threat posed by outsiders to the sanctity of their religion.

Gov. Querino Romero spoke next, lamenting that the Tribe had to wage a fight in order to be granted the right to worship in peace. He especially objected to having to worship "by permission" of the Forest Service. "We go in there by permission. This has been the thing that we don't like to see. We should not be going in there under any kind of a setup."[58] When Romero complained about restrictions on religious freedom, Anderson interjected, "Thus far you haven't illustrated anything that the Forest Service has done to cause you trouble in religious circumstances."[59] When he asked for concrete examples, Bernal, unfortunately, could come up with only one rather weak instance.

Metcalf then opened a hostile line of questioning. First he asked if the leaders of the Tribe were democratically elected, and then he wanted to know who had grazing rights and how they were obtained. He clearly was trying to prove that the Tribal Council had economic motives for regaining the watershed. Young Valentino Cordova, a tribal member living in Washington on an educational exchange program, explained the governmental process at Taos Pueblo. He said the Tribe was not yet politically sophisticated enough to hold democratic elections, relying instead upon a time-honored tradition of rule by the elders, who were chosen by their peers from within their religious clans. He denied that only tribal councilmen own cattle, an assertion subsequently proved by the Tribe when they provided the subcommittee with a list of the twenty-five tribal cattle owners, only nine of whom were councilmen.

Metcalf then asked how many tribal members actually made the Blue Lake pilgrimage. Linda Bernal, a young Taos Indian who worked for the BIA in Washington, testified that "Indians galore go up there every year." She said that a "large majority" of the Tribe went to Blue Lake, and that participation among the young was increasing. Paul Bernal supported this, claiming that seventy-five percent of the 1,400 members made the annual trek.

Metcalf's questions were so aggressive and leading that Senator Hansen, obviously embarrassed on their behalf, told the Tribe "I don't think it is up to you to have to say how many or what percentage of your people participate in a religious ceremony or activity."[60] He also stated that questions about democracy at the Pueblo were irrelevant, having no bearing on whether the Tribe deserved to be granted the land.

Dean Kelley strongly concluded the Tribe's case with a powerful statement on behalf of "small groups who are attempting to preserve their patterns of community life."[61] He gave a detailed explanation of why the Tribe needed the entire watershed, citing evidence from his article in the *Journal of Church and State*. Kelley asserted that the Tribe's religious attachment to the land justified their seeking its return rather than a cash settlement.

Now the serious attacks began. While Anderson and Metcalf had been adversarial in the extreme, they had left the real dirty work to the witnesses against H.R. 3306. The first was Jon Little, president of the New Mexico Wildlife and Conservation Association. He revealed that he was part of a group of five (including two Forest Service employees) that had ridden to Blue Lake just after the August ceremonials. "The Indians had left the area in a mess," said Little,

Querino Romero, one of the greatest of Taos Pueblo's leaders, whose character and determination proved crucial in the fight. C. 1960s. Photo by Dan Budnik.

who then went on to describe the "mess" at some length, documenting his asser-tions with photographs. "It was saddening and distressing to me," he continued,

> to see such a magnificent place being desecrated and abused by the very
> people who were ostensibly trying to protect it, their church, from such vio-
> lation. I couldn't help but think and feel that their abuse of the area was no
> way to treat a church.[62]

Further, Little professed surprise that the littering was not more extensive if, as the Tribe maintained, more than a thousand members had gathered at Blue Lake. One of the forest rangers who was with him had estimated that no more than forty to sixty people had camped there.

Little went on to assert that the members of the Tribe lived under the "tyranny" of the council and that the council was pushing the Blue Lake issue because many were cattle owners who wanted the area for grazing purposes. He said he believed that if the members of the Tribe could be polled "without fear of harassment by the council," most would chose to take the money awarded by the ICC because they cared neither about Blue Lake nor Indian religion.

Preston Gunter of the Sportsmen's Legislative Action Committee of New Mex-ico continued the assault.

> The proposed legislation would have the Indians own the land, and the poor
> old taxpayer take care of it for them, without the privilege of setting foot on
> it to see what he was paying for, if his skin was white instead of red.[63]

Gunter also took strong exception to the "secrecy" claim, saying that it was "very convenient" since it could not be challenged. He insisted that the reason for Indian secrecy was the immorality and obscenity of their religion. "The general shock and disapproval of the Indians by the early missionaries caused them to hide their religion, and is the basis of the secrecy today."[64] Gunter then further asserted that it was an "established fact that the Taos religion is a peyote cult."[65]

It was Gunter's conclusion that returning the land to Taos would only perpetu-ate the "Indian ghetto" there. He felt it was "high time" to stop looking at Indians "as a curiosity and something to be preserved in their natural state," when, in fact, preservation of Indian culture was the very thing that prevented their assimilation into mainstream America and made them "second class citizens."[66]

Elmer LaCome, vice chairman of the Taos County Commission, also spoke in opposition. Calling the bill a "giveaway," he expressed a concern that the Indians would use all the available water if they controlled the entire area. With respect to the ICC, LaCome said he thought its decision was misguided: the land at issue had not been stolen but fairly taken through conquest. He testified to his belief that the Indians were incapable of managing the land, citing serious past prob-lems with overgrazing. To the contention that the Indians needed the land more than the Forest Service, he replied that it was not the Forest Service but "the peo-ple of Taos County, the people of the State of New Mexico, and the people of the

United States who really need this land."[67]

La Come was followed by Louis S. Clapper of the National Wildlife Federation. He called the "giveaway" of the watershed "out of proportion." It would grant the Indians two million dollars worth of land to settle a three hundred thousand dollar claim. Where would such claims end? Citing similar cases waiting to be pressed by other tribes should Taos succeed, he said he feared they would "lay claim to a good part of the country if they were allowed."[68]

Kenneth Pomeroy of the American Forestry Association was the last speaker to testify for the opposition. He summarized their arguments concerning precedent, rights of downstream users, payment in cash and not land, grazing permits as vested interests, and protection of the watershed through Forest Service conservation. His remarks concluded what had amounted to so severe a collective assault it prompted Haley to send Bernal a telegram saying, "I am sorry that you received the kind of reception you did before the Senate Subcommittee."[69]

After the hearings, the Tribe did what it could to contain the damage. With regard to the charge of peyote use, Gunter's source had been the work of a professor of anthropology, Edward Spicer, who happened to be a member of the Blue Lake National Committee. Spicer throughly repudiated Gunter by showing that Gunter had misunderstood and misused the information in Spicer's work. The most damaging charge, that the Indians themselves left Blue Lake "a mess," the Tribe attempted to refute with a report from two members of the war chief's staff saying that they had inspected Blue Lake just after the ceremonials and "found the area very clean."[70] Schaab supplied the subcommittee members with the propitiatory suggestion that the littering may have been done by white campers after the inspection.

Respecting the other points made against them, the Tribe sent Senator McGovern a lengthy and detailed letter in refutation. They also wrote to the chief of the Forest Service, protesting in "the strongest possible terms" participation of Forest Service personnel in the "spy trip," and calling for removal of the cabin, corrals, directional signs, and all other evidence of Forest Service presence in the Blue Lake area. However, the damage had been done. The subcommittee took no action on any of the bills. Anderson had won.

Within the subcommittee, Anderson and Metcalf were clearly opposed to H.R. 3306, while Jackson and McGovern sided with Anderson more out of friendship than political or ideological conviction. Hatfield's questions had revealed his concern about precedent, and Fannin had not spoken. Hansen alone had displayed some sympathy for the Tribe's cause. Given this array of forces, the Haley bill had no chance.

The so-called "spy trip's" alleged discoveries about Indian littering had been especially damaging. If they were true and the Indians themselves were using Blue Lake so carelessly, then the charge that economics lay behind the title quest gained credibility. This suspicion, together with the strong arguments that had been advanced against H.R. 3306, gave Anderson his victory.

If Anderson had won, he also was hurting. At one point in the testimony he revealed that the "religious crowd" has been "belaboring me," saying, "Why don't you let them have their church?"[71] At another point he said, "I was sort of sorry some months past that some of the churches branded me as they did . . . .I was branded a thief, practically, of the grounds and lands."[72] It is clear that he had not enjoyed being the target of relentless pressure by religious groups and individuals. But still he had won.

Could the Tribe prevail? To do so required arousing enough sympathy for their religious plea to force the Haley bill out of the subcommittee and onto the Senate floor for a vote. In order to succeed, the Tribe realized that they now had to convince an even wider audience that the presence of outsiders was seriously threatening their ceremonials, that their mere presence, as Florence Hawley Ellis put it, provoked in the Indians "a horror such as a non-Indian Baptist might feel in seeing the baptismal pool of his fathers utilized as a wading pond, or a Catholic might sense if a casual visitor tossed orange peels into the font of holy water and pinched a wad of gum on the rim."[73]

8

Hemingway Luck

REFLECTING ON THE BATTLE FOR BLUE LAKE, Corinne Locker saw it as an instance of the Hemingway theory of luck: "You can't make your luck but you have to be ready for it when it comes."[1] Year in and year out the Tribe had been cultivating their readiness, and in the fall of 1968 the luck necessary for victory manifested as a remarkable confluence of persons and events.

One of their most unlikely champions was to be Wallace Newman, who had been a football coach at Whittier College in the early 1930s. Better known on campus as "Chief" because of his proudly worn Native American heritage, Newman had had a profound influence on one of his bench warmers. This was a bright young man from humble circumstances who had little athletic ability but a lot of determination. Of his football coach he said,

> I think that I admired him more and learned more from him than from any man I have ever known aside from my father. . . . .There is no way I can adequately describe Chief Newman's influence on me.[2]

Chief Newman's admirer had come a long way since Whittier College, and in the fall of 1968 was running for the presidency of the United States. Perhaps recalling his old football coach, Richard Nixon made it a point to stress Native American issues in his campaign.

On September 27, Nixon sent a message to the delegates of the National Congress of American Indians gathered in conference in Omaha, Nebraska. Its strong opening statement began, "The sad plight of the American Indian is a stain on the honor of the American people."[3] He ascribed that sad plight to "unwise and vacillating federal policies."[4] Nixon proposed a bold new plan for

Taos Pueblo member John Rainer: his inter-Tribal political influence helped make Blue Lake a pan-Indian symbol of cultural preservation. C. 1975. Courtesy of John Rainer.

Indian "Self-Determination," which would transfer responsibility for tribal affairs from the federal government to the Indians themselves. If elected, he promised that "The right of self-determination of the Indian people will be respected and their participation in planning their own destiny will be encouraged."[5]

Events were soon to join together as allies Richard Nixon and the Taos Indians, his policy of self-determination radically affecting the outcome of the battle for Blue Lake. As a precursor of that alliance, photographs of elders from Taos Pueblo were featured in the candidate's campaign literature.

Another contributor to Blue Lake luck was John Rainer, the first member of Taos Pueblo to graduate from college and a young man with political ambitions. Because of his education and ability, Rainer rose quickly in Indian politics, becoming chair both of the All-Indian Pueblo Council in New Mexico and the regional Interstate Indian Council. Tribal leaders on the national scene also recognized Rainer, electing him first vice president of the National Congress of American Indians. Through his position of authority in these organizations, Rainer helped secure resolutions from them in support of the return of Blue Lake. He was instrumental in making Blue Lake a pan-Indian symbol.

The governor of New Mexico, David Cargo, also found Rainer impressive, and appointed him director of the New Mexico Commission on Indian Affairs. Rainer lost no time in acquainting Cargo with the issue and with Blue Lake itself, taking him twice to Taos to learn first-hand of the quest's importance to the Tribe.

Left, *Governor of New Mexico, David Cargo, who rallied to the Tribe's cause during the last stages of the struggle, c. 1968. Courtesy of Mr. Cargo.* Right, *William Schaab, c. 1986, the attorney whose powerful advocacy proved crucial to the Tribe's eventual victory. Courtesy of Mr. Schaab.*

Cargo was immediately sympathetic, and began to devise practical measures for Blue Lake's reconveyance. As early as 1966, at a conference of new governors in Colorado Springs, Cargo discussed the issue with Spiro Agnew of Maryland, whom he convinced of the moral validity of the Tribe's claim. The friendship between the two deepened over the next few years when they met at meetings of the board of St. John's College, which has campuses in both Maryland and New Mexico.

Agnew's interest assumed national importance when the voters elected him and Richard Nixon to the highest offices in the land. Not long after their victory, Nixon and Agnew met with several Republican governors, including David Cargo. He used the opportunity to promote the Tribe's cause.

> We went to Palm Springs before Nixon was sworn in and they had seven or eight governors go in with him and Agnew. . . .We had a kind of closed meeting to talk about what they were going to do and I talked to Agnew that night. And the people from the *New York Times* were all there and Abe Rosenthal and Max Frankel and I and Dave Broder all had dinner one night and talked about Blue Lake at some length . . . .I kidded with them because they're all Jewish, all three, and I conversed with them a little in Yiddish and I told them that what they needed to do was to take care of one of the lost Tribes that wasn't from Israel.[6]

As vice-president, Agnew chaired the National Council on Indian Opportunity, established by Lyndon Johnson to advise on policy respecting Indians. The creation of NCIO was important for Indians. It was the first agency of the federal government to invite Indian leaders to sit as equals with members of the president's cabinet, its purpose being to oversee and recommend federal Indian policy.

At the time of Agnew's election, the executive director of NCIO was William Carmack, brought into government by Stuart Udall to develop the policy of self-Determination for Indian country. Originally an administrative assistant to Oklahoma Senator Fred Harris, Carmack came to the Department of the Interior, at Udall's invitation, to further initiatives Carmack had pioneered with Indians in Oklahoma. Harris recalls the political genesis of self-determination and Carmack's role:

> Once he and I and my then-wife LaDonna got together over at our house with Stewart Udall who was Secretary of the Interior under Johnson. And we told Stewart—we'd planned in advance just what we were going to say to him—what we thought ought to be done with regard to Indian policy, particularly in favor of self-determination, self-government, control of schools, and other programs by Indians. And Udall said, "I agree with all of that and we'll try to do it if you'll give me Bill Carmack." Well, we talked about it afterwards and decided that we had to do that. So Carmack went down there as Assistant Commissioner of Indian Affairs.[7]

Carmack, Udall, and the Harrises decided that a cabinet council devoted to tribal issues would be the most effective means of furthering Indian reforms. They convinced President Johnson, and NCIO was established. Vice-President Hubert Humphrey, who chaired the newly formed National Council on Indian Opportunity, hired Carmack as executive director. Carmack then set to work developing the specific programs to implement the self-determination policies.

When Agnew became vice-president, Carmack wrote him a detailed memorandum about self-determination and the steps that had been taken to that date to make it official government policy. Since his was a political appointment, Carmack fully expected Agnew to replace him. Instead, at a meeting in his office, Agnew told him, "Self-Determination sounds like good old Republican philosophy, moving power from the federal government down to the people. I'd like you to stay on."[8] Nixon agreed with the decision.

Nixon had become familiar with the basics of the self-determination policy before his 1968 campaign, and had supported it in his statement to the NCAI convention in Omaha. Soon after the inauguration, Agnew brought Carmack to the White House to give Nixon a detailed briefing on the nascent Indian policy. Nixon told Agnew and Carmack that the policy accorded well with his philosophy of government and that he had a special interest in doing something to help the Indians.[9]

From then on, the new administration strongly supported self-determination. Agnew gave Carmack easy access to discuss with him problems and developments relative to the new Indian initiative, and Carmack began taking the steps necessary to implement the policy. He was strategically well placed to do so since not only was he executive director of NCIO, with ready access to the vice-president, but he had also retained his position as assistant Indian commissioner at the Interior Department.

One of the problems facing those working in support of self-determination was tribal suspicion, especially since the new policy was now a Republican initiative. Indians remembered only too well that it was a Republican, Dwight Eisenhower, who had imposed on them the disastrous termination policy of the fifties which sought to abrogate the government's trust responsibility, destroy tribal sovereignty, and integrate Native Americans into the dominant culture. Tribes held the Republicans responsible for the horrors of that era, and were therefore extremely wary of any new proposals for Indians from that source. Ironically, this distrust of self-determination was soon to play a central role in the fate of the Blue Lake watershed.

Another factor contributing to eventual victory was the Indians' changed attitude toward voting. While the Taos Indians had remained resistant to voting throughout the sixties, their attitude changed, of necessity, when the subcommittee hearings made them fully aware of Anderson's power. To confront that power and gain much-needed political support, the Tribe began to exercise their franchise in 1968. Their first experience was a resounding success. Voting as a bloc in the Taos County Commission race, the Indians gave the victory to J.C. Cantu, an avowed supporter of reconveyance. Since the county commission had been one of the Tribe's most bitter enemies, the election had direct implications for Blue Lake. After the vote, Bernal issued a press release which called Cantu's victory "a decisive repudiation of the present commission's stand in opposition to the Pueblo."[10]

Despite the favorable new political developments, the Tribe still had to face the determined resistance of Anderson. While affected by the weight of unfavorable public opinion, Anderson nevertheless remained adamant. Flush with his victory before the subcommittee, he was emboldened to introduce, on January 29, 1969, a new bill, S. 750, which still further reduced the area permitted exclusively to the Tribe from 3,100 acres to a tiny parcel of 1,600 acres. The implication of S. 750 was clearly that, if the Tribe refused to compromise, there would be no bill at all.

Soon after the introduction of S. 750, the Tribe issued a press release attacking Anderson's new bill for ignoring the fundamental concept underlying the Pueblo's claim "that Taos Pueblo and the Rio Pueblo watershed form an integral organism of land and water and dependent plant, animal, and human life."[11] It said that Anderson's bill would destroy this relationship and open the area to timbering and outside intrusion. Calling S. 750 "torture for our people, from the oldest man to the youngest child," the Tribal Council asked:

> Is the dollar value of timber on a small tract of 48,000 acres, out of a million and a half acres in the Carson National Forest alone, more important to the

national interest than the spiritual life of an American Indian tribe and the honor of the nation?[12]

Anderson's new bill earned him a great deal of negative press and a deluge of critical letters, including one from Thelma Honey, reprinted in the *Albuquerque Tribune*. Describing herself as "shocked, disappointed and disillusioned," she went on to say,

> I am fully aware that bilking the Indians is an old and lucrative sport. But do you have to add your name to the list of infamous characters who have participated in this recreation for centuries?[13]

In addition to their concern about Anderson, three other problems occupied the Tribe. One was the old conflict between Bernal and Martinez. A visitor to the Tribe wrote Locker that things "at the Pueblo were quite sad and unpredictable. . . . the gap between Paul and Seferino is much too big for the good of the people. It will never be good between them again. More frustration and factionalism."[14]

Finances, also, were still a problem. Schaab's fees alone amounted to more than twenty-four thousand dollars for the previous year. That, in addition to the expenditures for getting the tribal delegation to the hearings in Washington, forced the Tribe to spend a considerable sum from their meager resources to carry on the fight. The legislative nature of their campaign precluded funding support from non-profit foundations. The small contributions that continued to trickle in to the NCC were of some help, but were altogether inadequate for the Indians' needs.

Another concern was the appointment of a new Interior secretary, Alaska Governor Walter Hickel. Udall, of course, had played a vitally supportive role in that position and the Tribe felt his loss keenly. While his agreement to join the Blue Lake National Committee was encouraging, the Tribe recognized that he could do far less for them without official status. Anxious about Hickel, Al Josephy wrote to Locker:

> I am terribly worried about the new Secretary of the Interior. He sounds like a real "spoiler" of the days of the 1890's. He knows practically nothing about Indians and appears to have a philosophy along the lines of "damn it, let's free the Indians from the reservations and give them a chance to become white men." He will bring frontier attitudes down with him from Alaska, and it's away we go back to the days of Custer.[15]

Upon his appointment, Hickel's attitude towards Indians had gotten some unfavorable publicity, and the Tribe and its backers hoped that he would see the Blue Lake battle "as an opportunity to counter this."[16]

Although Udall was gone and his replacement questionable, Haley kept faith with the Tribe, introducing on the first day of the legislative session H.R. 471, which was identical to H.R. 3306 of the previous year. The Tribe and its allies saw this early introduction as a "favorable development," since it would allow more time for action by Congress than in any previous session. In mid-March, the Tribal Council sent letters asking support of H.R. 471 to all of the newly elected Senate and House members on the Indian subcommittees. Especially important among these was New Mexico Republican Congressman Manuel Lujan (eventually to become secretary of the Interior under President Bush). Cargo for some time had been unsuccessfully seeking Lujan's support for the Tribe. According to Cargo, Lujan's reservations were political.

> His rationale was, well the Indians didn't vote Republican anyway and just as a political matter he was better off to go and seek the support of Hispanics than he was to go after the Indians or their interests.[17]

With the uncertainties of a new Congress and a new presidential administration facing them, the Tribe prepared for another round of hearings before the House Subcommittee on Indian Affairs. Haley called the hearings for May 15 and 16, 1969.

Anxiety about the position that Interior would take dissipated when, to the Tribe's great relief, Interior Undersecretary Russell Train sent Aspinall a letter affirming their continuing support for Haley's legislation. However, Agriculture Secretary Clifford Hardin also held firm to his department's earlier position: they were willing to concede, at most, an exclusive-use permit for a small area around Blue Lake.

While the Tribe had expected opposition from Agriculture, they were greatly disappointed when the Bureau of the Budget, representing the White House, came out against H.R. 471. It was the first indication of where the Nixon administration stood on the matter of Blue Lake.

Haley opened the hearings by holding up a handful of telegrams, letters, petitions, and resolutions in support of H.R. 471 that he had "just today" received. Saying that they were but a small part of the sum total, he declared that ninety-nine percent of his mail on the subject favored the Tribe.

Haley identified three issues for discussion:

1. Do the Indians have a need for the land?
2. Could their need be met adequately by a continuation of the special use-permit rather than by the conveyance of a trust title, or is a trust title necessary to meet their needs?
3. Would any public program be impaired by the conveyance of a trust title?[18]

Then Aspinall took the floor and pointed out that "we have a direct confrontation between the departments and the administration."[19] With Agriculture and Budget opposed and Interior in favor, the subcommittee was "in a very delicate position," he said. He was particulary concerned about the Bureau of the Budget, since they spoke for the White House. Given their opposition, "we have at least a threatened veto facing us if we pass this legislation through the Congress."[20] Turning to Harrison Loesch, the assistant secretary for public land management at Interior, Aspinall said it appeared this his department was "the underdog as far as the administration is concerned."[21]

Loesch was at the hearings to present the official position of Interior. It was encouraging to the Tribe that his remarks substantially recapitulated the points made by Udall at several earlier hearings. His central supporting argument was based on the fact that

> public and Forest Service uses have conflicted with the Pueblo's religious requirements and have effectively nullified the exclusiveness of the Pueblo's use of the permit area.[22]

While he was himself not "particularly religious," Loesch emphasized the right to religious freedom, and his conviction that "the religious need of the Pueblo for this land is no subterfuge dreamed up in order to get the ground, but is a true part and parcel of Pueblo life."[23]

While Aspinall welcomed these remarks, he was concerned with practical politics. He wanted to know if Loesch had been in close enough contact with Budget or "the Chief Executive himself" to know if action by the House was going to be "an effort in futility." Did Loesch have any idea what was going to happen if they passed the bill and "sent it down to the President for his signature?"[24] Referring to Nixon's statement, made in Omaha, about Indian policy, Loesch presciently replied,

> My only skill or knowledge of what we would do in this instance is drawn from his statement concerning his concern and ideas for the Indian peoples of the country when he made his statement last fall, and the repetitions which have occurred in his public utterances.[25]

Several of the subcommittee members then questioned Loesch on familiar issues such as precedent, the ICC case, the need for the entire 48,000 acres, and the relative merits of multiple use and exclusive use. Significantly, Rep. Lujan, picking up on Aspinall's "effort in futility" remark, asked if Interior had explored any compromises that might be acceptable to the Senate subcommittee.

Haley then defended the Tribe's unwillingness to compromise further. Noting that they had progressively reduced their request from 130,000 to 50,000 to 48,000 acres, he said he felt, "in all fairness," that the Tribe had "given about as much as they can and gone about as far as they can go."[26]

Loesch then took up two issues that had had a long and contentious history: water rights, and the Tribe's supposed commercial designs on the "Bowl's" timber. He stated unequivocally that H.R. 471 affected no existing water rights and precluded commercial uses by the Tribe since the land would, by congressional act, be designated wilderness in perpetuity.

The proceedings for the day ended with Haley's insightful summation of the conflict. Remarking that H.R. 471 would, in effect, simply transfer jurisdiction of the watershed from Agriculture to Interior, he then justified this measure to his fellow congressmen.

> The Secretary of the Interior really has more knowledge, and oversees more land belonging to the Indians than any other department of Govern-

ment. So we are not giving away land to the Indians to dispose of; we are merely putting the land under the jurisdiction of the department that we think can better handle it, and who would look out, you might say, for the Indians themselves.[27]

In his testimony of the next day, Schaab drove this point home. He said that Agriculture, by virtue of the fact that it was committed by law to the policy of multiple use, must always be in conflict with the Indian requirement for absolute privacy in the practice of their religion. When Lujan pressed him for further clarification, Schaab replied:

> The Interior Department, as we understand it, is not animated by a multiple-use philosophy in which forest land is deemed to be best applied to a multiple variety of uses. The BIA, whose Forestry Division would have a managerial responsibility over this land . . . .will not encourage tourists and recreationalists to come into the area, they will not threaten or contemplate the commercial sale of timber within the area. They will manage it as if it were truly trust land held for the benefit of the Indians, and in accordance with desires of the Indians with respect to its use. . . .[28]

Now it was Bernal's turn to explain this point from the tribal side. In what is unquestionably the strongest statement of the Indians' case to appear anywhere in the voluminous Blue Lake testimony, Bernal made plain the incompatibility of multiple use and tribal religion:

> The religious life of Taos Pueblo is organized around religious societies associated with our underground chambers, which are called "kivas." The many religious groups participate in the training of our young men to take their place in our community, and their members conduct religious ceremonies according to an ancient religious calendar throughout the year. Virtually all of those ceremonies are practiced in the Rio Pueblo watershed, but the places, times, and participants are secret.
>
> The ritual practices may involve only one Indian or a group of Indians. The ritual will frequently require a journey at a special time, by a special route, to a special place. The ceremony must be practiced in privacy; it will not be performed if outsiders are present.
>
> Here is where the Forest Service, the recreationalists it invites to the Rio Pueblo watershed, and the trespassers it fails to exclude, interfere with our religious practices. The presence in a part of the watershed of a Forest Service crew, recreationalists, or trespassers will require the Indian group which needs to be in that part of the watershed to detour or to discontinue its ceremony to avoid detection by outsiders. When our people are so interrupted in their religious practices, we do not tell the offenders of that fact; we do not approach them and ask them to leave because of our ceremony. We instead preserve our privacy and the sanctity of the ritual by avoiding contact with interlopers.
>
> For that reason, the Forest Service people do not know when they have interrupted our ceremonies. They have no way to know because our people are necessarily unobserved by them.[29]

Not only was multiple use destructive of religious privacy, he said, but it contradicted another tenet of tribal religion: preservation of the watershed in its primordial, God-derived naturalness. Bernal then delineated the philosophical differences at the heart of the conflict.

> In all of its programs the Forest Service proclaims the supremacy of man over nature; we find this viewpoint contrary to the realities of the natural world and to the nature of conservation. Our tradition and our religion require our people to adapt their lives and activities to our natural surroundings so that men and nature mutually support the life common to both. The idea that man must subdue nature and bend its processes to his purposes is repugnant to our people.[30]

Bernal went on to clarify the respects in which the permit violated the Tribe's religious freedom.

> We are probably the only citizens of the United States who are required to practice our religion under a "permit" from the Government. This is not religious freedom as it is guaranteed by the Constitution. Moreover, the permit covers only a portion of the Rio Pueblo watershed, while our religious practices take place also in the remaining area of the watershed. Outside the permit area we are at the sufferance of the Forest Service.[31]

Bernal then observed that permits are by their very nature subject to "administrative interpretations," interpretations which over time may change or vary. He informed the congressmen that in the fifties the Forest Service had issued permits without Pueblo permission, and pointed out that there was nothing to prevent them from doing so again. Referring to the Forest Service's "spy trip" of the previous fall, he charged that

> Forest Service participation in that effort leads us to believe that the field personnel of the Forest Service will invade our privacy in the future whenever they deem it convenient to do so.[32]

To give immediacy to the threat posed by the policy of multiple use, Bernal quoted from Forest Service testimony in 1968 which established that they planned to timber in the watershed and manipulate its vegetation to increase the water yield. "These plans," Bernal continued,

> tell us that the Forest Service will always be seeking ways to interfere with the natural ecology of the Rio Pueblo watershed and that it will claim the legal right to do so despite Indian rights under the 1933 act. Our religion is based upon the unity of man with nature in the Rio Pueblo watershed. Any outside interference with natural conditions of the watershed interferes with our religion.[33]

Bernal then dismissed the arguments of those who supported continued Forest Service conservation, saying, "We have found, over the years, that Forest

Paul Bernal pauses to pray on the shore of Blue Lake. His convincing testimony at the 1969 House Sub-committee Hearings at last made it clear that Forest Service management of the watershed was a threat to Indian religion. C. 1969. Photo by Dan Budnik.

Service conservation is destructive of nature."[34] He cited their practices of timbering in La Junta, lake dynamiting, and trail-cutting, and finally, constructing the loathsome cabin at Blue Lake, which was "a dilapidated eyesore and a source of filth."[35]

Both Bernal and Schaab had reached heights of eloquence and depths of clarity heretofore unprecedented in any of the hearings. This time the Tribe had succeeded in making a matter of permanent record arguments that had never before seemed to crystallize persuasively. Bernal, often praised for his eloquence, had been particularly cogent and inspired in finally explaining how it was that Forest Service control threatened tribal religion.

The testimonies of Gov. Lupe Sandoval and Seferino Martinez followed Bernal's, the former focusing on the Forest Service's desecration of the watershed, and the latter lamenting that the Tribe was tired of waiting for justice and the return of their land. Martinez, characterizing the Forest Service as "bad housekeepers," called for their departure on behalf of the Tribe.

Haley struck a further blow for the Indians by introducing a petition signed by 364 youths from Taos Pueblo. They had developed the petition to counter the charge, as Haley put it, "that the young people of Taos Pueblo are not interested in this bill. . . ."[36] The petition stated: "We the Indian youth of Taos Pueblo support the fight to reunite our tribe with the Blue Lake lands. We are participants in our Indian way of life which is very dependent upon the Blue Lake area."[37]

While the Tribe's arguments seemed to have taken on new life and clarity, the testimony of their opposition repeated the same old litany of charges. Edward Cliff, chief of the Forest Service, brought up the issues of grazing permits and precedent. Regarding the latter, he said that there were at least eight other Pueblo Indian tribes that used government land for religious purposes, and that indications were that they, too, wanted title to these shrines. Schaab denied that this was so, saying that the tribes in question were willing to accept cash settlements, and that a "very careful investigation" had made clear that no other New Mexico tribes were claiming land on religious grounds. Schaab then introduced into the record a letter from ICC chief counsel Harry Webb, verifying that the Taos claim was the "only petition filed" which asked for land instead of money.

After denying that the Forest Service had any management plans that would disturb the Indians' practice of their religion, Cliff contradicted himself by admitting that they wanted to leave open the possibility of cutting the 250 million board-feet of timber in the area. His chief reason for wanting the land to remain under Forest Service supervision, he said, was one of efficiency: the whole area was now one management unit and to "carve out an enclave" would create administrative problems.

Congressman Lujan then raised the old question of double compensation. Quoting from the act of 1933, he established that the use-permit had been given the Tribe in lieu of a cash payment for the land lost in the town of Taos. Schaab agreed, explaining that it would now be up to the ICC to determine the value of the permit and to offset that value against the financial award due the Tribe for the town lands.

Next to testify against H.R. 471 was Don Seaman, supervisor of the Carson National Forest. Haley promptly attacked Seaman for authorizing the covert "spy trip," and for excluding the Indians from the inspection.

Haley then asked Seaman to describe what the inspection party had found. Seaman did so, but admitted that he did not know who was responsible for the littering. Aspinall then interjected that "the whole matter is hearsay. And I object to the publicity being given to hearsay evidence."[38] Chastened, Seaman returned to his seat.

Haley then called two last witnesses, one for the Tribe and one against. Speaking for the opposition, Richard Pardo of the American Forestry Association waived his allotted time, submitting instead a written statement identical to the one provided by his group for the Senate hearings in the fall of 1968. Speaking for the Tribe was Michael Nadel, an executive of the Wilderness Society and editor of their quarterly magazine.

Nadel's testimony and the support of the Wilderness Society was a real coup for the Tribe and a significant difference from the 1968 hearings when the Society had not taken a stand. Nadel proved to be an eloquent backer of H.R. 471, asserting that

> the Taos Pueblo Indians are asking that the secret places of their soul be given back to them entire. They ask, not for a palliative in the form of a token boundary around Blue Lake, but for an ecological unit, a watershed, that would give them the environmental and spiritual security that was theirs from the beginning . . . .[39]

In conclusion, he said that the Wilderness Society supported passage of H.R. 471 "to restore their sacred land to the Taos Pueblo Indians for their sacred religious purposes and to maintain as a wilderness."[40]

Nadel's remarks completed the oral testimony. Haley then entered into the record pro-and-con statements from many groups and individuals. A great number of these had already appeared in previous proceedings. The statements in opposition were mainly from sportsmen's organizations and from old enemies like Elliott Barker who repeated his favorite charge: "I insist that, with the exception of the acreage immediately surrounding Blue Lake, religion is being used as a subterfuge to get the remainder of the lands."[41] Statements in support came mainly from religious groups and from old friends like Dean Kelley and Archbishop Davis.

The Indians left the hearings feeling that they had done well. They had reason to be satisfied. The Tribe had made its most convincing presentation to date, one which brought them many new supporters. The next hearing on the bill was not to be held until July of 1970. During the crucial intervening months, when many minds were being made up, the printed record of these May hearings was decisively influential, swaying many to the side of the Indians.

Perhaps the most important individual to be converted by the Tribe's eloquence was Congressman Manuel Lujan. Shortly after the hearings he
announced his support for H.R. 471, saying, "I believe that this achieves a settlement with which we can all live in the best of conscience."[42] Lujan's decision represented considerable political courage, since he represented a state that was
largely Democratic and often anti-Indian. Two highly placed elected officials
from New Mexico now stood with the Tribe: Lujan and Governor Cargo. That
they were both Republicans would prove to be important to the outcome of the
battle.

The summer of 1969 brought primarily good omens. At the end of May, the
Blue Lake National Committee sent out a powerful fund-raising letter which
reviewed the successes of the recent past and struck an optimistic note for the
future. It stimulated a spate of contributions.

Then, in early June, Haley's subcommittee passed H.R. 471 and got House
debate on the bill scheduled for September.

The next positive development was the Tribe's contact with the Washington
law firm of Wilkinson, Cragun, and Barker. They were experts in steering bills
through Congress and, as counsel for the National Congress of American
Indians, were well informed about Indian affairs. Tribal representatives held
encouraging discussions with Jerry Straus about the possibility of his firm
providing much-needed congressional liaison. There was even a possibility that
NCAI might pay the Tribe's legal fees.

July brought more good news in the form of an endorsement of H.R. 471 by
the Taos Town Council. That development, however welcome, could not com-
pare to another of far greater emotional and symbolic significance. After forty
years of pleading by the Tribe, the Forest Service finally removed the cabin, corrals, and outbuildings at Blue Lake. While their action undoubtedly was motivated more by a concern for public relations than for the Indians, to have these
symbols of Forest Service presence eradicated was a matter for profound satisfaction. Buoyed by the optimism of these developments, the Tribe looked forward to the upcoming debate in the House.

Aspinall opened the debate on September 9 by presenting a detailed history of
the Tribe's claim. He then defined the conflict: while the Forest Service argued
that the existing permit adequately protected the Indians' religious needs, in fact
it had led to years of protracted conflict. The issue was simply one of who had
greater need of the land, an issue that should be decided in the Indians' favor on
religious grounds.

> We are talking here about a different kind of culture than most of us recog-
> nize, the trees, the rivulets, the plants, and even the rock formations hold
> religious inspiration to the people of this particular tribe.[43]

Congressman Edmondson then rose to endorse Haley's position, saying, "We
do nothing but honor our own treaty commitments and equity and justice when

we enact this bill." He was followed by John Saylor of Pennsylvania. While Saylor had been one of the important supporters of H.R. 3306, it soon became evident that he had reversed his position.

Saylor advanced three reasons, later seconded by John Dingell of Michigan, for reconsidering his earlier vote for H.R. 3306: precedent, double compensation, and the ICC decision itself. He gave special attention to the issue of double compensation, pointing out that the act of 1933 compensated the Tribe for the land in the town of Taos "by giving a fifty-year permit which was accepted at that time by the Indians as a full settlement."[44]

Edmondson rejoined that the permit originally promised the Tribe was for an exclusive use they obviously had not received, and that therefore the settlement was unsatisfactory. His argument agreed with the findings of the ICC, which had earlier held that the permit granted the Tribe was not equal in value to the money owed them; and that they, therefore, were still entitled to financial damages, less the offsetting value of the usage of the land they had, to that date, already enjoyed under the terms of the permit.

Saylor then launched a complicated attack upon the ICC decision itself, an attack which Haley rose to refute. He made four points. First, he said, the ICC had agreed that Taos had aboriginal title to 130,000 acres that were taken from them in 1906 and for which they had not been paid. Second, the 48,000 acres covered by H.R. 471 were within the 130,000 acres for which the ICC formally determined the Tribe had not as yet been paid. Third, if H.R. 471 were enacted, the amount of cash to be paid the Tribe would be equitably reduced. Fourth, to say that the Indians already have been paid is to say that the ICC judgment itself is wrong. Since the Justice Department had not appealed the decision, Haley argued, they must have been satisfied of its correctness, a satisfaction confirmed by the judgement of counsel for the subcommittee, which had reviewed the decision at his request. Haley then dismissed Saylor's line of argument, saying that the House floor was not the place for debating the legal intricacies of questions that had already been adjudicated.

Congressman Morris Udall of Arizona, Stewart's brother, said it grieved him to see his friend from Pennsylvania "go so wrong." He suggested that "you never set a bad precedent when you do what is right,"[45] and proceeded to quote to Saylor his own words spoken the year before in support of the Pueblo.

Don Riegle of South Dakota followed Udall with a moving description of the native religion of the Taos Indians. "All that this legislation is attempting to do," he said, "is to provide in perpetuity a place where they may stand on their mother soil and pray to their God as they have from time immemorial."[46] He then introduced a bit of levity. Noting that the Forest Service is "full of chiefs," including the "Chief Forester" and lots of "deputy chiefs," he jibed, "Now, really it would not hurt the chiefs to give a few Indians a little bit of land that is now in the National Forest."[47]

Dingell, who had personal ties with Anderson and was working closely with him, then made a motion to amend H.R. 471 to conform essentially to the 1,600 acre bill introduced by Anderson in the Senate. Haley opposed this move. He stated candidly that when, in all likelihood, the Senate passed Anderson's bill, a conference committee of House and Senate members would meet to give both bills serious study and, if necessary, work out a compromise. Until then, he said, "I do not believe that the House is in a position to act favorably on the amendment and I would ask for its defeat."[48] The congressmen agreed with Haley, defeating Dingell's amendment by voice vote. The House then passed H.R. 471, with Dingell and Saylor the sole dissenters.

While elated by their victory in Washington, the Tribe was beset by a storm brewing at home. In early October, the Taos County Commission, in spite of Cantu's recent election, again came out publicly against transfer of trust title to the Indians. Their concern was with the water supply, specifically with a project known as the San Juan- Chama Water Diversion.

The purpose of the San Juan-Chama project was to deliver to New Mexico, through a series of trans-mountain tunnels, its share of water in accordance with the Colorado River Compact. If the diversion succeeded, Taos County stood to gain increased access to vital water supplies. For that reason, most in the county supported the diversion. For the project to proceed, however, the state of New Mexico had to adjudicate various water issues, and Taos Pueblo had to agree to be sued for the adjudication to take place. When the Tribe did not agree to be sued, they got blamed for holding up the project.

The Tribe's refusal incensed the county commission, which sent a letter bitterly critical of the Indians to Anderson. The *Taos News*, while disagreeing with the commission, reprinted their letter in full with a covering story. Noting that the Pueblo refused to participate in the adjudication, the commissioners wrote:

> This selfish action on the part of the Indians in regard to water is a very good example of what can be expected of the Pueblo Council. It is the very type of thing that responsible people of Taos County have been worried about happening, should the Blue Lake area be given to Taos Pueblo. The Indians have no regard at all for the water needs and water rights of the rest of us.[49]

Newspapers throughout a water-conscious state then took up the story, and charges flew back and forth between Interior, Justice, the State Engineer's Office, and the Tribe.

As it turned out, whether or not the Tribe agreed to be sued had no immediate bearing on the progress of the project. The special judge in the San Juan-Chama case let it be known that he could not consider the case until he had finished with a litigation involving another Pueblo (Pojoaque). In the meantime, the water to be adjudicated could be stored in the Heron Dam.

While the facts supported the Tribe, few of its opponents took the trouble to learn them. As a result, the Tribe received a good deal of negative press in the latter part of 1969. It came at a time when they could ill afford it, and over an issue, water, that is very sensitive in New Mexico. The controversy eventually died when the site proposed at Taos Pueblo for water storage proved geologically unsuitable.

In early October, Indian affairs were receiving coverage in the New Mexico papers for another reason: the National Congress of American Indians was holding its annual convention in Albuquerque. Tribal representatives from all over America were present, and important government officials came to address them. Among those speaking to the Tribes were two men who were to be important protagonists in the Blue Lake cause—Sen. Edward Kennedy and Interior secretary Walter Hickel.

Like his brother Robert before him, Edward Kennedy sympathized with the Taos cause. He became thoroughly familiar with the issue through discussions with the Taos leaders at the NCAI meeting in Albuquerque. In a gesture of personal good will, he invited Bernal and Schaab to ride with him to the airport as he departed.

During the ride, Bernal uncharacteristically choked up with emotion as he discussed with Kennedy the significance of Blue Lake. Later he explained the reason for this to Schaab, and Schaab relayed the story to Kennedy. Bernal's father, an important priest in the Taos religion, had died just before the Albuquerque meeting. According to Taos belief, Blue Lake is the home of the souls of the Tribe's departed: "Their living souls are present with the people in ceremonies at the Lake and throughout the watershed," as Schaab put it. Blue Lake is also a sort of Indian Valhalla, where the souls of non-tribal members may repose if they are persons of extraordinary courage, prowess, or spiritual insight. Schaab explained to Kennedy the significance of this belief in relationship to his assassinated brothers.

> When President Kennedy was killed, Mr. Bernal and his family were deeply affected by the loss. As a priest, he was moved to perform a special sacred ceremony which, in Paul's words, "made a place for John F. at Blue Lake." The ceremony involved Paul's whole family and touched Paul deeply. Then, during Senator Kennedy's campaign, Mr. Bernal had a premonition of tragedy the day before the assassination, and after the event he again performed the ceremony to "make a place for Robert" at Blue Lake. In the car behind you Paul became overwhelmed with a sense of the common loss of your brothers and his father and their common identification with Blue Lake.[50]

Convinced of the justness of the Pueblo's quest and personally touched by this story, Kennedy henceforward became a key factor in the luck of Blue Lake.

The Blue Lake quest drew the attention of Walter Hickel for a more practical reason. Hickel had come to Albuquerque to improve his image in Indian country. To achieve that, Hickel was looking for a symbolic gesture, a way of showing the Indians that the Republicans were on their side. Given the national importance the fight for Blue Lake had now assumed, H.R. 471 might provide Hickel with just the opportunity he needed.

Hickel was not unaware of the fact that of all of the tribes in the country, the nineteen Indian Pueblo peoples of New Mexico are the most conservative, and that Taos and Santo Domingo are the most conservative of these. Other tribes regard them as, in some special sense, the preservers of Indian tradition. An important reason for this is the special "holiness" of their locations. To quote David Cargo:

> A lot of people don't understand that [there are] two epicenters of Indian religion: one is Blue Lake and the other is at Santo Domingo. And they don't understand that . . . [Blue Lake] is a sacred place not just for Taos Pueblo but for all Pueblo Indians and Navajos and Zunis . . . . So it was something that was very critical because it reached out not just to the immediate area . . . . [51]

At the NCAI's Albuquerque gathering, Cargo confirmed Hickel's belief in the symbolic importance of H.R. 471, and Hickel announced his support for the bill. While Interior already had declared for H.R. 471 at the Haley Hearings, Blue Lake now had the personal support of its secretary.

The significance of the endorsement was not lost on Anderson, who immediately wrote Hickel a letter stamped: EXTREMELY CONFIDENTIAL—NOT FOR REGULAR FILES. He expressed his concern about newspaper articles reporting that the Nixon administration now backed Taos Pueblo. While he knew Interior favored H.R. 471,

> I was not aware that the Nixon administration was supporting this bill. On the contrary, I am advised that the Bureau of the Budget concurred in the views of the Department of Agriculture which submitted an unfavorable report on the bill. I assume that the newspaper article is in error on this score. [52]

Anderson lamented that Hickel was following the line taken by Udall, saying he had hoped that the Republicans would take a "fresh look" at the Blue Lake matter. He gave Hickel a list of reasons why he opposed H.R. 471, and offered to discuss the issue with him at any time. He also offered to make available his file on the subject, "probably the most complete history and copies of documents on this matter which exist in any one place."[53]

Through a covert source in New Mexico, Corinne Locker had obtained Anderson's confidential letter. Aware of the significance of this correspondence, both the Tribe and Schaab felt they needed the expertise of someone from the Washington scene to help them counter Anderson's pressure on Hickel. They turned to Jerry Straus, asking his help not only in dealing with the Anderson letter but also in contacting Hickel, the White House, the Bureau of the Budget, and the Department of Agriculture. Schaab pointed out that Straus could do this work under his contract, already approved by the Bureau of Indian Affairs. Despite the fact that the Tribe had raised only one thousand dollars towards paying their fee, Straus and the executive committee at Wilkinson, Cragun and Barker agreed to help the Tribe at a very favorable rate. The retention of Straus soon proved to be of significant strategic value.

The Republican National Committee now also became an important ally. In late November, Sue Lallmang, the American Indian advisor to the Republican National Committee, wrote a memo to Laszlo Pasztor, director of the RNC's Heritage Groups Division. She told him that both Hickel and Lujan had now spoken out in the cause of Blue Lake, and that it was important that other top Republicans, including the president, do likewise.

> It would benefit the party to support the Indians on Blue Lake because this is an issue that concerns all Indians and is one for which the Indians of New Mexico are willing to register Republican . . . . It is important not to underrate the importance of this issue.[54]

Not long after, Pasztor wrote to Hickel telling him that Lallmang had brought the Blue Lake issue to the attention of the RNC. Pasztor told Hickel he "wholeheartedly" supported Lallmang's view. Official Republican party support for the Indians' quest was now in the making.

One of the most important persons in creating that support was a young woman named Bobbie Greene, in Washington for a year as a White House Fellow. LaDonna Harris, the Comanche wife of Oklahoma Senator Fred Harris, sat on the committee that selected White House Fellows. When a group of them came to the Harris household for dinner one evening, LaDonna, striking up a conversation with Greene, learned of studies she had made of Indian education in Navajo country. They began discussing Indian issues, and a lifelong friendship was established between the Harrises and the young Washington visitor. Fresh from Yale Law School where she had drawn on her Navajo experience to do serious work on Indian education, Greene worked under John Erlichman, the domestic affairs counselor to President Nixon.

Soon after Greene came to the White House staff in the fall of 1969, Erlichman, aware of Greene's experience in Indian country, asked her help in formulating the administration's Indian policies. Working under the auspices of NCIO, she was to develop a comprehensive report on the general state of Indian affairs. LaDonna Harris, president of Americans for Indian Opportunity and a member of NCIO, collaborated with her young friend on this important document.

In January of 1970, the luck of Blue Lake began an unbroken run. Taos Pueblo helped its cause by selecting Querino Romero as governor, with Henry Lujan as his lieutenant, and Frank Marcus as secretary. They had been in office together in 1968, and were veterans of the pitched battles of that contentious year. Governor Romero and his men made the return of Blue Lake their top priority.

So, too, did the National Congress of American Indians. Meeting in Washington in January, the NCAI executive committee adopted a powerful resolution which made Blue Lake the symbol of a "dawning better day" for Indian Tribes.

> We call upon the Nixon administration to proclaim a new national policy, which recognizes and supports the existence of Indian cultures, the free practice of Indian religions, and authority of tribal governments and the exclusive, God-given right to use traditional ceremonial and holy

LaDonna Harris, President of Americans for Indian Opportunity and a member of NCIO, who saw to it that the quest for Blue Lake was brought to the attention of the White House. C. 1980. Courtesy of LaDonna Harris.

places. . . .The time has come to proclaim that policy and to confirm its adoption by supporting the Blue Lake bill of the Taos Pueblo. . . .The essence of a humane policy toward the American Indian minority is embodied in this legislation. We therefore ask the administration to take the lead in supporting and calling for the enactment in this Congress of H.R. 471 as a matter of first priority.[55]

Cargo, Rainer, and Straus rallied to this appeal. Cargo contacted the White House to inform them that, as New Mexico governor, he favored placing Blue Lake under the authority of the Indians. At about the same time, Rainer, through his position as chair of the Governor's Interstate Indian Council, persuaded that body to pass a resolution endorsing H.R. 471 "as evidence of a new day of respect and honor for the Indian culture and religion."[56]

In addition, Rainer and Straus met with Hickel to determine what effect, if any, Anderson's confidential letter had had. Hickel, obviously unmoved by Anderson's pressure, pledged his "unequivocal support," promising to do whatever he could to get H.R. 471 passed by the Senate, including testifying himself if necessary. He also worked with Rainer and Straus to devise a strategy to break the opposition of Agriculture and the Bureau of the Budget, saying he "thought he could get President Nixon to speak out favorably to the Taos position."[57]

To those backing H.R. 471, it became more and more evident that Nixon held the key to success. Only through his support could the positions of Budget and Agriculture be changed. If their opposition could be eliminated, Anderson would be left standing alone, and the Tribe would then have a good chance of swaying enough votes in the Senate to their side. The bait to attract Nixon was to suggest using Blue Lake as the administration's symbol of a new respect for and approach to Indian people. As Schaab explained to Straus, they needed to get Nixon to "commit the administration to an Indian policy which supports tribal cultures and religions, with enactment of H.R. 471 as the first step in the execution of that policy."[58]

The Indian members of NCIO now put pressure on Nixon to take that step. The occasion they chose was the presentation of the report on conditions in Indian country that Bobbie Greene and LaDonna Harris had been working on since the fall. The report made a series of policy recommendations for improving the quality of Indian life, and concluded with a request that Agnew and those in the president's cabinet give H.R. 471 "special attention" and support it at "every opportunity."

The Blue Lake issue made its way into the report through the friendship of Rainer and Harris. During the development of the report, he convinced her of the validity of the Tribe's claim, and she saw to it that a plea on behalf of H.R. 471 was included in the more general report on the state of Indian affairs.

Meeting in the Roosevelt Room at the White House, those assembled to hear the presentation by the six Indian members of NCIO included Vice-President Agnew as well as the president's cabinet secretaries for Interior, Agriculture, Commerce, Labor, Health Education and Welfare, Housing and Urban Development, and the director of the Office of Economic Opportunity. While Agnew was personally convinced of the Tribe's claim, he had not as yet made his commitment public. The Indian members of NCIO now urged him and the whole council membership to do so. Agnew gave the cabinet members of NCIO thirty days to respond to the Indian members' recommendations.

The importance of this meeting cannot be overemphasized. The Tribe's case had been effectively presented not only to the vice-president but to seven members of Nixon's cabinet, including Hardin at Agriculture. The report was circulated as an official document from NCIO and the office of the vice-president. Significantly, the frontispiece featured a quotation from Agnew:

> We are now learning the importance of the Indians' respect for nature; they however have not yet benefited from the ideals supposedly ours: 'liberty and justice for all.'[59]

Realizing that dealings with the White House had reached a critical juncture, the Tribe sent Bernal, Governor Romero, Schaab, and Locker to Washington to meet with chief decision-makers. Bobbie Greene arranged for them to confer with Brad Patterson, staff assistant to Leonard Garment at the White House executive offices. Jerry Straus also attended. Patterson was mainly concerned with the matter of precedent and, when the Tribe answered his questions to his satisfaction, he agreed that there was need for a "high level review" of the conflict between Agriculture and Interior. He promised to inform them of the White House decision when the review was completed.

To facilitate the review, one of Agnew's assistants, C.D. Ward, prepared for the vice-president a detailed memorandum summarizing the Blue Lake situation and its political implications. Noting that in the Tribe's own language Blue Lake signified "the Home of the Great Souls," he went on to explain that the watershed itself "is a natural cathedral containing the shrines, holy places and altars of their ancient religion . . . the oldest living religion in North America."[60] Ward then briefly reviewed the conflict between the Tribe and the Forest Service, and the presently conflicting views of Agriculture and Interior regarding H.R. 471.

He proposed four approaches to the matter of Blue Lake: 1. A "clear pronouncement" from the White House backing H.R. 471; 2. Release of such a pronouncement in the context of a general policy statement supporting "protection of Indian religious and cultural rights"; 3. A rebuttal of Agriculture's precedent concerns with a clear statement on the uniqueness of the Taos claim; and 4. Withdrawal of the present Interior and Agriculture reports on H.R. 471 until such time as the administration itself took a stand on the bill. Ward noted that Budget had "taken the unusual position" of supporting Agriculture while allowing Interior to report to Congress its endorsement of H.R. 471.

To encourage a favorable response from the vice-president, Ward listed the important partisans of H.R. 471, including Cargo, myriad religious organizations, the Wilderness Society, a majority of the press, and the "united Indian community." He then made clear the relationship between Blue Lake and the policy of self-determination:

Querino Romero, returned to office by the Tribal elders in 1970, provided inspired leadership in the final stages of the battle. 1970. Photo by Dan Budnik.

All tribes view the Blue Lake issue as a test of the sincerity and commitment of this administration to its policy of protection of the religious and cultural rights of the American Indians. Administration support would also tend to indicate that we mean what we say with regard to our policy of non-termination.[61]

Ward concluded with a review of the political implications of H.R. 471. Approval of H.R. 471 would give the Republicans in New Mexico a chance to capture two Senate seats, since "the Indian position is popular in the state and has the support of most newspapers . . . ." Such support also would help the party nationally, because it would accord with the opinion of "the vast majority of American citizens." It also would encourage the New Mexico Indians to back the Republican ticket, an important consideration, since their 70,000 votes could easily sway elections. Finally, endorsement of H.R. 471 would provide the administration with a means of demonstrating "without cost its support for minority group rights on a publicly non-controversial issue receiving wide-spread attention."

Ward's brilliant memorandum set the stage for the dramatic events to follow. It concisely summarized the situation, made clear its political implications, and set forth a practical plan of action. Its final recommendation concisely expressed the profound desire of all who had fought long and hard for the return of Blue Lake:

This administration should support legislation (H.R. 471) returning to the Taos Pueblo Indians of New Mexico their hereditary holy land known as the Blue Lake area.[62]

9

Year of Decision

I F THE PREVIOUS SEVERAL MONTHS HAD SEEN the luck of Blue Lake swelling, that luck now turned to magic. As Bobbie Greene said of the events of 1970:

> I think if you ask people who were involved in that fight they will tell you that it was the high point of their careers or of their lives. That there was something magical about it, that's precisely the right word, that never happened before and could never happen again.[1]

John Ehrlichman, assistant to the president for Domestic Affairs and Bobbie Greene's immediate superior, played an important part in these events. Soon after the NCIO presentation, she explained the current situation to Ehrlichman, telling him "At last we have a chance to be on the right side of something."[2]

Ehrlichman's position at the White House gave him the authority to approve provisionally the support of the Blue Lake matter, and he authorized Greene to proceed with resolving problems within the administration relative to the Blue Lake bill. He did so not only because it seemed to him "a good thing to do," but also because it accorded well with his understanding of Nixon's approach to Indian affairs. Ehrlichman says that while problems with other minorities seemed huge and intractable, this was a definable, finite,

> manageable problem where there were already federal handles on the Indian that we could grab. . . . I remember Nixon specifically saying "This is a minority that we can do some things for, that we can get some things done, that are not going to bite us back if we take hold of the problem and try and work with it." So I always felt like we had a green light in that sector to do whatever we could.[3]

Given Nixon's general receptivity to Indian initiatives, Ehrlichman felt comfortable authorizing Greene to begin working on the Blue Lake matter with C.D. Ward and Robert Robertson of the vice-president's staff, as well as with Nixon's advisor Leonard Garment and his assistant Brad Patterson.

Next to join the ranks of supporters was Sen. Fred Harris. While he had heard something about the Blue Lake matter from his wife LaDonna, he had not earlier given the issue much attention. At the end of January, however, the tribal delegation in Washington called on him and he remembers the effect of their visit:

> I was extremely impressed with these Taos leaders and absolutely convinced of how deeply they felt about the sacred nature and religious importance of this land . . . . So I told them I would help them. And then when they left the office, I said to Fred Gipson, if we don't do another damn thing while we're here in the Senate, let's help these people get back their land . . . . [4]

After the visit of the Taos elders, Harris made Blue Lake "a really fundamental cause, not just a kind of pro forma cause but something really fundamental, not only to push it but to win it . . . ."[5]

Immediately after the delegation's visit, Harris wrote to Sen. George McGovern, chair of the Senate Subcommittee on Indian Affairs, urging him to do "anything you can to speed action on this measure and bring it to the floor." He explained that because of "the great religious significance which Blue Lake holds for the Taos Indians, this bill has an importance to them which cannot be overestimated."[6]

Now Spiro Agnew, too, began to take action. While Cargo years earlier had made him aware of the significance of Blue Lake for the Indians, the NCIO report and Ward's memorandum forcefully brought home to him H.R. 471's wider political implications. Like Harris, Agnew began to take a personal interest in the bill, and in February started using NCIO's "interdepartmental muscle to get Agriculture to withdraw its opposition . . . ."[7]

In late February, Agnew called a meeting with Hickel, Agriculture Secretary Hardin, Budget Director Mayo, Brad Patterson, and C.D. Ward to review the status of the Blue Lake legislation. He made plain his personal support for H.R. 471, saying that he was gathering information on the bill "to pass on to President Nixon and to confer with him about it."[8]

Two weeks later C.D. Ward went to Taos on a fact-finding mission. He asked the Indians for answers to several questions raised by Hardin and Mayo at the meeting with the vice-president. Ward gathered the necessary information, and he told the Indians that

> the Vice-President's office is working very, very hard trying to get the Blue Lake situation resolved and reported out favorably, and that the Vice-President himself is very sympathetic and wants to do all he could [*sic*] to help the Taos Indians on their Blue Lake legislation.[9]

Senator Fred R. Harris (in his office at the University of New Mexico in 1989) put his political career on the line when he championed the Blue Lake Bill. Courtesy of the author.

While sympathetic, Agnew had not as yet made his views public, and in mid-March NCIO put strong pressure on him to do so. They sent Agnew a detailed seven-page memorandum (written largely by Robert Robertson, who by now had replaced William Carmack as executive director of NCIO and who was a strong proponent of H.R. 471) which reviewed the history of the title quest, the arguments for and against H.R. 471, and its political implications for the Republican party. The memorandum tied together Blue Lake, self-determination, and the administration's credibility among Indians.

> There is a pressing need for this administration to achieve credibility in the eyes of Indian people and their many supporters across the country; there is a need also to assure Indians that the philosophy of this administration is non-termination of the special relationship between them and their government. The fear of termination is holding back seriously the desire of Indians to get meaningfully involved in the process of self-determination. One issue which clearly unites all Indians and which can, if supported, garner credibility for the administration is the Taos Blue Lake legislation now in Congress.[10]

The memorandum concluded: "the equities of the situation favor the Taos Indians. This legislation should be supported by this administration."[11]

Robertson's NCIO memorandum accurately expressed the Indian perspective.

Tribes regarded H.R. 471 as a political litmus test both for the Nixon administration generally and for Agnew personally. The position of the vice-president on this issue was critically important because he chaired NCIO. For him to oppose H.R. 471 would be seriously to offend the Indian members of NCIO and, by extension, the entire Indian community. With LaDonna Harris an Indian member of NCIO, and her husband championing Blue Lake in the Senate, Agnew could ill afford a wrong move on H.R. 471.

According to C.D. Ward, Agnew was from the outset keenly interested in tribal affairs and supportive of initiatives to improve Indian life.[12] Like Nixon, he felt that this was an area in which he could have a real impact. Rainer recalls that, as chair of NCIO, "Agnew wanted to do something to make a mark and took up the cause of Blue Lake for that reason."[13] As Yakima chairman Bob Jim said when NCAI made the return of Blue Lake the "first priority" for 1970, "The future of all Indian tribes would be bleak indeed if so restrictive a measure as H.R. 471 to protect Indian religious rights cannot be passed."[14] The political implications for Nixon and his administration were clear.

The significance of H.R. 471 to all Indians persuaded Agnew that the administration ought to back the bill. On March 25, he informed President Nixon that a thorough review of the situation convinced him that "the equities lie with the Taos Pueblo Indians," and that the administration "should endorse H.R. 471" and "aggressively seek its enactment." Pointing to H.R. 471's "universal support from the Indian community," Agnew explained to Nixon the bill's wider political significance.

> This legislation . . .would symbolically serve as an indication of your understanding and desire to redress the many injustices which have been perpetrated upon the Indians. Additionally, it would greatly assist in creating the necessary climate to facilitate our long-term objectives of having the Indians assume increased responsibility and direction over programs affecting them.[15]

Walter Hickel agreed. The previous fall he had come to just that conclusion when, at the NCAI Albuquerque convention, he supported H.R. 471 in a pledge of his sincere desire to work on behalf of the Indians. It was that declared support which had occasioned Anderson's anxious letter of October 27 concerning the White House position on the bill, a letter to which Hickel finally replied in late February.

In his reply, Hickel explained to Anderson that since receiving his letter he had thoroughly studied the Indians' claim and was now "more convinced than ever that they should have the full use and enjoyment of this land that only a trust title will give them."[16] He then refuted all of Anderson's objections, and referred to Bernal's crucial 1969 testimony as to how Forest Service control threatened the Tribe's right to religious freedom. In the light of that testimony, he said, he wanted the enactment of H.R. 471 so that the Indians could "enjoy their freedom of unrestricted worship in the traditional manner."[17]

While Hickel's support had been expected, the support of Hardin of Agriculture came as a welcome surprise. At the time of the May 1969 subcommittee hearings, Hardin had vigorously opposed H.R. 471. His resistance had begun to weaken during the January NCIO presentation in the White House. By early April, under pressure from Agnew, he began an orderly retreat from the negative position taken by the secretaries of Agriculture for more than sixty years.

The first evidence of this reversal of position came in the form of his April 1 memorandum to the White House suggesting a minor amendment to H.R. 471, which would remove his department's concern about precedent by adding language to the bill that emphasized the uniqueness of the Taos claim. When H.R. 471's backers accepted his amendment, Hardin agreed to cooperate. Contributing to Hardin's decision was the knowledge that Ehrlichman at the White House supported the Indian cause.

The next important opponent to capitulate was the Bureau of the Budget. As a result of high-level meetings with representatives from Agnew's office and other interested agencies, James R. Schlesinger, now acting director at Budget, developed a new version of the Blue Lake bill and sent it for comment to Agriculture, Interior, Justice, the ICC, and NCIO. His draft demonstrated the willingness of the bureau to reach a compromise.

Because of his concern about precedent, Schlesinger wanted to qualify the Indians' possession by including in the bill a "reversion" clause. Under the terms of this clause, if the secretary of the Interior determined that the Indians were "no longer using the lands for religious purposes," or were failing to abide by that department's regulations, then "title to the property shall revert to the United States."[18] He also wanted the Tribe to forfeit the balance of the money due them under the ICC ruling if they received title to the watershed.

When Straus explained these proposals to the Tribe, they strenuously objected. They regarded the "reversion" clause as an insult, since it implied either that they were not going to use the land for religious purposes or that their religion might die out. Nor were they receptive to waiving their right to the remainder of their claim. As C.D. Ward summarized the Tribe's position:

> The Taos people should not be penalized for accepting the return of land rightfully theirs. They should receive their sacred lands and be paid for other lands taken from them.[19]

When Bobbie Greene made it clear to him that introducing a "fresh and significantly restricted bill" such as Budget wanted "would destroy any positive image benefits that the administration would otherwise gain among the Indian population,"[20] Schlesinger relented. He agreed to support H.R. 471 if the reference to grazing permits was eliminated and introductory language emphasizing the uniqueness of the Taos case was included. This agreement ended the long-standing opposition of his office to the return of Blue Lake.

While events were unfolding within the administration, Harris had been hard at work for H.R. 471 in the Senate. In an address there on March 4, he characterized the taking of Blue Lake as a "glaring example" of the "injustices perpetrated against American Indians," and "strongly" urged his fellow Senators to support H.R. 471. A month later, Harris introduced into the *Congressional Record* a letter to George McGovern calling for "prompt and favorable action on H.R. 471." It was signed by Harris, Alan Cranston, Walter Mondale, Edward Kennedy, Philip Hart, and Harold Hughes.

This letter increased Bobbie Greene's concern that Harris and the Democrats were stealing the administration's thunder on the issue. She felt immediate action was necessary if the administration was going to "get some positive exposure" for supporting Blue Lake. She recommended a presidential message backing the Tribe which would place "the blame for inaction where it really lies—i.e., in the Senate Committee. . . . It is the Democrats in the Senate who have been holding up a resolution of this issue."[21]

By this time, Ehrlichman had spoken with the president and Nixon had ratified the decision to proceed with support for Blue Lake. Accordingly, the White House staff prepared a brief presidential statement backing H.R. 471. On Wednesday, April 15, Ward called Locker in New Mexico to inform her that the statement would be issued the following day. The Taos elders rejoiced at this news.

On Thursday morning, the sixteenth, Garment sent the statement to Ken Cole in the White House with a note attached saying it was "proposed for release, hopefully today, in order to ensure that credit for this move accrues, where it belongs, to this administration."[22] The White House gave the statement to Bobbie Greene for release to the press. In a dramatic confrontation, Ken BeLieu, legislative liaison for the president, intercepted her on her way to the White House press room. Grabbing the statement from her hand, he shouted:

> We are not, we are not, we are not releasing this. Does the President know about this? We are going to lose Clinton Anderson on the ABM treaty. This is crazy, this is stupid, this is dumb. I've never heard of any nonsense like this, losing the ABM treaty over some damn lake in New Mexico.[23]

Through his contacts on the Hill, BeLieu had gotten word that if the White House went ahead with its support for H.R. 471, Anderson would withdraw his support for the ABM treaty, of vital importance to Nixon's foreign policy. Worse still, Henry Jackson, chair of the Senate Interior Committee, had made the same threat to Nixon himself at a state dinner the evening before.

Nixon promptly called in Ehrlichman to discuss the matter. Evidently upset, he asked, "What is Blue Lake?" Ehrlichman replied that

> it was the spiritual home of this Pueblo. And Nixon said, "No, no, I mean what is Blue Lake in terms of ABM, Clinton Anderson, Henry Jackson—we seem to have gotten badly out of position with important people in the Senate." And so I explained that it was cowboys and Indians and that we were on the side of the Indians. And he indicated that he was more of a John Wayne man himself, and that he thought that we may have made a serious mistake and wanted to know what could be done to make it right.[24]

Jackson's opposition was serious indeed, given the high regard Nixon had for him. The two had similar philosophies on defense, and, in fact Nixon had wanted

The fate of Blue Lake hung in the balance as Ehrlichman and Nixon discussed the political implications of opposition from Democrats in the Senate. C. 1970, courtesy of National Archives and Records Administration.

Jackson as his cabinet secretary for that department. Although Jackson had turned down the offer, Nixon had great respect for him, both personally and politically. To make matters worse, Jackson was a major supporter in the fight for ABM, for which Nixon was much in his political debt.

To further complicate this political tangle, Jackson and Anderson were extremely close, a closeness that increased as Anderson's health now began to fail. Ehrlichman explains the Jackson-Anderson connection:

> The tie here . . .was that Scoop Jackson's wife had at one time worked for Clinton Anderson, maybe at that time still did. But Scoop had a kind of power of attorney from Clinton Anderson as Anderson's health failed . . . .And so Jackson in effect ended up with two votes. And that's what made this even more important, because he was probably the only guy in the Senate who had two votes.[25]

With this inside knowledge, Ehrlichman considered the dilemma. "By then it was pretty much of an up or down situation for us," he recalls.

> I explained it to Nixon in those terms and he saw that it was much more of an esthetic matter than a political matter in the way that we got into it, and

that disappointed him because our orientation ought to be political in the first place. We should think these things through and decide on the basis of who were our friends and who were not.[26]

Uncharacteristically, Nixon suddenly dismissed the possible political consequences. He told Ehrlichman, "Well, as long as we're this far along, maybe we'd better tough it through."[27] He even volunteered to help in any way he could. As the meeting broke up, however, Nixon looked sternly at Ehrlichman and warned, "I don't like to get crosswise with Scoop, especially with all the help he's giving us on ABM. If we're going to buck him, just be sure we win."[28]

While agreeing in principle to back the Blue Lake bill, the White House decided to delay releasing the statement of support until BeLieu could gather more information from the Hill, sounding out key senators for their opinions. When Straus got the bad news, he telephoned Locker to let her know that there were problems. Hours later, Bob Robertson of NCIO called "to confirm that a snag had developed."[29]

Leonard Garment, Nixon's chief White House advisor on minority affairs, disagreed about the delay. On Friday, he sent the president a memorandum which warned that Harris and other Democrats were "moving to seize this issue." If McGovern opened hearings on H.R. 471 before the president backed the bill, it just might "finish the job of milking all credit away from us."[30] He pointed out to Nixon that Blue Lake was "now *the* single specific Indian issue and as such is of major symbolic importance."[31] Now that Agriculture, Interior, and Budget were in support of H.R. 471, he urged the president to issue his statement and use Blue Lake "as an opening gun in setting a new administration direction for Indians."[32]

He gave an additional reason for the statement's immediate release. Nixon was soon to go to New Mexico to attend the upcoming Republican Governors' Conference, "and silence on this matter will almost surely cause you embarrassment,"[33] especially since he had been invited to visit Taos Pueblo at that time. However, should Nixon issue the statement and visit Taos, "it would be of tremendous state as well as national impact."[34]

Garment was not naive. He recognized the importance of Anderson's vote on ABM, and that his "skittishness" on Blue Lake was making other important senators nervous. He asked BeLieu to write him a report concerning what he had found out on the Hill, and forwarded to the president BeLieu's report as an attachment to Garment's own memorandum urging immediate support for Blue Lake.

BeLieu learned that Anderson was "very, very strongly against" and would be "extremely unhappy" if the White House went ahead without consulting him further; that Jackson would not move the bill out of committee without Anderson's approval; that Gordon Allott sided with Anderson; and that Paul Fannin objected to H.R. 471, considering it "not important enough to jeopardize Anderson's ABM vote."[35] Alarmed at the threat to ABM, BeLieu scheduled a meeting with Anderson for the following Monday to discuss the matter in greater detail.

Aware of these political developments, Garment summarized the situation for Nixon:

> To be very candid, the question before you is not what happens to the bill; with the kind of opposition Ken BeLieu has reported, the answer seems to be: little chance. The question, however, is what position you as President should take, for both moral and political reasons.
>
> Here the dilemma is: to risk arousing Anderson's ire so much as to jeopardize the ABM vote *vs* [*sic*] to risk embarrassment in New Mexico and in fact to pass up an opportunity to seize this unique issue before or during your trip, even if the bill itself never moves out of the full Jackson-Allott Committee.[36]

Garment then related Blue Lake to the policy of self-determination: "A new Indian policy needs a starting point. Blue Lake is just that—strong on merits, and powerfully symbolic."[37] Garment recommended that the President "issue the statement soon."

Despite Garment's soundly reasoned urgings, the White House withheld the statement pending the outcome of BeLieu's meeting with Anderson. In that meeting, BeLieu learned that Anderson considered H.R. 471 a serious "mistake" because of the precedent it would set for other tribes. He "was chagrined," he said, that Interior supported the bill when it knew that he opposed it. Reiterating his opposition to the transfer, he gave BeLieu copies of various letters he had written that were critical of H.R. 471, and asked that the White House review their position in the light of his letters.

The following day, Jackson called BeLieu to say that, while he was sympathetic to the Indians, "now was not the time to rock the boat." In an unmistakable threat, he told BeLieu, "We have to decide whether it is ABM, or whether it is Taos Indians we opt for."[38]

Nixon now found himself in a very difficult position. On the one hand, he favored supporting the Indians and saw the relevance of H.R. 471 to the success of self-determination. On the other hand, he liked Jackson and needed him politically. In Ehrlichman's assessment, "I think you cannot overstate the problem of Henry Jackson being upset at that period of time."[39]

It was not only because of his friendship with Clinton Anderson that Jackson opposed H.R. 471. He was also angry with Fred Harris for promoting it in the Senate. In so doing, Harris was breaking two unwritten Senate rules which were virtually inviolable in 1970. The first was that junior senators did not oppose senior committee chairs from their own party. As LaDonna Harris says,

> You never went up against the Committee report and the Committee Chair, and to take them on was really kind of unorthodox . . . .[40]

Second, senators did not interfere with issues that affected the state of another senator. Harris's support of H.R. 471 was an invasion of Anderson's home turf. Several senators remonstrated with Harris, saying,

They didn't come into Oklahoma and try to tell me what to do in regard to Indians in Oklahoma and I ought not to come out to New Mexico and tell them what to do about New Mexico Indians.[41]

In particular, Harris had incurred the wrath of three very important people: Anderson, McGovern (the Indian subcommittee chair), and, most importantly so far as Nixon was concerned, Henry Jackson, chair of the Interior committee. They were incensed that Harris was breaching Senate etiquette in his attempt to "roll" their committees and force the bill onto the floor. Jackson's anger with Harris intensified the pressure he put on Nixon to withhold support for Blue Lake. Given that kind of opposition, the White House decided to let things cool down in the Senate and delay releasing support for H.R. 471 until Nixon, at a later time, would issue a broad statement on Indian policy. Then, too, the White House, for reasons unrelated to Blue Lake, had cancelled plans for the trip to New Mexico, removing any urgency from release of the presidential statement.

At Taos Pueblo, the Indians anxiously awaited the White House announcement. When, by April 20, no statement had been issued, they "felt that they could not sit back any longer, knowing that Senator Anderson was working against them,"[42] and called Cargo and Lujan for information and advice.

Cargo continued to prove his friendship. In January he had written to the White House to declare his support for the Indians. In February, he made the first official visit to Taos Pueblo by a New Mexico governor in 123 years, for the express purpose of giving H.R. 471 a widely publicized endorsement. Now he called the White House and learned that, while the president was planning to support H.R. 471, his announcement would be delayed for strategic reasons. Lujan informed the Tribe that the ABM/Jackson problem was causing Nixon's hesitation. Greatly disappointed, the Tribe decided that their only recourse was to increase the political pressure on Nixon.

To that end, they first appealed to the wider Indian community. In late April, nineteen Indian leaders from New Mexico sent Agnew a telegram which said that the signatory tribes were "DEEPLY DISTURBED BY FAILURE OF ADMINISTRATION AS OF THIS DATE TO RESPOND TO NCIO AND NCAI RECOMMENDATIONS TO DECLARE SUPPORT OF TAOS BLUE LAKE LEGISLATION."[43]

A month later, twenty-seven Indian leaders meeting in Denver sent Nixon a telegram which noted that he had been considering H.R. 471 since January and had had adequate time to reach a decision. They urged him to "ANNOUNCE YOUR SUPPORT AS SOON AS POSSIBLE."[44] NCAI followed up with a press release which stressed that those who had signed the telegram represented tribes throughout North America who were "asking the President to declare his support of H.R. 471 as part of a national policy that protects Indian religions and cultures instead of destroying them."[45] The signature list made it clear that virtually every major tribe and Indian organization endorsed passage of the Blue Lake bill.

The Tribe then turned to the non-Indian community. In late April, the formation of the Southern California Committee for Restoration of the Blue Lake Lands to the Taos Indians received wide publicity, as did a tribal delegation when it went to California to raise money and support. Other newly formed public support groups, too, increased the visibility of the Blue Lake quest, raising money by means of raffles, movie showings, and bake sales, while sending letters to key people in Washington.

The Tribe also used the press in an attempt to break the obstacles to H.R. 471 in McGovern's subcommittee. When McGovern made it clear, in early May, that the Subcommittee on Indian Affairs would not act on H.R. 471 without Anderson's approval, the Tribe sent him a letter complaining that their bill had been languishing in his subcommittee for eight months. They asked him to take immediate action on the bill lest it "die in your subcommittee without action on the floor for the third time since 1966."[46]

Not stopping there, the Tribe used excerpts from this letter in a late May press release which called upon Washington to give their bill "a fair chance this year." The Tribe wanted immediate Senate action, fearing that, unless the hearings were held at once, no decision could be made on Blue Lake before Congress adjourned. Wide coverage of the release by the media increased the pressure on the White House, McGovern, and Jackson.

At this moment of high tension, in early June, the Tribe, to break the deadlock between the White House and the Senate, turned to its ninety-year-old holy man, the Cacique, Juan de Jesús Romero. As the Tribe's "highest priest" in religious affairs, Juan de Jesús had a pressing schedule of religious observances to coordinate and oversee, leaving him no time for direct participation in outside political affairs. There also was a strong feeling within the Tribe that their spiritual leader should not be sullied by excessive contact with the profane outside world. For these reasons, the Cacique so far had taken no part in the external politics of Blue Lake.

Yet while Martinez and Bernal manned the battle on the political front, the Cacique had been tending the sacred flame. Year in and year out, decade after decade, he had been tirelessly at work to keep the sacred quest alive in the internal religious life of his people.

Juan de Jesús is described by tribal member Henrietta Lujan as the Pueblo's "first father." "He was the father to all the people of Taos Pueblo because he was our main leader, our Cacique."[47] In his capacity as "first father," he never let the people forget the vision of a Blue Lake restored to them. Through all of the years of disappointment, he had fanned the embers of hope within the Tribe and made sure that the people kept the Blue Lake quest in their hearts and in their prayers.

In addition to his religious duties, Juan de Jesús also played a crucial role in the internal politics of the Tribe. As Cacique, he functioned as the head of the Tribal Council. Tribal member Dave Gomez, then an assistant in the governor's office, vividly describes the Cacique's control of Tribal Council meetings.

He would sit there like he was asleep. He always had a cane and he would put it on his forehead and he would sit there with his eyes closed while everyone talked. Everybody, sometimes forty or fifty people would be in there talking. And when they finished he would ask them if there was any more to discuss. Then he would make a decision. He would be like your machine there [points to tape recorder], he would be recording everything they said and then he would say, "Well, this is what you want and this is the route that we're going to go." He had the Council in control.[48]

Through all of these many years, the Cacique had been guiding the Tribe's decisions regarding the fight for Blue Lake, and there can be no doubt but that his lifelong spiritual commitment to the cause had kept the title quest alive. His grandson, William Martinez, recalls the Cacique's devotion:

Every night and every morning . . . he used to pray in our way to get it back, he was impassioned about getting it back . . . . Every day, every day in the morning and in the evening . . . he also used to go to the river at five o'clock in the morning, he used to go down to the river even if it was cold, ice. He used to break the ice at six o'clock in the evening for the morning, he used to take a morning bath at five and pray, and then also in the evenings he used to go take a bath and pray.[49]

For all of these years the hidden power behind the quest, the Cacique suddenly came forth to assume control of the political battle. The Tribe now had a potent ancient threesome—Quirino Romero, James Mirabal, and the Cacique—to confront its political foes. Mirabal, who with Seferino Martinez and the Cacique was one of the Tribe's three most important religious leaders, had now taken the place of Martinez, who was too ill to continue the fight. Paul Bernal, of course, was another political warrior in the final battle.

Why did the Cacique, who had so long remained hidden, now decide to join the political fray? Perhaps he and his old ally Martinez knew of a tribal prophecy foretelling that 1970 would be the year of decision. What Tony Martinez has said of his father might equally well apply to the Cacique—that his

political behavior was motivated by his understanding of the tribal prophesies. He was very well versed in all aspects of tribal religious life, so he knew, like the older people, what was going to happen.[50]

Did Juan de Jesús and Martinez have some esoteric knowledge that the time of decision had come? The answer to that question is known only by the Indians themselves. Nevertheless, it is striking that only at this moment of apparently hopeless deadlock did the Cacique come forth to address the non-tribal world, creating by his presence the magic for victory.

At a press conference in Taos, James Mirabal, serving as interpreter, told the assembled reporters that "Juan is the most powerful man in our tribe . . . Juan speaks the truth. The only way to make Anderson believe us is to take him to look at him face to face . . . ."[51] And then the ancient Cacique spoke:

The Cacique, deep in thought. 1971. Photo by Dan Budnik.

> I want to be present with that white man . . . .He doesn't know us. . . .He does not visit our village, he does not come and speak to us face to face, man to man.[52]

Juan de Jesús then detailed the reasons why the Indians had "developed a dislike for the Forest Service," reasons which included timbering, spraying ("the birds, the little animals, the chipmunks, the grouse, the deer, and even the fish die"), cutting trails, and building cabins. He said that these activities compromised the sanctity of the watershed and directly threatened the Tribe. "Our Blue Lake wilderness keeps our water holy and by this water we are baptized. Without this, we have no life."[53] Firmly stating that the Tribe would accept no less than 48,000 acres, he concluded with a moving plea:

If our land is not returned to us, if it is turned over to the government for its use, then it is the end of Indian life. Our people will scatter as the people of other nations have scattered. It is our religion that holds us together.[54]

The Cacique's impressive presence and his words made the story irresistible. Scores of newspapers ran the story with such tags as: ancient spiritual leader (who hunted buffalo as a youth), Tribe's "secret weapon," makes first trip in airplane to confront powerful senator in Washington to obtain mountain shrineland.

The Cacique's entrance into the battle appeared to have an immediate effect. McGovern promptly announced that hearings on H.R. 471 would be held the following month. With the confrontation in the Senate looming, all eyes turned to Nixon. Would he now make good on his promise to back the Indians on Blue Lake?

Garment did his best to persuade Nixon to keep his word. In mid-June, he sent the president a memorandum which reviewed the developing self-determination proposals for Indian country, explaining that they were all based upon the principle of the "restoration of power and responsibility to the Indian people to the maximum extent."[55] He then stressed the propitiousness of the moment, saying that Nixon was in a position just then "to open a new deal for the American Indians. By speaking out now," he continued, "you can make these promising new initiatives your own and wrap all of these individual innovations into a Presidential new direction."[56] He reminded Nixon of the prior decision "to announce our support for H.R. 471," and tied that decision to the fate of self-determination:

> This is a decision of great symbolic as well as substantive significance to Indians everywhere; it is a key part of the message and is one of the reasons a message should be now rather than next winter.[57]

The press, too, soon picked up this theme, agreeing with the *Albuquerque Journal's* assessment of H.R. 471: "the whole concept of self-determination for the Indians is being put to a test on this bill."[58]

Nixon faced a difficult decision. His professional staffers were telling him to forget about that "damn lake in New Mexico" and concentrate on a real world issue like ABM. They derided the five amateur staffers—Ward, Robertson, Greene, Garment, and Patterson—who naively, in the professionals' judgment, supported the Indians. They considered the amateurs' bosses, Ehrlichman and Agnew, as wrongheaded as the others. Bobbie Greene describes their attitude:

> A lot of people in the White House laughed and thought this was absolutely ridiculous. Ehrlichman was spending his time and energy again on something that nobody would care about and that Richard Nixon was never going to get any good publicity [from,] because nobody liked him and the press was never going to give him a fair shake even on this . . . .[59]

Nor were the professional staffers happy about the strange alliances the amateurs were making because of this issue. Kennedy was one of the most liberal men in the Senate, and Harris was thought of as a radical populist. Serious friends like Jackson and Anderson should not be alienated, the professionals counseled, especially at the possible cost of ABM. Pragmatic politics, they insisted, dictated abandoning H.R. 471.

Nixon was not immune to such arguments, but, perhaps influenced by memories of Chief Newman, he also attached great importance to Indian affairs. He firmly believed that the right decisions for Indian country could really improve the lot of this neglected minority, and he just as firmly believed that the policy of self-determination would contribute significantly to that improvement. He also understood what Garment, Agnew, and Hickel were telling him: that if the administration failed to keep its promise on Blue Lake, Indians across the country would regard self-determination as nothing more than the old policy of termination in some nefarious new Republican disguise. The politics of the matter were simple: if the administration did not support H.R. 471, Indians would not support self-determination.

Intensifying Nixon's sympathy with the Indians was his general theory of race relations. Bobbie Greene described Nixon as,

> a president that was unique . . . in that he cared about the Indian community because they were not in favor of integration, they were in favor of self-determination . . . . He was not comfortable with the concept of integration . . . . He firmly believed, not in separate but equal necessarily, but in people doing their own things and not being forced together. And the Indian community's desire fit that beautifully—they wanted to be themselves, they wanted to have self-determination but not assimilation, they wanted to keep their culture and their heritage . . . . It fit his preconceived notion.[60]

Nixon knew that he could hardly represent himself as respecting Indian culture if he opposed legislation that Indians nationwide had themselves chosen as symbolic of that respect.

Finally, in a dramatic press conference with the Taos elders present, Richard Nixon declared his position in an important speech on Indian self-determination. To heighten the drama, Nixon delivered his address on the day before the Indian subcommittee opened the Senate hearings on Blue Lake. Recognizing that the success of self-determination required the trust in government of the Indian people, and that responding to just grievances was one way of establishing that trust, Nixon affirmed his support of H.R. 471 "as an important symbol of this government's responsiveness to the just grievances of the American Indians."[61] He continued:

> The restoration of the Blue Lake lands to the Taos Pueblo Indians is an issue of unique and critical importance to Indians throughout the country. I therefore take this opportunity wholeheartedly to endorse legislation which would restore 48,000 acres of sacred land to the Taos Pueblo people . . . . [62]

With the Nixon administration solidly behind the Tribe on Blue Lake, it was now, as the *Albuquerque Tribune* put it, a case of "Clinton P. Anderson seemingly against a great slice of the rest of the world."[63]

To the astonishment of the professional staffers at the White House, a front page story in the *New York Times* praised Nixon not only for his new self-determination policy but also for supporting the Blue Lake cause. Telegrams from across the country poured into the White House commending Nixon for his bold new vision. Bobbie Greene fondly recalls her reception by the professional staffers the day after the delivery of the historic message:

> The next day we had a picture on the front page of the *New York Times*, we had the entire message reprinted inside the *New York Times*. And I walked into the senior staff meeting which was at 7:30 in the morning, which Ehrlichman held . . .and those guys all stood up and gave me a standing ovation and said, "We don't believe it, he's on the front page of the *New York Times* doing something with a minority group that people like." They could not believe it.[64]

While buoyed by the favorable publicity as they drove to the Senate hearings, the tribal delegation could not but recall the harsh treatment meted out to them when they last testified before McGovern's Subcommittee on Indian Affairs in 1968. The list of opposing witnesses they were soon to face included the names of many familiar and bitter foes: Jean Hassell, the Carson supervisor; their old nemesis, George Proctor, flown in by the Forest Service to make a last-ditch stand; Jon Little, who had brought the charge of littering against the Tribe; and Louis Clapper, who had cautioned that the Blue Lake bill would lead to a "Pandora's Box" of further Indian claims. However, the Cacique seemed relaxed and jovial, and his companions took heart.

If the 1968 subcommittee hearings were rancorous, the 1970 hearings had elements of the grotesque. Metcalf was drunk and Anderson visibly unwell. Anderson's condition was by far more important to the Indians, although Metcalf's state received greater publicity. At the time of the 1968 hearings, Anderson was at the height of his political power and a very effective adversarial inquisitor. Now he was in a considerably weakened condition. His diabetes had gotten worse, he was suffering from a disease similar to Parkinson's, and that spring he had had a serious eye operation to counteract the effects of advancing glaucoma. As Myra Ellen Jenkins, who testified at the hearing, recalls, "Anderson was a sick man . . .it was almost impossible to understand [his speech]. And when you did understand his words, it didn't make any sense."[65]

Indeed, Anderson asked relatively few, although highly antagonistic, questions at the hearings, leaving most of the interrogation to his long-time aide, Claude Wood, an inveterate foe of Taos Pueblo. To the Tribe's advantage, Anderson's declining health inevitably diminished his political power and effectiveness. Referring to Anderson's sickly pallor, Bernal cracked that the day before they had seen Nixon, the "Great White Father," while today they were going to

(Left to Right) Paul Bernal, President Nixon, the Cacique, and Vice-President Agnew exchange congratulations following Nixon's press conference endorsing the Indians' cause. Courtesy of Saki Karavas.

face the "Great White Mummy."[66] If the remark was lacking in compassion, neither had Anderson displayed that quality toward the Indians in their many encounters.

Another signal change between 1968 and 1970 was that now there was support from Budget and Agriculture, previously implacable enemies. The reversal of Agriculture's position vitiated the force of Forest Service testimony, while support from the Bureau of the Budget underscored the White House backing of H.R. 471.

Presidential support also produced a considerable contrast to the character of the earlier hearing. Nixon's endorsement the day before of H.R. 471 was fresh in the minds of those who opposed the Tribe. His Indian message had made it plain that if the bill was passed by the Senate, it would receive his signature—there was no threat of executive veto.

Testifying first, Harris explicitly drew the connection between Nixon's self-determination message and H.R. 471. "I believe that the spirit of that message requires that if we believe in the spirit of that message that we also move with dispatch on this particular claim."[67] Stressing that H.R. 471 had "great significance for Indians throughout the country," he urged the subcommittee to approve the bill and give Congress the opportunity to make it law, "so that we may do right by the Indians of Taos Pueblo and also greatly lift the hopes and spirits of American Indians everywhere."[68]

Clifford Hansen then emphasized a point made by Nixon, that H.R. 471 was a "much needed symbol of this government's responsiveness to the just grievances of the American Indian."[69] He then moved to include the president's self-determination Blue Lake speech in its entirety in the hearing record.

For the Tribe, the presence at this hearing of the Cacique was incalculably valuable, not only because of what he said, but also, and perhaps more importantly, because of the effect his personal force had on others. La Donna Harris remembers: "He was of course so stately. . .there was really a majesty about him, a royalty that he always presented."[70] For Bobbie Greene "he had extraordinary spiritual power. . . .He had a presence about him, there was something about him that lit up a room."[71]

In his remarks to the subcomittee, the Cacique did not so much testify on behalf of the bill as weave a sort of spell. He spoke of his religious responsibility to pray for and "love the human being" without discrimination: "I include everyone, the white, the black man, the Indians, and what-have you in this world."[72] No resolution of the conflict could be reached by the antagonistic use of power, he said. It could be reached only through "love and care." He wanted to achieve a result based on understanding. "We want to talk peacefully. We want to talk as brothers. We want to talk as understanding of everything. And that is my desire."[73] Even Metcalf was moved, and praised the Cacique for his "splendid presentation."

The effectiveness of Bernal's testimony before the House subcommittee in 1969 also helped in this hearing. His earlier explanation of how the Forest Service had unwittingly interfered with the Tribe's religious rituals was cited several times, because it clarified the reasons for the lack of Forest Service documentation of such interference. To be sure of making this point, the Tribe introduced into the record thirty-five instances in which the Forest Service had interrupted religious rituals during the last ten years. Hickel, when pressed by Anderson to give examples of religious interference, humorously underlined the point with a reference to the Forest Service structures at Blue Lake: "I would have to go out there and pick up the outhouse and bring it in here."[74]

The youth of Taos Pueblo, too, contributed a new element to the 1970 hearings. In 1968, Metcalf and Anderson had charged that only the old councilmen had an interest in Blue Lake, an interest that was financially self-serving. Now Gilbert Suazo, as a representative of the Taos Pueblo youth, presented to the subcommittee a statement signed by almost all of the younger Taos Indians, calling for the return of Blue Lake.

An important new ally at these hearings was Dr. Myra Ellen Jenkins, whose testimony before the Indian Claims Commission had done so much to convince the government of the justness of the Pueblo's cause. When the Tribe asked her to testify at the subcommittee hearings, she had been concerned, as a profes-

The delegation from Taos Pueblo stands before the White House gates after President Nixon's historic 1970 speech supporting the return of Blue Lake to the Taos Indians. Front row, from left, John Marcus, Cruz Trujillo, the Cacique, Paul Bernal, Querino Romero, James Mirabal, Manuel Reyna, Gilbert Suazo, and John Rainer. Back row from left, Charles Hobbs of the Washington law firm Wilkinson, Cragun and Barker, and Bill Schaab. Photo courtesy of John Rainer.

sional historian and archivist for the state of New Mexico, about doing so. As a public employee, she had good reason to fear retribution from Anderson. To convince her to testify, the Tribe used their secret weapon—the venerable Cacique. When the Cacique personally asked for her help, she recalls, "that did it. With that marvelous old gentleman sitting there, there wasn't any way I could say no. Who could say no to that saint?"[75]

It was fortunate for the Tribe that Dr. Jenkins agreed, because her exchanges with Metcalf on exclusive use and precedent were highly important. Her testimony helped him to understand, perhaps for the first time, that the sacred area had originally been included in the forest reserves to protect it for exclusive Indian use. She also lucidly explained that money could not be considered an adequate compensation for sacred ground. After her discussion of this point, Metcalf enthusiastically exclaimed, "That is the kind of testimony we have to have."[76] Dr. Jenkins also clarified for the senators matters pertaining to Spanish/Indian population ratios and the precise meaning of historical documents with respect to Indian land tenure. In her highly effective testimony, she stood up impressively to Metcalf's badgering.

Other witnesses not present at the earlier hearing advanced the Pueblo's cause. Ernest Santistevan of the Taos Town Council gave a moving endorsement for H.R. 471, as did Andres Martinez, a member of the Taos Soil and Water Conservation District. Sue Lallmang testified on behalf of H.R. 471 as the American Indian advisor to the Republican National Committee, and La Donna Harris did her part as an Indian member of NCIO. Hickel, too, proved a strong new witness for the Tribe.

In addition, many old friends of the Tribe renewed their support. The most significant were Stewart Udall, Michael Nadel of the Wilderness Society, Thomas O'Leary of the Blue Lake National Committee, tribal member John Rainer, Lawrence Speiser of the ACLU, and Bruce Wilkie of NCAI. Several others, including such organizations as the National Council of Churches, sent supportive statements. Schaab's contributions were especially impressive. To every technical question he had an answer, backed up with citations from relevant documents or statements.

Testifying in opposition to the Tribe were Jean Hassell and George Proctor of the Forest Service, considerably restricted in what they could say because of the newly-reversed position of Agriculture. The usual array of sportsmen's groups opposed H.R. 471 on grounds they had covered before: precedent, downstream water users, conservation, and preservation of multiple use. They advanced no new arguments against the Tribe. In fact, the only new issue that came up in these hearings was that of including in the Blue Lake bill a "reverter" clause: if the Tribe ceased to use the watershed for religious purposes, ownership would revert to the United States.

North Dakota senator Quentin Burdick pressed Bernal on the issue, trying to ascertain under what conditions the Tribe might be tempted to exploit the area economically. If an economically valuable find were made in the area, he wanted to know, would the Tribe voluntarily give the land back to the government? Bernal succinctly replied, "We are not going to give this land back to nobody." This led to an exchange which became famous throughout Indian country.

> BURDICK: Just a minute. Your basis is one of religion.
>
> BERNAL: Yes; we base it on religious principle.
>
> BURDICK: But suppose a portion of the land ceased to be used for religious purposes?
>
> BERNAL: We are going to use it only for religious purposes, sir.
>
> BURDICK: Suppose it ceases to be used for religious purposes sometime?

Drawing about him the mantle of dignity woven by a thousand years of continuous religious practice, Bernal defiantly asserted, *"It Is Not Going To Be Ceased."*[77]

Metcalf's excitement, making him both petulant and querulous in his questioning, gave the hearings an ugly tone. Perhaps the best example of this came in an exchange with Bernal. At one point in the testimony, Bernal wanted to ask a question and Metcalf angrily cut him short, saying, "You are not supposed to ask questions; I am."[78] When he then allowed Bernal to proceed, Bernal asked Met-

calf if he believed in religion. Metcalf's reply was that Congress may not participate in any religion. He then added this gratuitously offensive remark:

> Maybe passage of this bill would be an encouragement and inspiration for a
> whole lot of Indian religions, and medicine men would spring up all over the
> country. I would hope not.[79]

This slur on Indian religion was typical of the tone set by the opposition at the
hearings.

As the proceedings drew to a close, the old Cacique, standing at the back of the
room, indicated that he wished to speak. Holding up his gnarled walking stick as
the symbol of his age, the Cacique intoned the hearing's last words:

> I want you to know this is an exhibit of the sacrifice and torture we have
> experienced in the last 65 years ever since your sovereign government took
> this beautiful land away from the Indians....Mr. Chairman, please do
> something about it and feel sorry for the American Indian. We want to
> encourage you. We want you to accept the principle that these people have
> long enjoyed before the beginning of time....[May] the Great Spirit give
> you the encouragement and understanding and inspiration to follow the
> steps that these people have presented for preservation of this Indian life.[80]

The conduct of the hearings was an outrage; the behavior of Anderson and
Metcalf disgraceful. John Bodine, professor of anthropology at the American
University in Washington, was present as an interested observer. His anger at
the treatment accorded the Indians prompted him to send a strong letter to Met-
calf, a letter that became an important addition to the record of the hearings.
Bodine describes the hearing and his reaction:

> I think the thing that really angered me the most and prompted me to go
> ahead and write the letter was the treatment that the Indians received. I just
> couldn't imagine that U.S. senators could be so callous towards someone
> appearing before their subcommittee. They were so patronizing, they were
> insulting, it was really appalling the way they were carrying on.[81]

Bodine was no casual observer of the proceedings. Although himself white, a
complex series of circumstances deposited him as a baby at Taos Pueblo, where
he lived for a number of his early years. He spoke the Indian language, and
wrote his doctoral dissertation on the interculture contact problems of the Taos
Indians. The Indians were "like family," and he also was a trained anthropologist,
giving him an unique advantage in understanding the situation. As he has said, "I
imagine that I'm the only person that has lived in the Pueblo who's also a social
scientist."[82]

As Bodine listened to the senators' hostile questioning, he perceived that their
fundamental problem was an inability to understand the Indians' religion. The
difficulty was cross-cultural, and it occurred to him that his professional training and knowledge of Taos culture might be useful in clarifying matters for the
senators. He recalls,

I felt the naiveté there in terms of their understanding of Indian religion was so apparent and so grossly obvious that this is what really prompted me to try to do something about it.[83]

As Bodine saw it, the senators' problems centered on their inability to grasp why it was that the Taos claim was unique. He sought to render this intelligible in his letter to Senator Metcalf.

The Taos claim is unique because if Blue Lake and the surrounding lands are not returned to the tribe it will effectively destroy Taos culture. No other Indian tribe can make that claim, because no other Indian group today relies to the same degree on shrines in a restricted area for the continuance of its religion.[84]

Bodine's letter continued with a knowledgeable description of the Taos Pueblo religion that supported his assertion that the loss of Blue Lake would destroy the Indians. It substantiated Bernal's 1969 testimony concerning the Indians' need for absolute religious privacy and became a key reference in the upcoming Senate debate.

If the hearings angered Bodine, the Tribe's reaction can be imagined. The *New York Times* printed a long article in which it was reported that the Pueblo leaders "were deeply impressed with President Nixon's reception of them and the dignity with which they were treated," but "came away [from the Senate hearings] with bitterness." Bernal, accusing Metcalf of being "under the influence of firewater," said that the whole affair "was shameful behavior, an insult, a mockery to the hearing audience."[85] He said that Metcalf's "medicine men springing up" remark "insulted all American Indians. He has hurt his constituents as much as the Taos Indians. He should apologize."[86] When Governor Cargo learned of Metcalf's behavior, he told the newspapers, "If he has no more respect for these people than that, he ought to disqualify himself. To ridicule anybody before a committee I think is uncalled for."[87]

Angered most deeply of all by the white man's behavior was Juan de Jesús Romero. The Cacique told reporters, "No person, society or government should ever act the way the subcommittee did. It is insulting to all and speaks very poorly of these people."[88] His grandson remembers the Cacique's return from Washington:

When he came back, he was pretty upset about something....And the night that they got back he spent most of the night in the *kiva*, he even stayed there overnight. And the next morning when he came down he was changed altogether. After that he started really praying....He put everything, all his whole life into it from that time on.[89]

The magic of Blue Lake was now fully in the making.

10

The Moment of Truth

THE MIGHTY RIO GRANDE TAKES ITS RISE in the Colorado Rockies as a tiny snow-melt rivulet. It gathers strength as it flows south toward New Mexico, reaching its fullest force when it joins the waters from the Sangre de Cristo Mountains. Its slow descent from the plains of Colorado abruptly ends as it enters New Mexico and the great fault rift which rends her northernmost reaches. There the mighty river becomes a white-water torrent as it gushes through the narrows of the 700-foot-deep gorge. The most intense white water in all the river may be seen just north of Taos, in a section known by rafters worldwide as the "Box."

The victory of Blue Lake is comparable to this passage down the mighty Rio Grande. It began as a small rivulet in 1906, when the Indians first wrote Washington to demand exclusive use of their mountain shrineland, and it gathered strength over all the decades that the Tribe persisited in its quest. Its momentum intensified, like that of the river in the Rio Grande Valley fault rift, when Nixon, Agnew, NCIO, and NCAI rallied to the Indians cause. On the night of the Cacique's passionate medicine making, we may imagine that their craft entered the waters of the "Box." H.R. 471 had now to run the perilous white water ahead.

Self-determination and Blue Lake were two interconnected issues. A Blue Lake victory was necessary to actualize self-determination because of tribal suspicion that the new policy was just termination in disguise. To allay their fears, Indians throughout North America asked the administration to grant them a symbol of good faith. The Indians made Blue Lake that symbol. They would accept Nixon's pronouncements on self-determination only if he backed them on Blue Lake.

H.R. 471 had become for all Native Americans a symbol of their cultural preservation. To the credit of Nixon and Agnew, they appreciated this, and their commitment to self-determination persuaded them to act on their understanding. In his historic July 8 message, the president made the return of Blue Lake his pledge of good faith on self-determination, and, by extension, expressed his support for the preservation of Native American culture and religion.

The policy of self-determination was important to the proponents of the Blue Lake quest because of the "home state noninterference" rule: by tradition, senators from other states would not vote for a measure if the senator whose home state the vote affected had some objection. The unwritten rule was put to a critical test when, as in this instance, the senator concerned, namely Anderson, sat on the two committees with direct oversight over the matter in question (the Indian Affairs Subcommittee and its parent Interior Committee) and was a political power. In the case of H.R. 471, the Senate was particularly reluctant to oppose Anderson, because he, along with Barry Goldwater, were considered the Senate experts on Indian affairs. The majority of the Indian population was to be found in the states these two men represented.

When Nixon joined the fate of Blue Lake with the policy of self-determination, H.R 471 lost its home state status and became a national issue. Senators could now in good conscience approve it without feeling they were violating Senate tradition and crossing Anderson. To appreciate their reservations on this score, a political fact supplied by LaDonna Harris is helpful. She remembers Walter Mondale warning the White House team

> how careful we had to be about how you would take on Anderson, because he was so elderly, and he was very strong. He dominated that Senate, he was one of the few leftovers, like Bob Kerr and others, Lyndon Johnson and others who just dominated. Particularly through their committee, they could do all kinds of things.[1]

With Nixon's support making Blue Lake a national issue, senators were freed to vote according to their best judgment, without violating the tradition of "home state non-interference," which would have constrained them to side with Anderson. In 1970, the fear of crossing Anderson was quite strong. "He was like Carl Hayden," LaDonna Harris says of Anderson. "Carl Hayden kind of shuffled in, they were like two old dinosaurs. Anderson was . . . frightening in lots . . . of ways."[2]

With the senators free to vote their conscience, it was up to the Lakers at the White House to convince the solons that their conscience told them "yes" on H.R. 471. After the close of the subcommittee hearings, the Lakers—Garment, Robertson, Ward, Greene, and Patterson—commenced lobbying in earnest. Their zeal compensated for their inexperience, and they were supported all along the way by the astute counsel, coordinational skills, and political savvy of Jerry Straus. Greene reported on developments to Ehrlichman, Ward, and Robertson to Agnew, and Garment and Ehrlichman kept the president

On board Air Force 2: Leonard Garment (left), Counselor to the President, and Bobbie Greene (center), White House Fellow to the President, on their way to the celebration at Taos Pueblo, July 27, 1970. Courtesy of Bobbie Greene Kilberg.

informed. Nixon, Agnew, and Ehrlichman provided direction from the White House. If they were indeed going to "roll" Anderson and Jackson, they were going to have to go all out. "Just be sure we win," Nixon had said.

To cement relations with Nixon and Agnew, the Tribe held a second Justice Day on July 25 in their honor. Present to represent the administration were C.D. Ward, Greene, Garment, and Bob Robertson. The special guest of honor was Agnew's teenage daughter Kim. She brought with her a cane sent by Nixon, which Garment said "should be taken to symbolize the Taos Pueblo's right to religious and cultural self-determination." With this talisman from the president, the Tribe prepared to face the Senate rapids.

Three especially intense sections of Senate white water lay ahead. First there was McGovern's Subcommittee on Indian Affairs, which had just concluded the hearings on Anderson's S. 750 and Haley's H.R. 471. The second was Jackson's Interior committee, which would receive the subcommittee's recommended bill. Finally, the full Senate would vote on the bill which emerged from Jackson's Interior committee. H.R. 471 could be sunk as it rafted any one of these perilous sections.

Manning the frail craft, in addition to Straus, the Lakers, and the White House, were Bill Schaab, Corinne Locker, the Taos elders (Governor Romero, James Mirabal, and the Cacique), and Paul Bernal. Unfortunately, during this time of crucial test, Bernal was undergoing and then recovering from major surgery. In spite of ill health, he continued to devote his available energies to the cause. The partisans of Blue Lake, for all their differences of background and culture, worked as one to achieve the long sought for goal.

Fred and LaDonna Harris were possessed of the same spirit, and were indispensable allies. LaDonna, who had brought Blue Lake through NCIO and worked closely with Greene to secure White House backing, now put in long hours with the White House Lakers in lobbying the Hill. Her husband had spearheaded the Senate offensive in the spring when he pressured the subcommittee to report out H.R. 471. In so doing, he had violated the home state rule and challenged the seniority system. For this he earned his seniors' censure, and put his political career at risk. LaDonna remembers:

> I know that Fred said that several times all the staff in his office couldn't understand, and senators as well, why he would want to get into this kind of fight with Anderson. Career-wise in the Senate it wasn't one of those things you did. You got along—to get along you went along much like McGovern did. But he chose not to do that because of the feeling that he got, that we both got, as a matter of fact, from the Taos people.[3]

The political courage and ability of Harris now guided H.R. 471 forward. Ted Kennedy, too, was active; his keen interest leading to a minor conflict with Harris over who should lead the fight on the Senate floor. Harris won because of his closer involvement with Indian affairs.

Harris needed all the political acumen he could muster, since it was clear that Anderson was going to do everything in his power to block H.R. 471. An aide to McGovern pointed out to the Lakers "how powerful and cagey Anderson is," warning that he "is going to use all of his wiles and collect as many debts as he can to avoid losing face."[4] Anderson was soon to demonstrate that the physical infirmities plaguing him during the summer had not dimmed his ability to wield power and to strategize.

The initial problem confronting Harris was McGovern's deference to Anderson. As chair of the Indian Affairs Subcommittee, McGovern had the power to determine the fate of H.R. 471. Normally, the subcommittee members did not vote on bills. They would hold hearings and discuss a bill, and if McGovern wanted the full Interior committee to vote on it, he simply sent the bill on to Jackson. Anderson had kept the pressure on McGovern not to report the bill out, and McGovern complied.

However, the lobbying efforts of the White House Lakers, of Harris and Kennedy, of Nixon and Agnew, and the glare of unfavorable publicity, now made it almost impossible for Anderson and McGovern to continue to stonewall. As the pressure mounted, Anderson attempted to kill the initiative in the Senate by intimidating Harris. To that end, he asked McGovern to invite Harris and Kennedy to a special meeting on H.R. 471. Kennedy's opening tactic was to deliver a powerful plea on behalf of Blue Lake the day before this unusual meeting. Harris remembers the meeting clearly:

> A very unprecedented thing happened. The Chairman asked me, not a member of that committee, to meet privately. . .with the democratic members of that committee, who were in the majority. . . . Basically what [McGovern] did was to turn to Anderson for a statement and Anderson said to me, very pointed[ly] to me, he sat just opposite me at the table, that if I did not accept the bill that he wanted to pass . . . then there wouldn't be any bill.[5]

Undaunted, Harris replied, "Senator Anderson, there is no way you can prevent a vote on the floor. If your committee holds up H.R. 471, I will attach it as an amendment to any bill that comes out of the Interior committee."[6]

As Anderson well knew, Harris could make good his threat, since Senate rules permitted the attaching of a "rider" to any bill even if the rider itself was not germane to the bill it was amending. Using this tactic, Harris would be able to insure a Senate vote on H.R. 471. The problem with this approach was that it would require a major lobbying effort, and the bill would have to go back to the House for approval since H.R. 471 would then be a "tack-on amendment."

Recognizing that Harris refused to be intimidated, Anderson then tried another ploy. To appear the reasonable compromiser, he now repeated an offer previously rejected by the Tribe: to give the Indians trust-title to 30,000 acres with the balance of the watershed remaining under Forest Service control. Harris said he doubted that the Indians would accept anything less than the entire "Bowl," but invited McGovern to contact them to find out.

McGovern promptly called Bernal at the hospital where he was recovering from surgery, and Bernal unhesitatingly turned down Anderson's offer. He reminded McGovern "that back in 1968 the tribe had flatly refused that proposal, so the Indians are not accepting any other proposal except 48,000 acres."[7]

After the Indians' rejection of his proposal, Anderson countered with another strategy. If Harris attached H.R. 471 as a rider and secured a successful Senate vote, the bill would have to go back to the House for ratification. Anderson now threatened Harris that he would block the bill if it went to the House. Blue Lake's supporters doubted that Anderson could make good his threat, given the support of Haley and Aspinall. However, Anderson's influence was so great that they could not take his threat lightly.

Harris called the bluff. He made it clear that he and Kennedy would see to it that H.R. 471 reached the Senate floor as a tack-on amendment if Anderson kept it in the subcommittee. If they got a favorable Senate vote, they were ready to take their chances in the House. Harris told Anderson that he had better act quickly or he would soon be facing a vote on H.R. 471 as a rider. "Harris says the pressure is enormous down there," one of Straus's aides reported, "and Harris is inclined to wait a little longer before starting floor action to let the pressure

Kim Agnew wears the shawl and admires the ceremonial drum given her by Taos Pueblo. Seated in front row (left to right) New Mexico Governor David Cargo, C.D. Ward, Robert Robertson, and two unidentified participants. Pete Concha, the present Cacique of Taos Pueblo (with braids) stands at far right. 1970. Photo by Dan Budnik.

build up a little more."[8] Faced with the imminent embarrassment of Harris "rolling" their subcommittee, Anderson and McGovern conceded. They passed H.R. 471 out of Indian Affairs to Jackson at Interior. The Blue Lake bill was freed from the eddy in which it had been trapped for four long years.

While McGovern sent H.R. 471 on to the Interior Committee, he did so in a decidely equivocal fashion. "I called him the chicken from South Dakota after that,"[9] says Myra Ellen Jenkins. McGovern earned from her that sobriquet by reporting out not only H.R. 471, but S. 750, Anderson's 1,600-acre bill, as well. In other words, the subcommittee, as the newspapers put it, "refused to take decisive action." On August 27 they had "recommended two different bills to the full Senate Interior Committee for consideration." If Interior was unable to decide between them, then "both could be directed to the Senate floor."[10]

Now the pressure was on Jackson and his committee to decide between the Anderson and Haley bills. The Interior committee had seventeen members. A simple majority of nine would defeat H.R. 471, and when Straus last counted, Anderson had at least six other senators solidly with him. If a vote took place without all of the members present, then an even smaller total could defeat the bill. The Lakers worried that Anderson might call in some of the "many, many favors" owed him and persuade "some people who are otherwise for the bill to be absent."[11] Threatened by this possibility, the Lakers proceeded vigorously to lobby the senators uncommitted to, or in favor of, H.R. 471.

While more than two weeks passed without any action by the Interior committee, an important breakthrough had by then occurred. Harris had persuaded McGovern, who, like Anderson, sat on both the Indian Affairs Subcommittee and the Interior committee, to work with him on behalf of Blue Lake. McGovern's conversion made the prospects in the Interior committee look much more favorable, and there was now a good chance to move the bill forward if the committee could be persuaded to meet in executive session. Harris and McGovern planned to press Jackson for early action after he returned to Washington from a short trip.

McGovern, however, fearful that Anderson would manage to block H.R. 471 if they pressured the Interior committee to report it out, came up with a scheme to fool the wily old New Mexican. The committee would report out S. 750 and, when it got to the Senate floor, Harris and McGovern would co-sponsor an amendment which would substitute H.R. 471 for Anderson's bill. If it turned out that they couldn't get the committee to act even on Anderson's bill, then they would fall back on the plan to attach H.R. 471 as a rider to another Interior committee bill.

Harris and McGovern met with Jackson as planned when he returned to Washington, and Jackson agreed that the committee had to take a stand. He promised a September 30 vote on H.R. 471. When Straus made an estimate of the vote, he came up with eight senators in favor, six opposed, and three undecided. Since two of those who were undecided were Republicans, subject to White House influence, Nixon and Agnew made efforts to secure from them a favorable vote.

By now, the newspapers were commenting on what the *Washington Star* called the "coalition of peculiar political bedfellows" supporting H.R. 471. Noting that Nixon, Agnew, Harris, McGovern, and Kennedy were backing the bill, the *Star* observed: "The plight of the Taos is probably one of the few issues on which such an alliance could ever come together." The story informed its readers that "Nixon and Agnew have been waging an unprecedented lobbying effort on the Indians' behalf," and quoted the old Cacique as saying, "Like Job in the Biblical story, our people have patiently endured great hardship and deprivation fighting to save the religious heritage embodied in this holy land."[12]

To assist the Blue Lake cause, Agnew wrote an unprecedented personal letter to the Republican members of the committee urging them to vote for H.R. 471 "as a vivid attestment to our determination to implement the programs and policies called for by the President,"[13] that is, self-determination. He sent a copy of the letter to Minority Whip Robert Griffin. Nixon also met with Griffin to explain to him the relationship between self-determination and Blue Lake. Blue Lake's significance to the entire Indian community convinced Griffin to back H.R. 471. Just two days before the Interior committee vote, Griffin told his fellow senators,

> Because enactment of this legislation would go far toward restoring Indian trust and confidence in the federal government at a time when many new

and far-reaching proposals are before them, I strongly urge the passage of the Taos-Blue Lake legislation.[14]

With the advent of Griffin's support, Anderson knew he was in political trouble. Now that both the Senate Republican whip and the White House backed H.R. 471, there was every likelihood that the two undecided Republicans on the Interior committee would vote against him and tip the balance in favor of Haley's bill. Anderson asked Jackson to delay the vote for a week while he pondered his strategy.

Anderson then displayed the political expertise that had made him such a power in the Senate. Faced with the likely defeat of S. 750 in committee, he revived an idea he had been keeping up his sleeve since the previous spring. On October 2, in a masterstroke of political maneuvering, he wrote to Jackson that he was making "a final effort to do what is fair and reasonable." He explained that he planned to propose to the Interior committee an entirely new bill in place of H.R. 471. Under this bill's provisions, the entire watershed "will become embraced within a special ranger district required to be staffed by Taos Indians to assure the privacy essential to the survival of their religion." Anderson felt that staffing the watershed with Indians would eliminate "the frictions and uncertainties that have plagued them for decades."[15] At the same time, his new bill would avoid the bad precedent of giving the Indians title by leaving ownership with the Forest Service.

Clearly, Anderson's "Ranger bill" was a last-ditch effort to save face and keep the watershed under Forest Service control while appearing to give the Indians the religious protection they desired. Even the *New Mexican*, long a Pueblo supporter, found Anderson's compromise reasonable because it "wisely avoids setting a precedent" while giving the Indians "exclusive use."[16] So reasonable did Anderson's bill seem that Schaab had to persuade at least one member of the Blue Lake National Committee not to support it. If the support of a Blue Lake National Committee member had nearly been lost, what would the members of Anderson's own committee do?

On October 5, the day before the vote, Nixon asked Garment to write to the Republican senators on the committee explaining to them the White House position. The White House objected to Anderson's last-minute "compromise" because the Ranger bill itself set an undesirable precedent. While national forests and parks were for the benefit and use of all, "to sequester the use of a section of such lands, by statute, yet still call it a National Forest seems to be an inconsistency, compounded by the fact that the result is misleading to the public." The letter further explained that the "clean way" to insure exclusive use for the Indians was to give them title: "This is what H.R. 471 does and the President hopes you and your colleagues will support it tomorrow morning."[17]

The following day, the vote was called. Despite the efforts of the White House, four Republicans broke with the administration, and the Interior committee voted eight to five in favor of the Ranger bill, and reported it out of committee to

Under the vast New Mexico skies, the Tribe celebrates the White House decision. 1970. Photo by Dan Budnik.

the full Senate. The day after, two Forest Service signs in the Carson National Forest were blown up by plastic explosives. Although responsibility for the bombings could not be fixed with certainty, a caller to the Forest Service said they were to protest the Interior committee's vote. Days later, there was a second bombing. Tensions were running high.

The Tribe's supporters swung into action to discredit Anderson's bill, planning their strategy during the Senate adjournment for election break in the latter part of October and early November. Schaab did yeoman service during this hectic three-week period, developing the Tribe's opposition to Anderson's latest ploy. Nevertheless, he required payment for his efforts, and informed the Tribe that by the end of the year they would owe him and Straus nearly twenty-five thousand dollars more than they had been paid to date. While the Blue Lake National Committee had raised nearly nineteen thousand dollars during the previous several months, all of it had been spent. The Tribe was now going deeply into debt to keep the fight alive.

Financial worries, however, did not deter the Tribe from continuing to pursue their long quest. On November 7, they sent Jackson a letter condemning the Ranger bill on the grounds that it did not convey trust title; left the Forest Service in administrative control; infringed upon the Tribe's water rights; contained a "reversion" clause according to which their use-rights could be terminated without notice; and inadequately protected the Pueblo's religion, because it left open the possibilities of recreational use and vegetational manipulation. In their final objection, they said that the bill's assurance of Indian staffing was "illusory," because such staff had to be "qualified" by the Forest Service, which the Tribe feared would simply reject all Indian applicants. Signed by the Taos Pueblo governor, the letter was also affixed with the old Cacique's mark (a scrawling "X" attested to by Bernal's initials), the first time he had signed any tribal document.

Anderson had been waiting for the Tribe to reveal its reactions to his bill. After he knew their objections, he had the Ranger bill hastily rewritten ("apparently without any authorization" from the Interior committee) to take them into account. The rewrite of the Ranger bill deleted the initial version's restrictions on the Pueblo's water rights and some of the qualifications on exclusive use, but it retained the provision for Forest Service control and the highly objectionable reversion clause. For these reasons, the bill remained unacceptable to the Tribe.

Aware that to review all of these details with busy senators would be an almost impossible task in the short time available, the Lakers lobbied on the simpler objection already raised by the White House: that the Ranger bill "would carve out a piece of the national forest to create a sequestered district for the exclusive use of a special group." They argued for H.R. 471 on the grounds that it was "cleaner" simply "to restore the land to its Indian users and cease the pretense that it is public land."[18]

To make their case, H.R. 471's primary Senate backers—Harris, Kennedy, and McGovern—sent a letter to their colleagues denouncing Anderson's bill as "unworkable," and reaffirming that conveyance of title was the only "sound" way to preserve the Indians' religion. The letter explained that an "amendment will be offered on the floor of the Senate which would substitute the original House-passed bill for the committee approved bill."[19]

Anderson returned fire with a letter of his own, warning his fellow senators of the bad precedent set by H.R. 471. If they gave land instead of cash to the Taos Indians, they would have to honor similar requests from other tribes; further, many already settled claims might have to be reconsidered. Assuring his colleagues that he "wholeheartedly" wanted to protect the Taos religion, he urged them to vote for his bill because it not only protected the Indians but also avoided setting a potentially troublesome precedent.

As both sides were vigorously lobbying, H.R. 471 received invaluably favorable publicity when National Educational Television aired a program devoted to the Taos quest. Called "The Water Is So Clear that a Blind Man Could See," the program was written by an ardent Taos supporter, Stan Steiner. The program cast Anderson in a distinctly negative light, and emphasized the threat posed by Anderson and the Forest Service to the timber in the watershed. Aired nationally, and more than once in many communities, the program generated a flood of letters to the Senate in support of H.R. 471. One of these, exemplifying the passionate partisanship the issue had aroused, was sent to Anderson by Curtis Lucy of East Point, Georgia.

You are just one of the millions of stupid, selfish, murderous, bastards who doesn't give a damn for the earth or life. Some day, when it's too late, S.O.B.s such as you may get the message the Indians have always known. I could cry for your stupidity except that you are murdering the Indians and what is theirs. The worst descriptive name is too good for you. I expect you imagine yourself as being well versed in Rights—Bull Shit![20]

In the program, Anderson had been quoted as saying that the logging interests would be kept out of the watershed "only over my dead body." David Albright of Wynnewood, Pennsylvania took up this point in his letter to Anderson: "After hearing your boast, a fellow viewer remarked: 'I hope to God that event will happen before it is too late for the Indians.'"[21] Albright's letter echoed a remark of Dean Kelley's, that it seemed to him during the heat of the fight that success for H.R. 471 "would have to await one well-placed funeral before it could progress much further."[22]

Shortly after this program aired, minority whip Robert Griffin, at the urging of the White House, approached Harris about co-sponsoring H.R. 471 as an amendment to the Ranger bill. While Griffin had already declared himself for H.R. 471, his proposal to co-sponsor it made the support for the bill truly bipartisan. Harris recalls that "with Nixon on board, and his leader in the Senate on board, that made it into a really serious effort . . . ."[23] The momentum accelerated when, on November 25, Griffin spoke on behalf of H.R. 471, saying that it was

the first of President Nixon's recommendations in the area of Indian affairs to reach the floor of the Senate. By enacting this legislation in the form recommended by the President we will be according justice and demonstrating commitment to a group of Americans who have been neglected in many respects for too long.[24]

With the the Republican whip's co-sponsorship, H.R. 471 became known as the Griffin-Harris Amendment.

Then the Senate majority leader, Mike Mansfield, announced his support for H.R. 471. This was a coup, not only because he was majority leader but also because he was from Montana, the home state of Lee Metcalf who, with Anderson, was the Tribe's major opponent. With the Senate vote now imminent, Metcalf and Anderson made their final move, entering into the *Congressional Record* for November 30, 1970 a lengthy statement opposing Blue Lake's return.

The Anderson/Metcalf statement took the precedent issue for its chief argument, warning the Senate members that, if H.R. 471 passed, other tribes would soon "bog Congress down in a morass of claims that could not possibly be settled by payment in land."[25] Anderson and Metcalf asserted that the Tribe had not convincingly demonstrated that without trust title their culture and religion would "vanish." They pointed out that the Tribe had not had control of the watershed for sixty years, yet by their own admission their religion was stronger than ever. The statement charged that the Indians' motivation was, in fact, economic, that they themselves were planning to develop Blue Lake as a financially lucrative recreational reserve.

This lengthy statement was Anderson's final assault, and it exemplified his political prowess. It masterfully interwove history and contemporary testimony in such a way as to obscure the facts and the Indians' valid grievances, while at the same time impugning their motives. Anderson and Metcalf presented themselves as wise and diplomatic legislators who were responsive to the Indians' religious needs, and who opposed the bill only because it would establish a dangerous precedent and give leave to the Indians to put something over on the government.

The Senate scheduled the debate on Blue Lake for December 1. Straus and the lakers estimated the vote at forty-seven in favor, thirty-one opposed, and twenty-two unknown or undecided. The *Albuquerque Tribune*'s prediction was that "Anderson will win this one in the Senate arena. A big win for him. He will get some vital Republican defections from the White House camp."[26]

On the first day of the debate, the Senate floor and gallery were packed. The Blue Lake battle was by now a cause célèbre in Washington. Many people attended to find out why the White House was backing an Indian bill closely identified with such liberals as Kennedy and Harris, especially when it was widely known that in supporting the Indians Nixon could be imperiling one of his favorite defense strategies, ABM.

Harris, referring dramatically to the widespread national interest in Blue Lake, opened the debate by declaring that "millions await our decison." He emphasized the fact that the issue on which the Senate would be voting had implications much greater than the question of the welfare of the Taos Indians. Blue Lake was a symbol for all Native Americans.

> Justice for the Taos Indians will mean that Congress really has begun to declare a century of wrongs suffered by Indians enough, that it recognizes the unique worth of American Indian culture and American Indian heritage.[27]

Harris then took up the most controversial aspect of H.R. 471: the possibility of it establishing a potentially troublesome precedent. Offering reasons why the Taos case was unique and would not, in fact, establish such a precedent, he then masterfully played on the precedent issue by reversing its implications.

> If the Senate wishes to dwell on precedence, then it should be reminded of the precedence [*sic*] for destroying the culture, heritage, religion and pride of the American Indian—precedence [*sic*] for this is plentiful. Let's now set a precedent for justice in the individual and unique case of the Taos Pueblo.[28]

McGovern then took the floor to focus on the "spiritual issue." He had just returned from a Thanksgiving visit to his daughter who lived in Taos. While there he had met with the Indians, who convinced him that what "really is involved here is a deeply spiritual and religious matter, which goes right to the

Young men and women of the Tribe dressed in their ceremonial best on the second Justice Day. On the left, Esther Winters, center George Flying Eagle, and on the right an unidentified Indian from Taos. 1970. Photo by Dan Budnik.

heart of freedom of religion and freedom of conscience in our country." He referred to Forest Service actions in the watershed as "an incredible violation of the respect that we have under our system of government for freedom of conscience and religion," and said that successful passage of H.R. 471 would be like "throwing the money changers out of the temple. Our concept of freedom of religious expression," he said, compels passage of H.R. 471, adding that the Taos case was the only one on record in which Indians were asking for land to "be used for religious purposes only."[29]

Kennedy spoke next, also on the issue of precedent. It was unjust, he maintained, to turn down the valid claim of the Taos Indians solely on the grounds that passage of H.R. 471 might encourage other Indians to seek the return of sacred land. If H.R. 471 represented justice, it ought to be passed on that basis alone, without consideration of its effects on other possible Indian cases. Kennedy expressed confidence that Congress had the ability to weigh any future Indian claims and determine their validity. To vote against Blue Lake for fear of setting a precedent was, he said, "to abdicate our function and responsibility to look at each bill on its own merits, important in and of itself."[30] He then pointed out that the ranger bill set a bad precedent, making public land available for exclusive use by one group.

Harris then rose to enter into the record his arguments as to why H.R. 471 would not set a precedent. McGovern spoke again, offering an impressive list of the individuals and organizations supporting the Taos Indians. The debate continued until almost six o'clock. Harris, Kennedy, and McGovern were optimistic, but they knew that tomorrow they would have to face the opposition.

An even larger crowd attended on December 2, aware that the final vote would be that day. The mood of anxious expectation was heightened by editorials which had appeared that morning in the *Washington Post* and the *New York Times* unequivocally supporting H.R. 471. The *Times* said that the Senate vote could "right an old wrong," and "perhaps start the country back on the long road toward regaining the trust of the first Americans."[31] The *Post* saw the vote on H.R. 471 as "an acid test" of the government's sincerity on self-determination and "the policy of respecting the Indians' rights and allowing them the cultural freedom that other ethnic groups in the country enjoy."[32]

Bobbie Greene was doing some last-minute lobbying in the Senate anteroom when Barry Goldwater walked in. His stand on Blue Lake was critical, given the respect he enjoyed as one of the senators most knowledgeable on Indian affairs. When he refused to reveal his position, Straus listed him in the "undecided" column of his projected vote tally. A smiling Goldwater greeted Greene, and said, with an enigmatic look, "You listen good, girl."[33]

Jackson opened for the opposition, stressing the precedent issue. Metcalf, speaking next, said that the issue was one of transferring the land from the jurisdiction of the Department of Agriculture to the Department of Interior. He warned against the transfer, saying that Interior was "notorious" for its incompetence in managing land resources. (Ironically, just days before this state ment, Metcalf had entered into the *Congressional Record* a study which bitterly indicted Forest Service "clear-cutting" policies in his home state of Montana.)[34] Jackson then spoke again, citing alleged "other known Indian religious interests in national forest lands" which might present problems in the future. The combined effect of Metcalf's and Jackson's presentations must certainly have raised questions in the minds of those who were still undecided, and occasioned concern that passage of H.R. 471 could lead to serious complications.

At this decisive moment, the distinguished senator from Arizona rose to speak. Goldwater informed the Senate that he knew a bit about Indian affairs — nearly a third of his state was Indian land on which lived forty percent of the nation's Indian population. "I can understand the feelings of the Indian tribes, having lived among them all my life . . . ," he told the Senate.

> I think we are overlooking one important thing here. This will not establish a precedent . . . . I think we can control this, because what these Indians are asking for. . .is the use of land that we would say is religious land.

Goldwater then began a fascinating discourse on Indian religion and its relationship to the land. His central point was that land is sacred to the Indians, and if a tribe made a claim for land that was genuinely of religious significance, then the government should be willing to grant it to them. The decision on such requests should hinge on the proof of its religious significance: "No lands will be given or even allowed to be used . . .unless they are wrapped up in some religious meaning to the Indians." Goldwater made it plain that he would like to see the Indians receive their rights

> to these religious lands, just as we have the right to go to the church of our choice. They should have the same rights, even though their religions, I must say, are completely different to ours.[35]

Goldwater's remarks proved a turning point at this critical stage of the debate, significantly influencing the opinions of the fence-sitters. Goldwater counterbalanced the opposition of Anderson, partly because both were highly regarded senators from southwestern states with large Indian constituencies. Even more important was Goldwater's widely recognized pre-eminence in Indian affairs. While Anderson certainly commanded respect in this area, Goldwater was thought to be the Senate expert. As Allott from Colorado said, "I am sure that no member of the Senate is as knowledgeable over all of Indian history and Indian lore as the distinguished Senator from Arizona."[36] As the debate over precedent continued, many of the senators simply concluded that if Goldwater favored H.R. 471, then it must represent the right decision. Anderson's and Metcalf's arguments could not outweigh for them those of this respected and expert Indian authority.

Goldwater also contributed another strong point. To inflame the fears of precedent, Metcalf had entered into the record pages of potential Indian claims to public land on religious grounds. He then alleged that the Taos Indians were unable to articulate their religious claim, using as evidence the letter written to him by the anthropologist John Bodine.

In his letter, Bodine had said that the subcommittee hearings of the summer before had left him "frustrated by the inability and/or unwillingness of the witnesses called on behalf of the Taos" to explain why their case was unique. Metcalf quoted this statement from Bodine's letter out of context, and Goldwater countered by saying that he wished Metcalf had read the entire letter into the record.

Goldwater then referred to another statement in Bodine's letter: that when his doctoral committee asked him what would he do if he wished to destroy the Taos culture, he had "replied unhesitatingly that I would destroy Blue Lake."[37] Goldwater entered into the record all of Bodine's letter, with its crucial explanation of the Taos religion and its importance to the preservation of Taos culture.

There can be no question of the importance of Bodine's letter, since it illuminated for many senators how it was that the loss of Blue Lake threatened the Indians with cultural, and perhaps even social, extinction. The letter resolved the problem of cultural "translation" that the Indians faced in articulating their own case. With the exception of Bernal in his House testimony in 1969, they seemed unable to make their point precisely because of their reticence to discuss the details of their religion. "I am willing to do so," Bodine had written to Metcalf, "even though I realize that I am divulging information which could damage me professionally, but which no Taos Indian could possibly divulge."

To make the case for the religious uniqueness of Blue Lake, Bodine doubtless revealed in his letter more about their religion than the Indians would have wished. However, not to have done so might have meant their defeat in the Senate. As Bodine told Metcalf:

> Unless the structure of Taos religion is bared, then there is little basis for understanding why an exception should be made for them. There is no reason to understand why the area could not continue to be protected and administered by the United States Forest Service.

Faced with a difficult choice, Bodine had written in candid detail. "I have carefully maintained silence about their religion," he explained to Metcalf, "because I never wished to betray the confidence and trust they have extended to me. I know that the Taos required that I speak out, in spite of the consequences."[38]

Bodine's letter now proved an effective instrument. Even Metcalf admitted that "Professor Bodine made the most important and the most eloquent argument in behalf of this bill contained in this entire hearing record."[39] The credit is Goldwater's for bringing the letter to the attention of the Senate at this crucial time.

When Metcalf argued that the Taos situation was no different from the other potential Indian religious claims he had just cited, Goldwater cooly replied: "Who had this land in the first place? . . .The Indians were on these lands thousands of years ago."[40] He reiterated his earlier point, that the Taos case did not

The canes symbolizing Taos Pueblo's sovereignty. The cane on left was given to Taos Pueblo by Abraham Lincoln in 1863; center, the cane presented by Kim Agnew on behalf of President Nixon; the last cane is from the King of Spain. 1970. Photo by Dan Budnik.

pose a threatening precedent, because if other such claims arose "the committee can require proof of religious aspects of the land, and I do not think that is difficult to prove."[41]

Mondale now struck a blow for the Indians, pointing out that under the Ranger bill the Indians have only an "exclusive use" that could be terminated without notice. He then asked this rhetorical question of Harris. If he were representing "a client who brought in a deed which extended to him an exclusive use, subject to termination at any time without notice, what would he recommend that the client pay for the right?"[42] Harris played his part, saying such a right would be of dubious value and hardly a right at all.

Now the senior senator from New Mexico rose to speak. Perhaps his thoughts were ranging back to 1957, when he introduced the first bill concerning Taos Pueblo. Perhaps he was remembering the bulging files in his office, the thousands of pages he had gathered and written, the press conferences he had held, the hearings he had conducted, the politicking he had done, all with one purpose in mind: to keep the Indians from getting control of the land and retain the land as part of the National Forest, open to all under multiple use.

The informed members of his audience who were now intently watching Anderson might have reasonably wondered why the issue had mattered to him so much. McGovern's answer was this: "I really don't know all the reasons, but I think with Anderson, it is a question of long allegiance to the Forest Service and to the feeling of the government playing a trustee role."[43] If the old Cacique was in the Senate gallery watching from above, Gifford Pinchot was on the Senate floor, speaking through Clinton P. Anderson.

Anderson had long been committed to Pinchot's Forest Service and Pinchot's policy of multiple use. He had learned these principles well as Truman's secretary of agriculture, and he never lost his affection and respect for the Forest Service's "fine band of men" who were dedicated to carrying out the ideals of Gifford Pinchot. As he had once said in a newspaper interview:

> It may be that I spent just long enough in the Department of Agriculture to appreciate the Forest Service; but I have been, am now, and perhaps always will be a staunch supporter of the fine band of men who protect our forest areas and preserve them for coming generations.[44]

Anderson also genuinely doubted that the title quest had been undertaken for religious reasons. He was convinced that the Indians had economic designs on the land. His thinking was that the watershed was genuinely of religious significance only to a few older tribal members, and that when these men died there would no longer be a need to protect the "Bowl" for religious reasons. The land could then revert to control under conventional Forest Service multiple-use policies. Finally, on a more unconscious level, Anderson was probably influenced by old New Mexico frontier attitudes: he just plain was not going to get beat by a gang of Indians.

Anderson gave his all in the Senate debate, marshalling his physical strength in a last-ditch effort to defend the Forest Service. Though he lacked the vigor of his earlier years, his mind was still sharp, and he was able effectively to distill all of his objections into a carefully reasoned and hard-hitting speech. While he introduced no opposing arguments that had not been heard before, he invested his remarks with all of the passion that his age and infirmity allowed.

Anderson's central contention was that his Ranger bill was a "genuine and valid compromise" which protected Indian religion while establishing no adverse precedent affecting public lands. He said he was genuinely concerned that passage of H.R. 471 would set off a nationwide Indian "raid" on the public domain, and undo all of the work done by the Indian Claims Commission. Blue Lake had "become a symbol of the plight of the American Indian," he said, and as such had attracted "adherents who are well-meaning but who are not fully conversant with the real issues involved."[45] Blue Lake's backers had made the quest a symbolic and emotional issue but, in his judgment, few of them understood its implications for the federal land system. "It is my hope," he said, "that Congress can agree to settle the issue on its true merits rather than on a generalized desire to 'do something' for the Indians." In summation, he defended his Ranger bill:

> With the present legislation the Taos Indians can continue to receive the protection for their religious shrine that they rightfully deserve—without a disturbing precedent with national implications being established.[46]

The final speaker, Charles Percy of Illinois, the assistant minority leader, used his opportunity effectively, drawing the connections between the policy of self-determination and the case of Blue Lake. While he backed the Blue Lake cause on its merits alone, he made it clear that it had "a significance [with] wider [application] than [to] a single tribe in a single state."

> Our past Indian policies of subordination and paternalism are now just as outdated as the conquest policies of the ancient past. We must establish a new policy for American Indians: a policy of self-determination.
>
> Today we begin to write a new slate, in a new time. We should restore trust title to the Blue Lake lands because it is morally right to do so, but we should take this action also because of what it will become. It will become a signal to the future, a sign that this Congress considers Indians not only as first Americans, but as equal Americans, whose institutions and beliefs are to have the same independence and respect which we non-Indians have for our own.[47]

With Percy's moving remarks concluded, the senators prepared to vote. The question before them was whether or not to approve the Interior Committee's substitution of the Ranger bill for H.R. 471 as originally passed by the House. The roll was called, and the Ranger bill was defeated by a vote of 56 to 21.

With the rejection of Anderson's "compromise," the next issue under debate was the Griffin-Harris amendment, which substituted H.R. 471 for the Ranger bill which the Interior committee had approved. Robert Dole spoke on the president's support for H.R. 471, and Alan Cranston, following, reviewed the issue that had been at the heart of the conflict for decades: "the [incompatibility of the] multiple use policies applicable to the Carson National Forest . . .with the religious uses of the land."[48] Griffin had the last word:

> Cathedrals, mosques, and temples are generally respected as structures of sanctity and significance because they are important in the religious lives of men and women. What the Indians of Pueblo de Taos are asking is that equal consideration—no more and no less—be extended to the shrine where they have performed their religious obligations for at least as long as the famed cathedrals of Europe have been in use . . . .I strongly urge enactment of this legislation in the form as passed by the House.[49]

Now the moment of truth was at hand. In Agnew's absence, Goldwater was the Senate's presiding officer. "On this question," he announced, "the yeas and nays have been ordered, and the clerk will call the roll."[50] In the top row of the Senate gallery sat the old Cacique with Governor Romero, James Mirabal, and Paul Bernal. They huddled together, chanting softly, making medicine, and "communicating with the spirits of those strong departed ones who dwell at Blue Lake. They asked for strength, not to punish the government which had taken their sacred land, but to achieve justice by recovering the sacred area."[51] After so many years of work, so many trips to Washington, so many heartbreaks and defeats, they listened intently as the voting began: Aiken—"Yea," Allen—"Yea," Allott—"Nay," Anderson—"Nay." When the "yeas" and "nays" were counted, H.R. 471 had successfully shot the rapids—seventy in favor of Blue Lake, twelve opposed, eighteen absent. The interminable quest was at an end; the Blue Lake victory had been decisively won.

The enthusiasm in the gallery was uproarious. Goldwater had already had to gavel the gallery to silence after Harris had made a particularly telling point, and now the pent-up emotion of the supporters burst forth. Shouts of victory rang out, tears began to flow, hugs were exchanged, and fists upraised in triumph. The enduring image of victory is remembered by Bobbie Greene: the old Cacique, standing joyfully in the Senate gallery, holding aloft the Tribe's three symbolic canes. "When the thing passed," she vividly recalls,

> the hallways were in a frenzy. When you walked out of the Vice President's gallery . . .the place was in tears, there were Indians coming out all over, I mean it was really strange in the sense that nobody had ever seen anything like it before . . . .[52]

Epilogue

YOU ARE MY CHILDREN," said the old Cacique to the tribal councilmen gathered in Albuquerque to greet the delegation's triumphal return from Washington. "I bring you the victory." Hundreds of Indians were at the airport, including the leaders of many tribes from throughout the Southwest. New Mexico Governor David Cargo was among the non-Indian dignitaries also present. "God has given us this land back," the Cacique told the crowd. "The spiritual things that we said about our land are true . . . .we are going to use it like we said, the religious way."[1]

The victorious warriors' motorcade was greeted at the entrance to Taos Pueblo by hundreds of tribal members. Bill Schaab describes the scene:

> The bells of the old church pealed out their welcome, there were prayers, embraces, crys of rejoicing and a euphoria that showed the blessing of God.[2]

Ironically, the tribal elders and the rest of the joyous throng pressed into the Pueblo's old Catholic church to give thanks for the return of their "pagan" sacred ground.

Indians throughout the country rejoiced, convinced that the return of Blue Lake initiated a new era of justice for all Native Americans. "It was a dramatic decision for Indians everywhere," said the *Christian Science Monitor* of the Blue Lake vote.

> In Indian eyes it was the righting of one wrong that has marked most white relations with the red man. All Indians take heart that it now is possible to seek justice at either end of Pennsylvania Avenue and get it.[3]

At the press conference, the Taos Indians solemnly attend to the Cacique's words. From left, Frank Marcus, John Reyna, Teles Goodmorning (partially hidden), John Marcus, Teresino Jiron, Ben Marcus, Cruz Trujillo, Daisy Romero (seated), and Sam Martinez. 1970. Courtesy of John Rainer.

The *New York Times* made the return of Blue Lake front-page news, and papers around the country covered this moving story. *Time* magazine focused on the victory's wider implications.

> The bill's passage indicates that President Nixon is keeping his pledge, made last July, to open "a new era in which the Indian future is determined by Indians acts and Indian decisions." The measure would never have got to the Senate floor without presidential pressure . . . . [4]

Since passage of the Blue Lake bill symbolized the administration's new approach to Indian affairs, and was the first of Nixon's Indian legislative proposals to become law, the White House wanted the event to be widely known. It therefore invited several prominent Indian leaders, as well as key members of Congress and the White House staff, to the signing ceremony. The guests of honor, of course, were the Taos Pueblo elders, accompanied by Bill Schaab, Corinne Locker, and Jerry Straus.

Something of a dust-up developed when the professional staffers at the White House objected to inviting Ted Kennedy and Fred Harris. Bobbie Greene told Ehrlichman that since the two liberal Democrats had been key supporters of the bill, to exclude them would be unconscionable. Nixon agreed, saying to Ehrlichman that, "I'm happy to have them at my house." [5] The Blue Lake fight's bipartisan cooperation carried over into the signing ceremony as well.

The ceremony was held at the White House in the State Dining Room ten days before Christmas. Prior to the signing, Ehrlichman briefed the president on protocol. Nixon had another appearance scheduled soon after the signing, and he told Ehrlichman that he hoped the Blue Lake matter would not take long and that he would only be speaking briefly.

As the President entered the State Dining Room, however, the magic of the Cacique's presence exerted itself and he and Nixon greeted each other warmly.

*Nixon addresses the joyful throng gathered in the State Dining Room at the White House for the sign-
ing of the Blue Lake Bill. 1970. Courtesy of National Archives and Records Administration.*

"This sure is an interesting day," the President began, "to be signing a bill where
the chief sponsors were Fred Harris and Ted Kennedy."[6] Nixon continued,

> I want to welcome all of you here on this very special occasion during the
> Christmas season . . . .We are here for a bill signing ceremony that has very
> special significance. The Taos-Blue Lake Bill . . .is a bill which could be inter-
> preted particularly in the Christmas season, as one where a gift was being
> made by the United States to the Indian population of the United States.
> That is not the case.[7]

Nixon went on to emphasize that the return of Blue Lake represented not a gift,
but long overdue "justice."

"This bill also involves respect for religion," Nixon explained, adding:

> Long before any organized religion came to the United States, for 700 years,
> the Taos Pueblo Indians worshipped in this place. We restore this place of
> worship to them for all the years to come.[8]

"And finally," the President said,

> this bill indicates a new direction in Indian affairs in this country, a new
> direction in which we will have the cooperation of both Democrats and
> Republicans, one in which there will be more of an attitude of cooperation
> rather than paternalism, one of self-determination rather than termina-
> tion, one of mutual respect.[9]

He hoped, he said, that the return of Blue Lake would mark a time in America when, after "a very sad history of injustice," we "started on a new road" of just treatment for the first Americans. In conclusion, he said of the signing of the Blue Lake bill into law, "I can't think of anything . . . that could make me more proud as president of the United States."[10]

Then the ancient Cacique, with all of the dignity of his ninety years and his spiritual position, rose to speak. He revealed to his White House audience that in his role as the Pueblo's religious leader, his devotions at Blue Lake and other tribal shrines included all of America and all Americans.

> The life that I live belongs to the American people . . . . I have exercised within my Indian power and my spiritual way to do exactly what I have been told by the forefathers beyond my times. My responsibilities include all America and its people, and what we have in this good country of ours . . . in my prayers and in my daily talks in my spiritual ways . . . In telling you the truth I go to Blue Lake with my little package of worship, with the thing that I have to give and offer to the spiritual way . . . . I know myself when I do this it will be included in all the walks, in all the lives of this country.[11]
>
> The Cacique agreed with the president that the signing of the Blue Lake bill marked not only a "new day" for Taos Pueblo but for all of America. It would be a new day marked by brotherhood and understanding, which would enable the nation's leaders to succeed in their responsibilities. "And this responsibility," he made clear,
>
> is [to] more than the material things . . . [It is] to protect the life and to protect what this America is, really beautiful, peace, honesty, truth, understanding, consideration.

The Cacique concluded with thanks to Nixon ("the greatest father that we have"), to "each and every one of the American public," and to "the nicest people who have been with us"—

> Congressman Haley, Barry Goldwater, Senator Griffin and Senator Harris, and other people, who have sacrificed with the Taos Pueblo . . . to find a place for the Indian people of this country. We wish you a Merry Christmas. We are going to enjoy from here on out a happy New Year every year. Thank you very much.[12]

On the desk in front of Nixon lay Public Law 91-550, the official act of Congress which formally conveyed trust title to the Tribe. "Now I will sign the Blue Lake bill," the president told those assembled, adding that, since it was Christmas, the White House would make a gift of pens symbolizing the signing to all those present. "But the one that I sign it with, I believe you would all agree, should appropriately go, rather than to one of the senators, to the spiritual leader of the Taos Indians, Mr. Romero."[13] Nixon then signed P.L. 91-550 with a flourish, and handed the instrument of final victory to the beaming Cacique.

Quieting the din of enthusiastic applause, Nixon asked for attention for some concluding remarks. He explained that he was going from the Blue Lake signing to another ceremony, and he wanted everyone to appreciate a special "perspective [on] the two ceremonies that I participate in today as president of the United States. Today," Nixon told his rapt audience,

> the United States passes one trillion dollars in terms of its national economy. . . .That one trillion shows one side of the strength of America. But today, in the eloquent comments of Mr. Romero, we saw another side, a side that money cannot measure—eloquence, a deep spiritual quality, and the strength that the Indian people, the first Americans, have given to America generally in their contribution to this nation. . . .On this occasion, as we look at that one trillion, we want to remember that the Indians in the United States of America have contributed something that no trillion dollars could ever possibly estimate.[14]

Appropriately, Nixon ended with a reference to the "strong, indomitable character" of his old football coach, Chief Newman, in expressing his gratitude to America's Indian peoples. Just as Chief Newman had influenced the Whittier football squad through his strong character, so had the first Americans "given great character to so many parts of our country."

By now the president was late for his next appearance, but he seemed unable to leave, held by the magical aura of this special signing. Dwight Chapin kept catching the president's eye and pointing to his watch, but Nixon, waving him off, continued to converse warmly with the Taos elders. Bobbie Greene recalls that,

> Richard Nixon, who usually had a burr under his saddle and did not like to sit still for anything, just sat there and listened and was very mesmerized and when he spoke he was really choked up.[15]

The signing ceremony remains vivid for LaDonna Harris as well.

> It was really a beautiful thing . . .and it was again the Taos people that did it. It was the dignity and the reverence that they held, and the joy of the occasion, that moved [Nixon], because it was unlike any other signing that anybody had ever been to. . .and the day was so beautiful. . . .There was a different satisfaction [felt] than [with] any piece of legislation that people had been involved in. . . .There was such a human element and the [Taos] people showed that they were so directly affected by the return [of Blue Lake] as to who they were and how they saw themselves continuing that it captured everyone. And I think that's what [affected] Nixon: he just got carried away with the moment because everyone was. . . .[16]

Fred Harris also recalls the signing ceremony with deep emotion.

> It was just a marvelous ceremony, just the most moving thing. It moved everybody to tears, I think, it did me. There's something about those Taos Pueblo people, they are such generous warm people, and you felt the spiritual strength of these people and I think that that's what sort of grabbed

ahold of Nixon in that ceremony as well. He could feel that very strong spiritual feeling and depth of the Cacique and these elders.[17]

By now Chapin was frantic, and the president reluctantly rose to leave. Bobbie Greene, who walked part of the way with him from the State Dining Room, recalls their conversation.

> "Boy," he said, "HEW can wait, that was a wonderful thing." It was very clear to me that he traded off, that he was late to HEW but that was alright . . . because that had meant a lot to him and he was glad that he had stayed . . . .[18]

The battle for Blue Lake was now finally and irrevocably won. While the victory had been achieved through many means, from the medicine of the Cacique to the funds donated in support of the Blue Lake cause, the greatest political contributions had been made by Richard Nixon and Fred R. Harris. It is of interest that both regard the Blue Lake victory as a special event in their political careers. Nixon has said, "I consider the signing of Public Law 91-550 one of the most significant achievements of my administration."[19] Harris is equally unequivocal.

> I've said since I left the Senate that . . . . getting Taos Pueblo back its Blue Lake lands [is] one of the things that I'm most proud of as a result of my service in the Senate.[20]

Perhaps the pride shared by Nixon and Harris stems in part from Blue Lake's wider political implications. The self-determination intitiative finally did become law on November 18, 1975, when Congress passed P.L. 93-638. This law arguably has done more to benefit Indian people than any other single piece of government legislation, Collier's Indian Reorganization Act not excepted.

The other major political consequence was just what Anderson feared when, shortly after the Senate vote, he had warned, "we can look forward to some of our public lands being jeopardized by similar claims."[21] During the twenty years after passage of P.L. 91-550, millions of acres were returned to Indian tribes by judicial or legislative action. These successful claims were based in part upon the precedent set by Blue Lake.

Whether or not the Blue Lake bill can be considered to have set a precedent for long overdue justice depends largely on one's perspective on Indian affairs. One thing, however, is certain. The story of the Blue Lake battle sets a precedent for aspiration in the conduct of human life. It shows, as Bobbie Greene has said, that "if you have a mission, and if you capture the imagination of the people . . .and you have a cause that really is just, sometimes good really does prevail."[22] It shows that the impossible can be made possible by even a small group when its members are spiritually inspired, politically determined and individually brave.

Obituary: The *New York Times*, July 31, 1978

TAOS TRIBE LEADER, IN WEST, AT AGE 103
JUAN DE JESUS ROMERO, A SPIRITUAL HEAD
OF NEW MEXICO INDIANS

TAOS PUEBLO, N.M., July 30 (AP)—Juan de Jesus Romero, the spiritual leader of Taos Pueblo, died here today and, in accordance with tribal custom, was buried the same day. He was 103 years old.

Mr. Romero had been hospitalized in early June and was discharged Wednesday from Presbyterian Hospital in Albuquerque.

He will be succeeded as cacique, or religious leader of the Taos Indians, by Juan Concha.

Mr. Romero was the prime backer of a move that resulted in December 1970 in the award to the community of its sacred Blue Lake and 48,000 acres as a wilderness area for religious observances.

The Federal Government had taken the land in 1906 and Mr. Romero began a campaign that year to regain title to the lake and surrounding area. He eventually took his tribe's case to Washington and spoke with President Nixon.

Responsible for Spiritual Life

The cacique of the Taos Pueblo is a hereditary position. Only the cacique, who is responsible for the tribe's spiritual life, knows the ritual and myth that has preserved the continuity of the Taos Indians since their beginning, which they believe was their emergence from Blue Lake.

Mr. Romero became the cacique when his grandfather died.

Before the Government's return of Blue Lake to the Pueblo, Mr. Romero predicted: "If our Blue Lake land is not returned to us, then it is the end of our Indian life. Our people will scatter as the people of other Indian nations have scattered. It is our religion that holds us together"

After the return of the lake, Mr. Romero said, "Now when I die, I will die at peace."

The Cacique and the President share a moment of joy after the signing ceremony. Courtesy of Bobbie Greene Kilberg.

Notes

Citations for all information other than that to be found in special collections conform to standard usage. Information from special collections is cited in the following manner. All citations from special collections begin with a capital letter. The capital letters used to cite these collections are: **A** = Anderson Papers; **D** = Duke Papers; **N** = Northern Pueblos Agency Files; **P** = Princeton University Papers; **S** = State of New Mexico archives; **T** = Taos tribal records in the office of the War Chief.

In the case of all citations except those from the New Mexico State archives and the Princeton papers, the format is a capital letter followed by the date of the document cited. For example, "A: 3/11/69" refers to a document dated March 11, 1969, to be found in the Anderson papers. All of the collections except the Princeton papers and the records from the New Mexico State archives are in roughly chronological order. To locate the document cited in one of these collections, the researcher need only go through the collection cited until the proper date is found.

Both the records in the New Mexico State archives and the Princeton papers are filed in folders that are to be found in specially labeled expandable files or boxes. The key to their usage is as follows.

Citations beginning with an "S" indicate that the document is to be found in the Paul J. Bernal Papers at the New Mexico State archives. The citation then directs the researcher first to the expandable file and then to the specific folder in which the document is located. The final information provided is the exact date of the document, and the page number from which the citation derives. If there is no page number, either the document cited comprises only one page, or else the citation itself comes from page one of the document. For example, "S-3-28, 9/24/48, p. 3" means that the citation comes from the New Mexico State archives, Expandable 3, Folder 28, September 24, 1948, page three. Information within each of the folders in the State archives is not arranged in exact chronological order.

In the case of the Princeton papers, if the citation derives from the Blue Lake collection, it is cited in the same manner as documents in the State archives, except that the beginning capital letter will be a "P." For example, "P-3-26, 11/18/47, p. 3," means that the citation comes from the Princeton Blue Lake papers, Expandable 3, Folder 26, November 18, 1947, page three. The papers of the American Association on Indian Affairs are arranged either according to the subject covered or are identified by the name of the person whose papers are included in the collection. All of the citations from AAIA come from the papers of Corinne Locker or Oliver La Farge. If the citation derives from the Locker papers, it will be prefaced with the capital letters "PCL." If the citation derives from the La Farge papers, it will be prefaced with the capital letters "PLF." For example, "PCL-Ex1-F1, 1/11/55, p. 2" means that the citation derives from the Corinne Locker papers in the AAIA collection at Princeton, Expandable 1, Folder 1, January 11, 1955, page two. In the case of the La Farge papers, "PLF-Ex4-Box: Taos 1947—, 9/14/55" means that the citation derives from the Oliver La Farge papers in the AAIA collection at Princeton, Expandable 4, to be found in the box labeled Taos 1947—, September 14, 1955.

Finally, information or quotations derived from conversations recorded in the Albuquerque home of Suzie Poole, among the principals in the Blue Lake fight, are cited as "Suzie Poole tapes." Interviews conducted by the author are cited according to the name of the individual interviewed, place of interview, and date. If the interview was by phone rather than in person, it is so cited.

Chapter One

1. Edward H. Spicer, *Cycles of Conquest: The Impact of Spain, Mexico and the United States on the Indians of the Southwest, 1533-1960.* (Tucson: University of Arizona Press, 1962) pp. 160-161.

2. *Taos Pueblo-Blue Lake, Hearings Before the Subcommittee on Indian Affairs of the Committee on Interior and Insular Affairs,* House of Representatives, Ninety-first Congress, First Session, on H.R. 471, May 15 and 16, 1969, p. 13.

3. Myra Ellen Jenkins, "Development Potential of Taos Pueblo Area in 1906," pp. 5-8. (Unpublished manuscript loaned to author.)

4. *Taos Indians-Blue Lake, Hearings Before the Subcommittee on Indian Affairs of the Committee on Interior and Insular Affairs,* United States Senate, Ninetieth Congress, Second Session, on H.R. 3306, S. 1624, and S. 1625, September 19 and 20, 1968, p. 103.

5. Ibid.

6. Ibid.

7. S-3-26a, 11/23/03.

8. S-3-26a, 10/21/04, p. 2.

9. Theodore F. Rixon, "Report on an Examination of the Taos Forest Reserve, Territory of New Mexico," *United States Geological Survey,* 1905, pp. 27-28.

10. S-3-26a, 10/30/06.

11. Elsie Clews Parsons, *Taos Pueblo,* (New York and London: Johnson Reprint Corporation, 1936) p. 14.

12. *Taos Indians-Blue Lake Amendments, Hearings Before the Subcommittee on Indian Affairs of the Committee on Interior and Insular Affairs,* United States Senate, Ninety-first Congress, Second Session, on S. 750 and H.R. 471, 9 and 10 July 1970, p. 299.

13. Op. cit., *Senate Subcommittee Hearings,* September 19 and 20, 1968, pp. 103-104.

14. Ibid., p. 103.

15. Ibid.

16. S-3-26a, 12/14/10, pp. 2-3.

17. Ibid., p. 7.

18. Ibid., p. 13.

19. S-3-26a, 10/19/12, p. 4.

20. S-3-26a, 3/10/14, p. 2.

21. S-3-26a, 9/23/16.

22. S-3-26a, 10/6/16.

23. Joe S. Sando, *The Pueblo Indians,* (San Francisco: The Indian Historian Press, 1976) p. 75.

24. S-3-26a, undated, c. 10/15/26, p. 3.

25. S-3-26a, 5/26/27, p. 2.

26. S-3-26a, 6/29/27.

27. S-3-26a, 8/19/31.

28. S-3-26a, 5/28/27, p. 2.

29. S-3-26a, 9/28/27.

30. S-3-26a, 12/15/27.

31. S-3-26a, 1/12/29.

Chapter Two

1. John Collier, *From Every Zenith: A Memoir and Some Essays on Life and Thought,* (Denver: Sage Books, 1963), p. 128.

2. Ibid.

3. Ibid., p. 193

4. S-3-26a, 5/9/33, p. 17.

5. S-3-26a, 6/30/33.

6. S-3-26a, 4/27/35, p. 2.

7. S-3-26a, 8/1/39, p. 2.

8. Ibid.

9. S-3-26a, 10/31/39.

10. Ibid., p. 3.

11. S-3-26a, 12/9/39, p. 2.

12. S-3-26a, 12/27/39.

13. S-3-26a, 10/27/39.

14. Ibid.

15. S-3-26a, 8/6/40.

16. S-2-17, 10/24/40, p. 2.

17. S-3-26a, 10/27/39.

18. Ronald P. Archibeck, University of New Mexico M.A. thesis, "Taos Indians and the Blue Lake Controversy," 1972, p. 111.

19. S-3-28, 9/24/48.

20. S-3-28, 9/24/48, p. 3.

21. Ibid.

22. *Taos Indians-Blue Lake, Hearings Before the Subcommittee on Indian Affairs of the Committee on Interior and Insular Affairs,* United States Senate, Ninetieth Congress, Second Session, on H.R 3306, S. 1624, and S. 1625, September 19 and 20, 1968, p. 155.

23. S-3-28, 6/22/50.

24. S-3-28, 9/24/48, p. 2.

25. S-3-28, 11/10/48, p. 14.

26. Ibid., pp. 14-15.
27. Ibid., p. 21.
28. S-3-28, 9/22/52, p. 4.
29. S-3-28, 9/22/55.
30. S-3-28, 12/16/48.
31. Frank Waters, *New Mexico Magazine*, Winter, 1972, pp. 18-19.
32. Ibid., pp. 19-20.

33. Ibid., p. 17.
34. D'arcy McNickle, *Indian Man: A Life of Oliver La Farge*, (Bloomington: Indiana University Press, 1971.) p. 91.
35. Quoted in, Ibid., p. 192.
36. PLF-Ex2-No file number, 1948, p. 5.
37. S-3-28, 12/16/48.

Chapter Three

1. S-3-28, 9/12/53, p. 2.
2. S-3-28, 9/12/53.
3. S-1-1, 10/13/53.
4. Larry W. Burt, *Tribalism in Crisis: Federal Indian Policy 1953-1961* (Albuquerque: University of New Mexico Press, 1982) p. 5.
5. PCL-Ex1-F1, 1/11/55, p. 2.
6. Ibid., pp. 1-2
7. Ibid., p. 1
8. PCL-Ex1-F1, 1/11/55, p. 2.
9. PCL-Ex1-F1, 1/21/55.
10. S-3-28, 1/25/55, p. 2.
11. Ibid.
12. S-3-28, 5/6/55.
13. S-3-28, 6/7/55, p. 2.
14. Ibid., p. 3
15. S-3-28, 5/6/55.
16. S-3-28, 4/13/55.
17. Ibid., p. 2
18. Ibid., pp. 2-3
19. Ibid., p. 4
20. PCL-Ex1-F1, 5/20/55.
21. S-3-28, 7/12/55.
22. PLF-Ex4-Box: Taos 1947—, 9/14/55.
23. PLF-Ex4-Box: Taos 1947—, 10/7/55.
24. PLF-Ex2-No file number, 12/9/55.
25. Ibid.
26. Ibid.
27. Ibid., pp. 2-3
28. PLF-Ex4-Box: Taos 1947—, 1/9/56.
29. PLF-Ex4-Box: Taos 1947—, 1/8/56.
30. S-3-28, 1/24/56.

31. Ibid., p. 7
32. PLF-Ex4-Box: Taos 1947—, 2/24/56.
33. Ibid.
34. PLF-Ex4-Box: Taos 1947—, 3/6/56.
35. PCL-Ex1-F1, 7/21/59.
36. S-3-28, 3/24/58.
37. Ibid., p. 2
38. S-3-26, 4/4/60.
39. S-1-1, 3/7/61.
40. S-3-26, 6/8/61.
41. S-3-26, 7/11/61.
42. S-3-26, 7/31/61.
43. S-3-26, 12/1/61.
44. PCL-Ex1-F1, 12/8/61.
45. S-3-26, 1/31/62, p. 2.
46. Ibid., p. 3
47. S-3-26, 2/7/62.
48. PCL-Ex1-F1, 6/18/62.
49. S-3-26, 8/22/61, p. 2.
50. Ibid., p. 3
51. S-12-113, 3/18/62.
52. S-1-1, 4/3/62, p. 2.
53. S-3-26, 8/10/61.
54. PCL-Ex1-F1, 10/31/61, p. 3.
55. PCL-Ex1-F1, 6/24/63, p. 5.
56. S-3-27, 4/11/61.
57. S-3-26, 9/15/61.
58. PCL-Ex1-F1, 12/22/61.
59. PCL-Ex1-F1, 11/7/61.
60. S-1-3, May-1961.
61. S-3-26, 7/16/63.
62. Ibid., p. 2

Chapter Four

1. Author interview with Tony F. Martinez at his office, Eight Northern Indian Pueblos Council, San Juan Pueblo, 1/8/90.
2. S-1-5, 10/24/63, p. 3.
3. S-1-5, August-1963, p. 3.
4. Ibid., p. 4.
5. Ibid.
6. S-1-5, 12/20/63, pp. 1-2.
7. S-1-5, 1/2/64.
8. S-1-5, 12/20/63, p. 2.
9. Suzie Poole tapes.
10. S-1-5, 10/31/63, p. 2.
11. S-1-5, 12/2/63, p. 2.
12. S-1-5, 12/20/63.
13. S-1-5, 10/24/63, p. 2.

14. Ibid., p. 3.
15. S-1-5, 2/14/63.
16. S-1-5, 2/4/64.
17. S-1-5, 1/5/64.
18. S-1-5, 2/14/64.
19. Ibid., p. 2.
20. Ibid., p. 3.
21. S-1-5, 2/24/64.
22. S-1-5, 4/10/64.
23. S-1-5, 12/2/63.
24. S-1-5, 12/20/63, p. 2.
25. S-1-5, 1/3/64.
26. S-1-5, 1/27/64.
27. S-1-5, 7/24/64.
28. S-1-8, 4/22/65.

29. S-1-5, 8/17/64.
30. S-1-5, 2/3/64.
31. S-4-31, 1/24/65.
32. Suzie Poole tapes.
33. S-1-5, 9/25/64, p. 2.
34. S-1-5, 9/17/64.
35. S-1-8, 2/6/65.
36. Op. cit., interview with Tony F. Martinez.
37. S-1-5, 12/10/63.
38. S-3-26, 1/15/65.
39. S-3-26, 3/2/65, p. 2.
40. PCL-Ex1-F1, 10/13/64.
41. S-1-5, 12/22/64.
42. S-1-8, 11/9/65.
43. S-3-26, 6/13/61.
44. S-3-26, 6/20/61.
45. Author interview with Florence Hawley Ellis at her home in Albuquerque, NM, 11/3/89.

46. Ibid.
47. Ibid.
48. Pueblo of Taos, "Petitioner's Findings of Fact and Brief," Before the Indian Claims Commission, Docket #357, p. 80.
49. Ibid., p. 12.
50. Ibid., p. 77.
51. 15 Indian Claims Commission 666, Docket # 357, "Opinion of the Commission: Pueblo of Taos, Petitioner v. The United States of America, Defendant," September 8, 1965, p. 692.
52. Ibid., p. 694.
53. Ibid., p. 695.
54. Ibid., p. 697.
55. Ibid.
56. Ibid., pp. 700-701.
57. Ibid., p. 701.

Chapter Five

1. S-7-66, 1/13/66.
2. S-1-10, 2/7/66, p. 2.
3. S-1-10, 1/17/66.
4. S-1-2, 3/15/66, p. 3.
5. S-3-26, 2/1/66.
6. Ibid., p. 2.
7. S-12-113, 1/4/66.
8. S-1-2, 4/5/66.
9. S-1-10, 2/7/66.
10. S-1-2, 4/5/66.
11. A: 4/12/66.
12. S-1-2, 5/11/66.
13. S-5-40, 5/9/66.
14. S-1-2, 5/11/66.
15. S-5-40, 5/11/66.
16. S-1-2, 4/16/66.
17. S-1-2, 4/19/66.
18. Ibid.
19. S-12-112, 3/29/66.
20. S-4-35, 4/24/66.
21. S-1-2, 4/25/66.
22. Ibid.
23. Ibid.
24. Ibid.
25. S-1-10, 4/25/66.
26. S-11-96, 5/27/66.
27. S-1-3, May-August 1966, p. 2.
28. S-1-10, 5/9/66.
29. S-1-2, 5/11/66.
30. Ibid.

31. *Taos Indians—Blue Lake Bill, Hearings Before the Subcommittee on Indian Affairs of the Committee on Interior and Insular Affairs* on S. 3085, United States Senate, May 18 and 19, 1966, p. 9.
32. Ibid., p. 10.
33. Ibid., p. 16.
34. Author interview with Richard Romero, at his home, Taos Pueblo, New Mexico, 10/18/89.
35. Ibid.
36. Op. cit., *1966 Subcommittee Hearings*, p. 89.
37. Ibid., pp. 89-90.
38. Ibid., p. 90.
39. Ibid., p. 91.
40. Ibid., p. 96.
41. Ibid., p. 94.
42. S-2-17, May 1966.
43. Ibid., p. 11.
44. S-7-67, 5/27/66.
45. Op. cit., *1966 Subcommittee Hearings*, pp. 49-50.
46. Ibid., p. 48.
47. Ibid., p. 42.
48. Ibid.
49. Ibid., p. 50.
50. Ibid., p. 67.
51. Ibid., p. 68.
52. A: 4/4/66.
53. Ibid.
54. A: 4/6/66.
55. S-3-26, 6/17/66, pp. 1-2.

Chapter Six

1. Author interview with John Rainer at his home, Taos Pueblo, New Mexico, 10/13/89.
2. S-1-10, 6/23/66.
3. S-5-40, 6/8/66, p. 2.
4. S-1-2, 6/13/66.
5. S-1-10, 7/18/66.
6. S-5-39, 10/21/66, p. 2.
7. S-2-17, 8/22/66.
8. S-1-10, 10/22/66.
9. S-1-10, 10/23/66.
10. S-2-12, 11/18/66, pp. 23-24.
11. Ibid., p. 30.
12. Ibid., p. 33.
13. Ibid.
14. Ibid., p. 34.
15. S-1-10, 8/26/66.
16. Ibid.
17. S-2-11, 2/20/67, p. 13.
18. Ibid., p. 14.
19. S-2-18, 2/9/67.
20. S-2-18, 2/10/67.
21. S-2-24, 4/30/67.
22. S-2-18, 5/3/67, pp. 1-2.
23. S-2-21, 5/9/67, p. 8.
24. S-2-24, 7/11/67, p. 3.
25. Author interview with Rev. Dean Kelley at his office, National Council of Churches Headquarters, New York City, 11/29/89.
26. Ibid.
27. Ibid.
28. Ibid.
29. Reprinted in *Taos Indians—Blue Lake, Hearings before the Subcommittee on Indian Affairs of the Committee on Interior and Insular Affairs,*
United States Senate, on H.R. 3306, S. 1624, S. 1625, September 19 and 20, 1968, pp. 210-211.
30. S-2-17, 1/6/67.
31. S-2-17, 1/16/67.
32. S-12-110, 1/23/67.
33. S-3-26, 5/16/67, p. 2.
34. S-12-113, 5/11/67.
35. S-2-24, 5/25/67, p. A-2.
36. S-1-8, 12/2/65, p. 2.
37. S-2-24, 7/28/67.
38. S-4-32, 7/28/67.
39. S-5-38, 8/24/67.
40. Ibid., p. 4.
41. Ibid., p. 1.
42. Author interview with Richard Romero at his home, Taos Pueblo, New Mexico, 10/18/89.
43. S-12-111, June 1967, p. 3.
44. Ibid., p. 3.
45. S-5-40, 7/5/67.
46. Author interview with Bruce H. Rolstad at his office, New Mexico Community Council, Santa Fe, New Mexico, 11/17/89.
47. Ibid.
48. S-5-40, 10/30/67.
49. S-4-32, 7/28/67.
50. Op. cit., Rolstad interview.
51. S-2-24, 9/22/67.
52. A: 9/19/67.
53. S-2-24, 7/15/67.
54. S-4-32, 12/16/67.
55. Suzie Poole tapes.
56. Ibid.
57. S-2-24, 10/3/67.
58. Ibid.

Chapter Seven

1. S-4-32, 2/13/68.
2. S-5-51, 1/31/68.
3. S-6-62, 2/14/68, p. 9.
4. S-6-54, 4/16/68, p. 3.
5. S-5-46, 4/1/68.
6. S-5-46, 3/28/68.
7. S-5-46, 4/1/68.
8. S-4-32, 5/1/68.
9. S-10-88, 5/9/68, pp. 1-2
10. Ibid., p. 29.
11. Ibid., p. 59.
12. Ibid., p. 86.
13. Ibid., p. 87.
14. Ibid., p. 88.
15. Ibid.
16. Ibid., p. 89.
17. Ibid., p. 90.
18. Ibid., p. 119.
19. S-4-32, 5/23/68.
20. S-9-87, 6/18/68, II 5056.
21. Ibid.
22. Ibid.
23. Ibid., II 5057.
24. Ibid.
25. Ibid.
26. Ibid., pp. II 5057-5058.
27. S-7-69, 6/18/68.
28. S-12-112, 6/22/68, p. 2.
29. Ibid., p. 3.
30. S-4-35, 6/24/68.
31. S-12-112, 6/27/68.
32. S-2-24, 7/16/68.
33. Author interview with Tony Reyna at his home, Taos Pueblo, New Mexico, 10/16/89.
34. Charles Reich, *The Greening of America,* (New York: The Penguin Press, 1971) p. 1.
35. S-2-24, 7/17/68.
36. S-5-40, 7/17/68.

37. S-2-24, 7/30/68.
38. S-9-87, 7/30/68.
40. S-6-60, 8/29/68.
41. S-13-118, August 1968, pp. 1-2.
42. Ibid., p. 4.
43. S-5-43, 9/10/68.
44. S-3-26, 5/26/61.
45. S-3-26, 6/2/61.
46. *Taos Indians—Blue Lake, Hearings Before the Subcommittee on Indian Affairs of the Committee on Interior and Insular Affairs*, United States Senate, Ninetieth Congress, Second Session, on H.R. 3306, S. 1624, and S. 1625, September 19 and 20, 1968, p. 60.
47. Ibid., p. 61.
48. Ibid., p. 62.
49. Ibid., p. 63.
50. Ibid., p. 71.
51. Ibid.
52. Ibid., p. 88.
53. Ibid., p. 87.

54. Ibid., p. 101.
55. Ibid., pp. 101-102.
56. Ibid., p. 121.
57. Ibid., p. 122.
58. Ibid., p. 161.
59. Ibid., p. 162.
60. Ibid., p. 186.
61. Ibid., p. 202.
62. Ibid., p. 128.
63. Ibid., p. 141.
64. Ibid., p. 143.
65. Ibid.
66. Ibid., p. 144.
67. Ibid., p. 153.
68. Ibid., p. 213.
69. S-7-69, 9/24/68.
70. Op. cit., *1968 Senate Hearings*, p. 192.
71. Ibid., p. 165.
72. Ibid., p. 211.
73. Ibid., p. 199.

Chapter Eight

1. Suzie Poole tapes.
2. Richard Nixon, *The Memoirs of Richard Nixon* (New York: Grosset & Dunlap, 1978), pp. 19-20.
3. S-12-111, 9/27/68.
4. Ibid.
5. Ibid., p. 2.
6. Author interview with David Cargo at his office, Albuquerque, New Mexico, 10/27/89.
7. Author interview with Fred R. Harris at his office, University of New Mexico at Albuquerque, 10/27/89.
8. Author's telephone interview with William Carmack, 3/15/90.
9. Ibid.
10. S-13-120, 11/14/68.
11. S-7-71, 2/14/69.
12. S-13-120, 2/16/69.
13. S-7-71, 2/22/69.
14. S-13-117, 3/8/69.
15. S-13-117, 12/23/68.
16. S-4-32, 12/26/68.
17. Op. cit., David Cargo interview.
18. *Taos Pueblo-Blue Lake, Hearings before the Subcommittee on Indian Affairs of the Committee on Interior and Insular Affairs*, House of Representatives, Ninety-first Congress, First Session, on H.R. 471, May 15 and 16, 1969, p. 23.
19. Ibid., p. 24.
20. Ibid., p. 25.
21. Ibid.
22. Ibid., p. 26.
23. Ibid., p. 28.
24. Ibid., p. 29.
25. Ibid.
26. Ibid., p. 35.
27. Ibid., p. 36.

28. Ibid., p. 71.
29. Ibid., p. 65.
30. Ibid., pp. 67-68.
31. Ibid., p. 66.
32. Ibid.
33. Ibid., p. 67.
34. Ibid.
35. Ibid.
36. Ibid., p. 39.
37. Ibid.
38. Ibid., p. 63.
39. Ibid., p. 86.
40. Ibid., p. 87.
41. Ibid., p. 80.
42. S-11-94, 5/20/69.
43. *Congressional Record*, House Debate on H.R. 471, Ninety-first Congress, September 9, 1969, p. H7698.
44. Ibid.
45. Ibid.
46. Ibid., p. H7702.
47. Ibid.
48. Ibid., p. H7705
49. S-12-113, 10/9/69.
50. S-7-71, 10/10/69.
51. Op. cit., David Cargo interview.
52. S-7-72, 10/27/69.
53. Ibid., p. 3.
54. S-5-40, 11/25/69.
55. S-5-49, January 1970, pp. 1-3.
56. S-5-40, 1/23/70.
57. S-6-54, 1/7/70.
58. S-6-54, 1/8/70, p. 2.
59. S-6-56, 1/26/70.
60. S-7-72, 1/29/70.
61. Ibid., p. 2.
62. Ibid., p. 1.

Chapter Nine

1. Author interview with Bobbie Greene Kilberg at her office, Old Executive Office Building, Washington, D.C., 11/28/89.

2. Suzie Poole tapes.

3. Ibid.

4. Author interview with Fred R. Harris at his office, University of New Mexico at Albuquerque, 10/27/89.

5. Ibid.

6. S-6-54, 1/30/70.

7. S-7-72, 2/20/70.

8. S-5-39, 3/10/70.

9. Ibid.

10. S-7-72, 3/18/70.

11. Ibid.

12. Author's telephone interview with C.D. Ward, 3/12/90.

13. Author interview with John Rainer at his home, Taos Pueblo, New Mexico, 10/13/89.

14. S-5-39, 2/6/70.

15. S-7-72, 3/25/70.

16. S-7-67, 2/27/70.

17. Ibid., p. 3.

18. S-7-72, 3/31/70, p. 4.

19. S-7-72, 4/8/70, p. 2.

20. S-7-72, 4/15/70, p. 2.

21. S-7-72, 3/12/70, p. 2.

22. S-7-72, 4/16/70.

23. Op. cit., Kilberg interview.

24. Suzie Poole tapes.

25. Ibid.

26. Ibid.

27. Ibid.

28. Author interview with John Ehrlichman at his home, Santa Fe, New Mexico, 3/7/90.

29. S-5-49, 4/18/70.

30. S-7-72, 4/17/70, p. 2.

31. Ibid., p. 1.

32. Ibid., p. 2.

33. Ibid., p. 3.

34. Ibid.

35. S-7-72, 4/17/70.

36. S-7-72, 4/17/70, p. 3.

37. Ibid.

38. S-7-72, 4/22/70.

39. Suzie Poole tapes.

40. Author interview with LaDonna Harris at her office, Americans for Indian Opportunity, Washington, D.C., 11/28/89.

41. Op. cit., Fred Harris interview.

42. S-8-75, 4/20/70.

43. S-5-49, 4/28/70.

44. S-7-72, 5/26/70.

45. S-12-100, 6/3/70.

46. S-8-76, 5/21/70.

47. Author interview with Henrietta Lujan at her home, Taos Pueblo, New Mexico, 10/18/89.

48. Author interview with David Gomez at his office, Taos Pueblo, New Mexico, 10/17/89.

49. Author interview with William Martinez at his shop, Taos Pueblo, New Mexico, 10/30/89.

50. Author interview with Tony Martinez at his office, Eight Northern Indian Pueblos Council, San Juan Pueblo, New Mexico, 1/8/90.

51. S-12-112, 6/11/70.

52. Redacted from S-4-33, 6/70/78 and S-8-76, 6/14/70.

53. S-4-33, 6/7/70.

54. S-8-76, 6/14/70.

55. S-7-72, 6/13/70.

56. Ibid.

57. Ibid.

58. S-4-33, 6/22/70.

59. Op. cit., Kilberg interview.

60. Ibid.

61. S-5-49, 7/8/70, p. 5.

62. Ibid.

63. S-4-33, 7/2/70.

64. Op. cit., Kilberg interview.

65. Author interview with Myra Ellen Jenkins at her home, Santa Fe, New Mexico, 10/27/89.

66. Ibid.

67. *Taos Indians—Blue Lake Amendments, Hearings before the Subcommittee on Indian Affairs of the Committee on Interior and Insular Affairs*, United States Senate, Ninety-first Congress, Second Session, on S. 750 and H.R. 471, July 9 and 10, 1970, p. 15.

68. Ibid., p. 16.

69. Ibid., p. 17.

70. Op. cit., LaDonna Harris interview.

71. Op. cit., Kilberg interview.

72. Op. cit., *1970 Subcommittee Hearings*, p. 107.

73. Ibid.

74. Ibid., p. 33.

75. Op. cit., Jenkins interview.

76. Op. cit., *1970 Subcommittee Hearings*, p. 86.

77. Ibid., p. 131.

78. Ibid., p. 129.

79. Ibid.

80. Ibid., p. 257.

81. Author interview with John Bodine at his office, American University, Washington, D.C., 11/27/89.

82. Ibid.

83. Ibid.

84. Op. cit., *1970 Subcommittee Hearings*, p. 298.

85. S-12-112, 7/16/70.

86. S-11-95, 7/16/70.

87. Ibid.

88. Ibid.

89. Op. cit., William Martinez interview.

Chapter Ten

1. Author interview with LaDonna Harris at her office, Americans for Indian Opportunity, Washington, D.C., 11/28/89.
2. Ibid.
3. Ibid.
4. S-11-99, 8/21/70, p. 3.
5. Author interview with Fred R. Harris at his office, University of New Mexico at Albuquerque, 10/27/89.
6. Ibid.
7. S-8-80, 8/21/70.
8. S-11-99, 8/21/70.
9. Author interview with Myra Ellen Jenkins at her home, Santa Fe, New Mexico, 10/27/89.
10. S-8-80, 8/27/70.
11. S-11-99, 8/21/70.
12. S-4-37, 9/28/70.
13. S-8-75, 9/10/70.
14. S-11-96, 9/28/70.
15. S-8-75, 10/2/70.
16. S-12-112, 11/5/70.
17. S-5-49, 10/5/70.
18. S-5-52, 11/16/70.
19. S-8-75, 11/17/70.
20. A: 11/22/70.
21. A: 11/22/70.
22. Author interview with Rev. Dean Kelley at his office, National Council of Churches Headquarters, New York City, 11/29/89.
23. Op. cit., Fred Harris interview.
24. S-8-75, 11/25/70.
25. S-10-80, 11/30/70.
26. S-14-124, 11/27/70.
27. *Congressional Record—Senate*, December 1, 1970, p. S 19157.
28. Ibid., p. S 19159.
29. Ibid.
30. Ibid., p. S 19166.
31. S-8-75, 1/2/70.
32. S-8-75, 1/2/70.
33. Author interview with Bobbie Greene Kilberg at her office, Old Executive Office Building, Washington, D.C., 11/28/89.
34. S-8-77, 11/18/70.
35. *Congressional Record—Senate*, December 2, 1970, p. S 19225
36. Ibid., p. S 19226.
37. Ibid., p. S 19230.
38. Ibid., p. S 19231.
39. Ibid., p. S 19232.
40. Ibid., p. S 19231.
41. Ibid., p. S 19232.
42. Ibid., p. S 19233.
43. S-14-124, 12/3/70.
44. S-7-67, 8/20/68.
45. *Congressional Record—Senate*, December 2, 1970, p. S 19238.
46. Ibid., p. S 19239.
47. Ibid., p. S 19240.
48. Ibid., p. S 19241.
49. Ibid., pp. S 19242-19243.
50. Ibid., p. S 19244.
51. S-8-75, 12/8/70.
52. Op. cit., Bobbie Greene Kilberg interview.

Epilogue

1. S-14-124, 12/5/70.
2. S-6-62, 12/8/70.
3. S-12-112, 12/6/70.
4. S-8-75, 12/14/70.
5. Author interview with Bobbie Greene Kilberg at her office, Old Executive Office Building, Washington, D.C., 11/28/89.
6. Ibid.
7. S-5-49, 12/15/70.
8. Ibid.
9. Ibid.
10. Ibid., p. 2.
11. Ibid.
12. Ibid., p. 3.
13. Ibid.
14. Ibid., p. 4.
15. Op. cit., Bobbie Green Kilberg interview.
16. Author interview with LaDonna Harris at her office, Americans for Indian Opportunity, Washington, D.C., 11/28/89.
17. Author interview with Fred R. Harris at his office, University of New Mexico at Albuquerque, 10/27/89.
18. Suzie Poole tapes.
19. S-7-72, 8/14/70.
20. Op. cit., Fred Harris interview.
21. S-14-124, 12/4/70.
22. Op. cit., Bobbie Greene Kilberg interview.

Resources and Bibliography

The most important of the primary resources for research on Blue Lake is the Western Americana Collection at Princeton University's Firestone Library. In this collection are the originals of most of the papers on Blue Lake and of the papers of the American Association on Indian Affairs. The New Mexico State Records Center and Archives in Santa Fe has a duplicate set of Princeton's Blue Lake Papers, but not the papers from AAIA. Two additional collections of relevant papers are to be found at the University of New Mexico Library in Albuquerque. These are the papers of Clinton P. Anderson, and the Duke Papers, a series of interviews conducted with principals involved in the Blue Lake struggle. Further information on Blue Lake can be found at the Northern Pueblos Agency of the Bureau of Indian Affairs in Santa Fe. Finally, the papers on Blue Lake at the War Chief's Office of Taos Pueblo contributed significantly to telling the Tribe's side of the story.

Secondary sources consulted by the author include Edward H. Spicer's *Cycles of Conquest: The Impact of Spain, Mexico and the United States on the Indians of the Southwest 1533-1960* (Tucson: University of Arizona Press, 1962), an excellent foundation for study of the Indians of the Southwest and the impact upon them of European expansion. It was especially helpful in its explication of religious themes.

For the history of Taos at the turn of the nineteenth century, an unpublished research paper by Dr. Myra Ellen Jenkins of Santa Fe, New Mexico, "Development Potential of the Taos Pueblo Area in 1906," was informative. Also helpful was the "Theodore F. Rixon Report, 1905" from the archives of the Bureau of Biological Survey.

Three secondary sources were useful for an understanding of New Mexico Pueblo culture, especially that of Taos. These were Joe S. Sando's *The Pueblo Indians* (San Francisco: The Indian Historian Press, 1976), Elsie Clews Parsons's *Taos Pueblo* (New York and London: Johnson Reprint Corporation, 1936), and John J. Bodine's doctoral dissertation at Tulane University, "Attitudes and Institutions of Taos, New Mexico: Variables for Value System Expression," published on demand by University Microfilms, Ann Arbor, Michigan, 1967. The information on Gifford Pinchot was derived primarily from Volume 2 of Roderick Nash's *From These Beginnings: A Biographical Approach to American History* (New York: Harper & Row, 1978).

For information on John Collier, his *From Every Zenith: A Memoir and Some Essays on Life and Thought* (Denver: Sage Books, 1963) was indispensable. D'arcy McNickle's *Indian Man: A Life of Oliver La Farge* (Bloomington: Indiana University Press, 1971) provided information on this crucial figure. I am most indebted to an article by author Frank Waters detailing his contribution to the Blue Lake cause, published in the Winter 1972 issue of *New Mexico Magazine*. A very helpful resource on the Blue Lake struggle, especially in the forties and fifties, was the master's thesis of Ronald P. Archibeck, "Taos Indians and the Blue Lake Controversy." It can be found in the library at the University of New Mexico in Albuquerque.

For background on the termination era, Larry W. Burt's *Tribalism in Crisis: Federal Indian Policy 1953- 1961* (Albuquerque: University of New Mexico Press, 1982) was most helpful. The Indian perspective on this era derived from Vine Deloria's *Custer Died for Your Sins: An Indian Manifesto* (New York: Avon Books, 1970). Information on the sixties came from Charles Reich's *The Greening of America* (New York: The Penguin Press, 1971) and from Jay Stevens's *Storming Heaven: LSD and the American Dream* (New York: Harper & Row, 1988). Nixon's *The Memoirs of Richard Nixon* (New York: Grosset & Dunlap, 1978) provided background on his personal life and presidential administration.

For information on the developments within Congress relative to Blue Lake, the author consulted the May 18 and 19, 1966 hearings in the Senate Subcommittee on Indian Affairs; the hearings held by the House Subcommittee on Indian Affairs on May 9 and 10, 1968; the House debate of June 18, 1968 published in the *Congressional Record*; the hearings held on September 19 and 20, 1968 by the Senate Subcommittee on Indian Affairs; the House hearings of May 15 and 16, 1969 in the Subcommittee on Indian Affairs; the House debate of September 9, 1969 published in the *Congressional Record*; the hearings of the Senate Subcommittee on Indian Affairs of July 9 and 10, 1970; and the Senate debate of December 1 and 2, 1970, also published in the *Congressional Record*. All of these documents can be found in the Library of Congress, Washington, D.C., and many of them also are included in the Blue Lake Collection at Princeton University and the New Mexico State Records Center.

In addition to the printed primary and secondary sources, the development of this book depended heavily on the author's personal interviews with key persons involved in the struggle. The tapes of these interviews have been deposited with the Western Americana Collection at Princeton University and duplicate copies are available at the School of American Research, Santa Fe, New Mexico. Informative also were tape recordings of the reflections of principals involved in the battle for Blue Lake recorded by Suzie Poole at her Albuquerque home and now deposited with the Western Americana Collection at Princeton University.

Index

A

AAIA. *See* Association on American Indian Affairs

Abbott, F.H., 15

Aberle, Sophie, 31

ABM treaty, 177-81, 185, 186, 205

Accent show, 60-61, 65

Acequia Madre del Prado ditch association, 69, 88

Acequia Madre del Rio Lucero ditch association, 69, 88

ACLU. *See* American Civil Liberties Union

Agnew, Kim, 196, 210; photo of, 199

Agnew, Spiro, 150-52, 173, 174, 176, 181, 185-86, 194, 195, 196, 197, 200, 213; H.R. 471 and, 175; NCIO and, 151, 168-69, 175; photo of, 188

Albright, David, 204

Albuquerque Council of Churches, 109

Albuquerque Herald, 47

Albuquerque Journal, 110, 136, 185

Albuquerque Tribune, 153, 187, 205

All-Pueblo Council, 25-26, 43, 68, 109, 149

Allott, Gordon, 179, 208

American Civil Liberties Union (ACLU), support from, 109, 133, 191

American Forestry Association, 146, 160

American Indian Defense Association, 26

Anasazis, viii, 4

Anderson, Clinton P., xi, xiii, 47, 48, 55, 61, 87, 111, 115, 118, 121, 136, 138, 141, 147, 162-63, 165, 168, 175, 177, 181, 182, 186, 190, 192, 195, 196, 200, 208, 211-12: ABM and, 179-80; compromise by, 125,
212; criticism of, 153, 203-4; H.R. 471 and, 200; H.R. 3306 and, 137-38; health of, 178, 187-88; influence of, 198; negotiations with, 113-14, 119-20; opposition from, 4, 49-51, 122, 129, 137, 140, 142-43, 146, 152-53, 187, 197-98, 204-5; photo of, 48; Ranger bill and, 201-2; S. 1264, S. 1265, and, 120; S. 3085 and, 88, 91, 96, 103-6, 110; timbering and, 62, 104-5

Apaches, 6; Jicarilla, 109

"Appeal for Emergency Funds" (Locker), 139

"Artists and Writers Protest, The," 17-18

Aspinall, Wayne, 107, 109, 121, 131, 154, 155, 160, 198; role of, 134-35

Assimilation, 45, 145, 186

"Association and the Taos Blue Lake, The" (Locker), 111-12

Association on American Indian Affairs (AAIA), 46, 56, 63, 68, 72-74, 85, 87, 93-95, 111-12, 114-15, 126; role of, 41-42; support from, 66-67, 96; withdrawal of, 116

Austin, Mary, 23

B

Bailey, Vernon, 10, 14

Barker, Elliott, 15-16, 37, 90-91, 103, 160

BeLieu, Ken, 177, 179-80

Belindo, John, 141

Benet, Stephen Vincent, ix

Bennett, Robert, 97, 109, 129; testimony of, 130

Benson, E.T., 55

Bernal, Paul J. 39, 44, 45, 52-54, 56-57, 63, 65-69, 72-73, 84, 93, 104, 111, 112, 114, 121, 124, 127, 143,
146, 152-53, 164, 169, 182-83, 187, 197, 198, 203, 213; photo of, 40, 58, 82, 84, 89, 94, 95, 97, 117, 158, 188, 190; testimony of, 101, 105, 106, 132, 133, 156-57, 159, 175, 189, 191-93, 209

Bernal, Linda, 143

Berry, Congressman, 131

BIA. *See* Bureau of Indian Affairs

Blue Lake: desecration of, 21-22, 139-40, 145, 146, 159; importance of, 9, 50, 72, 80, 92, 102, 173; location of, 3; photo of, vi, 21, 29; protecting, 11-12, 15; return of, ix, 42, 63, 71-72, 79, 104, 189, 194, 217. *See also* Sacred watershed

Bodine, John: quote of, 13, 192-93, 209

Boldt, L.G., 36

Boundaries: defining, 81; inaccuracy of, 37-38

"Bowl, The," 58, 101, 119, 132, 142, 198; photo of, 58; protection for, 62, 118, 211

Brandborg, Stewart, 103

Brett, Dorothy, viii

Broder, Dave, 150

Brody, J.J., 77-78

Brooks, Charles, xi, 59

Brooks, Mary, 59

Brophy, William, 31, 33, 34, 37, 43; quote of, 30, 32, 38

Brown, Harry, 31

Budnik, Dan, 93

Bunker, R.M., 37

Burdick, Quentin, 96, 191

Bureau of Indian Affairs (BIA), 33-36, 38, 43, 47, 55, 111, 156, 165

Bureau of the Budget, 111, 131; opposition from, 129-30, 154, 165, 168; support from, 176, 188

Burke, Charles, 16-19
Bursum, Holm O., 17
Bursum Bill, 17-18, 21, 23, 25-26
Byler, William, 67, 71-72, 85, 91, 92, 103, 111, 112, 114-17; photo of, 71, 94, 97; testimony of, 101, 102

C
Cabot, Ted, x
Cacique. *See Romero*, Juan de Jesús
Cantu, J.C., 152, 163
Capulin Livestock Association, 90
Cargo, David, 125, 149, 150, 161, 168, 169, 173, 181, 193, 214; photo of, 150, 199; quote of, 154, 165
Carmack, William, 174; role of, 151-52
Carson National Forest, viii, xi, 15, 28, 39, 49, 79, 80, 88, 152, 213; arson in, 202; establishment of, ix; land transfer to, 36
Carter, Russell, 72, 107, 109, 117, 128; photo of, 117
Cash settlement, 53, 75, 113; refusing, 21, 76, 131, 132, 142
Castellano, Louis, 132, 133
Cather, Willa, 23
Chapin, Dwight, 218, 219
Chapman, Oscar, 31-32
Charles V, King, vii
Chavez, Dennis, 49, 51
Christian Science Monitor, 214
Church groups. *See* National Council of Churches
Claims Commission Act of 1946, 44-45; provisions of, 42-43
Clapper, Louis S., 102-3, 146, 187
Clark, Ramsey, 76
Clayburgh, Mark, 72
Clear-cutting, 36, 105, 118, 124, 142, 208. *See also* Timbering
Cleaver, Eldridge, 136
Cliff, Edward P., 159; testimony of, 131
Cochiti Pueblo case, 79
Cochrane, Walter, 19
Cohen, Felix, 42, 43
Cole, Ken, 177
Colgrove, Jim, xi, 70
Collier, John, Sr., xi, 25, 30-32, 41, 58-59, 65, 70, 128, 142, 219; appointment of, 22, 27; influence of, 64, 66; opposition from, 62-64, 74; photo of, 26, 60; quote of, 28, 62
Collier, Lucy: photo of, 26
Colorado River Compact, 163
Comanches, 6
Compromises, 119-20; benefits of, 87-88
Concha, John (Juan), 76
Concha, Pete: photo of, 199
Concurrence clause, 59
Congressional Record, 177, 204, 208
Conservation, xi-xii, 72, 85-88, 90, 92, 104, 110, 126, 133, 191; Forest Service and, 87, 138, 146, 157, 159
Considine, Bob, 91-92
Coolidge, Calvin, 20
Cooperative Agreement of 1927, 19-21, 30, 28, 37-38
Cordova, Juan, 52
Cordova, Manuel, 76
Cordova, Valentino, 143
Cornell, Dudley, 37, 72

Coronado, Francisco de, 6
Cottam, Louis, 35
Crane, Leo, 57
Cranston, Alan, 177, 213
Cultural pluralism, 136, 137
Cutting, Bronson, 27

D
Davis, James P., 124, 133; support from, 91, 128, 160
Dempsey, John J., 49, 51
Department of Agriculture, 7-8, 19, 30-33, 47, 57, 59, 66, 95, 111, 131, 169, 207, 211; multiple use and, 156; opposition from, 55, 56, 103, 129-30, 140, 154, 165, 168; support from, 188
Department of Justice, 56, 76, 78, 162
Department of the Interior, 20, 30-31, 47, 70, 95, 100, 111, 133, 152, 169, 207; support from, 56, 59, 129, 154-55
Derivation of Apache and Navajo Culture (La Farge), 41
Dingell, John, 162, 163
Dismuke, Dewey, 38, 47
Dodge Luhan, Mabel, vii, viii, xviii, 23, 25; photo of, 24, 25
Dole, Robert, 212
Double compensation, 159-60, 162
Dunham, Harold H., 80, 81, 83
Dwire, C.R., 20-21

E
Easley, Mack, 90
Eastern Association on Indian Affairs (EAIA), 41
Edmondson, Congressman, 161-62
Ehrlichman, John, 166, 173, 176, 180, 185, 187, 195, 196, 215; photo of, 178; quote of, 172, 177, 178-79
Eisenhower, Dwight, 152
El Crepusculo, ix
Ellis, Florence Hawley, 147; photo of, 77; testimony of, 76-77, 80, 81, 83
Encomienda system, 6
Ernst, Roger, 55, 56, 115, 116
Eviction, 17, 27, 42
Exclusive use, 14-16, 28, 30-33, 49, 59, 62, 65, 83, 87, 90, 130, 131, 135, 141, 142, 154, 201, 203, 211. *See also* Multiple use
Expert witnesses, testimony of, 76-78, 80, 83

F
Fall, Albert B., 23, 25
Fannin, Paul, 96, 140, 146, 179
Farrar & Rinehart, ix
Fee-simple title, 47
Fernandez, Antonio M. x, 36, 49, 51, 53-55
Field Foundation, 130
Flying Eagle, George: photo of, 206
Forbes, Henry, 109
Forbes, Hildegard, 116, 126
Forest Management Act (1897), 7
Forest preserves, creation of, 7-9, 11
Forest Reserve Act of 1891, 7, 8, 131
Forest Service, 14, 15, 18, 28, 30, 31, 42, 45, 47, 57, 61, 62, 64, 65, 69, 90, 95, 110, 122, 124, 131, 132, 134, 143, 156, 157, 161, 169, 175, 188,

203, 207, 211, 212; concessions by, 33; criticism of, 20-21, 73, 74, 133, 146; desecration by, 32-33, 142, 159, 184, 189; development of, 9; exclusion of, 99; H.R. 7758 and, 55; multiple use and, xi, 13, 135; opposition from, 85-86, 100-101, 103-4, 140; Ranger bill and, 201, 202; S. 903 and, 56; timbering and, 36, 99; tourism and, 37, 58, 59; use agreement with, 50, 67
Foster, A.L., 73-74
Franciscans, repression by, 6, 13
Frankel, Max, 150
Freeman, Duane R., 57, 139
Freeman, Orville, 56
From Every Zenith (Collier), 23
Fund-raising, 161, 182, 202

G
Gallagher, Bill, 90
Garment, Leonard, 169, 173, 177, 179, 180, 185, 186, 195, 196, 201; photo of, 196
Gaspard, Evelyn: photo of, 25
Gaspard, Leon: photo of, 25
"Gathering of the Tribes, The," 136
Gipson, Fred, 173
Goldwater, Barry, 195, 207, 213, 217; support from, 4, 208-9
Gomez, Dave, 182
Gomez, Star Road, x, 45
Goodmorning, Teles: photo of, 215
Goodwin, Mary, xi
Gordon-McCutchan, R.C.: photo of, xiii
Grant, Ulysses S., 4
Graves, C.L., 38
Grazing, 14, 15, 30-35, 37, 38, 49, 79, 90, 98, 100, 131, 145, 146, 159
Greeley, Arthur W.: testimony of, 100-101, 104-5, 141, 142
Green, Keith, 70, 92, 99
Greene, Bobbie, 166, 168-69, 173, 176-77, 189, 195-97, 207, 215; photo of, 196; quote of, 172, 185, 186, 187, 213, 219
Greening of America, The (Reich), 137
Grey, Zane, 17
Griffin, Robert, 4, 200-201, 217; quote of, 204, 213
Griffin-Harris Amendment, 204, 212-13
Groefflo, Malcom: photo of, 25
Gunther, Preston, 109-10

H
Hagerman, H.J., 18
Haley, James A., 107, 119, 124, 125, 128, 129, 146-47, 153-54, 159, 160, 162, 163, 196, 198, 217; hearings by, 130-34, 154; praise for, 135-36
Hansen, Clifford, 4, 140, 143, 146, 189
Hardin, Clifford, 154, 169, 173, 176
Harris, Fred R., 166, 174, 188, 198-200, 203, 204-5, 207, 211, 213, 215-17; H.R. 471 and, 176-77, 180-81, 197; photo of, 174; quote of, 151, 173, 198, 205, 218-19; support from, 4, 186
Harris, LaDonna, 151, 166, 168, 173, 175, 189, 191; photo of, 167; quote

of, 180, 195, 197, 218
Harris, Will Ed, 38
Hart, Philip, 177
Hassell, Jean, 187, 191
Hatfield, Mark, 140, 146
Hayden, Carl, 195
Heron Dam, 163
Hetzel, Theodore, 101
Hickel, Walter, 166, 168, 175, 186, 189; appointment of, 153; H.R. 471 and, 164-65; support from, 176, 191
Hobbs, Charles: photo of, 190
Hobert, Lee, 124, 128; testimony of, 133, 141
Honey, Thelma, 153
Hopi, xii
House Agriculture Committee, 134
House Concurrent Resolution 108, 45
House of Representatives Bill 471, 153, 197; amendment of, 162-63; debate on, 161-63; delay for, 179, 182, 198; hearings on, 196; Interior committee and, 199-200; lobbying for, 203; opposition to, 154, 160, 162, 165, 179, 180; passage of, 163, 171, 195, 200, 207, 208, 212-13; self-determination and, 188, 194, 195; significance of, 171, 173-75; support for, 154-56, 160-62, 168, 169, 171, 173-74, 176, 177, 181, 185, 186, 188, 191, 201, 204, 207, 208, 212-13
House of Representatives Bill 2656, 38
House of Representatives Bill 3306, 124, 153, 162; debate on, 134; defeat of, 146-47; importance of, 141; opposition to, 129, 132-34, 140-41, 143, 145-46; passage of, 135-36; reintroduction of, 119; support for, 129-31, 133-35, 137-38
House of Representatives Bill 4014, 27
House of Representatives Bill 7758, 51, 53, 54, 55
House of Representatives Bill 15184, 107, 109
House Rules Committee, 134
Hughes, Harold, 177
Hughes, Henry, 44, 53
Hummon, Serge, 101-2
Humphrey, Hubert: NCIO and, 151

I
Ickes, Harold, 26, 28
Indian Affairs Office, 15
Indian Bill of Rights, x-xi
Indian Bureau, 21, 30
Indian Claims Commission (ICC), xiii, 43, 46-48, 51, 52, 56, 65, 67, 80, 88, 92, 93, 100, 104, 108, 113, 131, 155, 176, 212; decision by, 71, 79, 81, 83, 85, 87, 102, 132, 162; establishment of, 42; hearings of, 44-45, 63, 74-79
Indian Claims Commission Act, 75, 80
Indian Defense Association, 27, 41
Indian Investigating Committee, 26
Indian New Deal, 26
Indian Reorganization Act (1934), 26-27, 219

"Indians Need Blue Lake, The" (New York Times), 137
Interior committee, 201, 202, 212; H.R. 471 and, 199-200; hearings of, 196; Ranger bill and, 203
Interstate Indian Council, 149, 168

J
Jackson, Henry, 90, 140, 182, 186, 196, 197, 199-201; opposition from, 4, 146, 177-80, 207-8
Jaramillo, Luis D., 91
Jenkins, Myra Ellen, 81, 199; photo of, 78; testimony of, 78, 80, 83, 187, 189-91
Jim, Bob, 175
Jiron, Teresino: photo of, 215
Johnson, Lyndon B., 130, 131, 195; NCIO and, 151
Johnson, Marcus, 70
Johnson, Spud, vii
Joint Efforts Group, 43, 46, 72, 113
Josephy, Al, 111, 153
Journal of Church and State, 118-19, 143
Justice Day, 135, 196

K
Karelsen, Frank, 43, 72, 85-87, 110, 114, 115; charges against, 111-13
Kelley, Dean, 117, 124, 130, 133, 134, 204; photo of, 117; support from, 118, 119, 126, 128, 160
Kennedy, Edward M., 177, 198, 200, 203, 205, 215, 216; support from, 4, 164, 185-86, 197, 207
Kennedy, John F., 56, 76, 164
Kennedy, Robert F., 93, 96, 136, 164; photo of, 94
Kerr, Bob, 195
King, Martin Luther, 136
Kingsley, Darwin, 43-46, 73, 79, 80; charges against, 112, 113; firing of, 51-54
Kivas, 6, 156

L
LaCome, Elmer, 145-46
La Farge, Consuelo, 124, 127, 128
La Farge, Oliver, xi, 46-53, 55, 59, 65-66, 70, 72-73, 83, 84, 113; death of, 63-64, 66; photo of, 43, 63; quote of, 41-42, 45-46, 54, 58, 61-63, 76-77, 139-40
La Junta Canyon, timbering in, 35-37, 62, 94, 99, 142, 159
Lallmang, Sue, 166, 191
Land, interrelationship with, 13
Lands Board. See Pueblo Lands Board
Land-use patterns, 78
Las Cruces Arroyo, 69; easement for, 70, 88, 107
Laughing Boy (La Farge), 41
Lawrence, D.H., 17, 23
Lawrence, Frieda: photo of, 25
Leopold, Aldo, 122
Le Sage, Robert, 110, 111, 119, 122, 124, 142; Anderson and, 105-6, 121
Lindsay, Vachel, 17
Little, Jon, 143, 145, 187
Livestock, impounding, 35
Locker, Corinne, 63, 67, 70-71, 83-87, 93, 110, 130, 153, 165, 169, 177,

179, 197, 215; appeal by, 139; charges by, 111-13, 115; dedication of, 126; firing of, 114, 116, 126; photo of, 82, 97; problems with, 72-73; quote of, 119, 128, 129, 133, 148; reinstatement of, 114-15; role of, 68-69, 125-27, 166
Loesch, Harrison, 154-55
Long Drought, viii, 4
Los Angeles Times, 3
Lucy, Curtis, 203-4
Luhan, Tony, vii, viii, 23, 25, 39; photo of, 25
Lujan, Henrietta, 182
Lujan, Henry, 166
Lujan, Julian, 76
Lujan, Manuel, 154, 155, 159-61, 166, 181

M
McArdle, Richard E., 56-57
McClure, Representative, 131
McConnell, Robert, 129
McGovern, George, 138, 146, 173, 177, 179, 181-82, 185, 187, 197-200, 203, 205, 207, 211
McKinley, William, 8
McKinney, Robert, 70
McMillan, Ross, 14
Mansfield, Mike, 204
Man Who Killed the Deer, The (Waters), viii, ix-x, xi, xiii, 39
Marcus, Ben: photo of, 215
Marcus, Frank, 166; photo of, 215
Marcus, John: photo of, 190, 215
Martinez, Albert, viii
Martinez, Andres, 191
Martinez, Clara, viii
Martinez, Pascual, viii, 39
Martinez, Roberto, 90
Martinez, Sam: photo of, 215
Martinez, Seferino, x, 33, 34, 36, 44, 46-47, 51-53, 56-57, 64-67, 73, 92, 93, 119, 121, 153, 182, 183; H.R. 7758 and, 54; opposition to, 44-45, 68, 74; photo of, 34, 89, 94, 95, 97, 117; testimony of, 62, 76, 101, 132-33, 142, 159
Martinez, Tony, 183
Martinez, William, 183
Masters, Edgar Lee, 17
Mauldin, Bill, 128
Mayo, Budget Director, 173
Merriam, C. Hart, 10, 14
Metcalf, Lee, 96, 104, 189-92, 209; criticism of, 187, 192-93; opposition from, 4, 140-43, 146, 204-5, 207-8
Miccosukees, 109
Mining, 31; protection from, 20, 30
Mirabal, Antonio, 34, 76
Mirabal, James, 53, 183, 197, 213; photo of, 190
Mitchell, Stephen A., 53, 60, 69, 70, 72-73, 85-87, 110, 126; charges against, 111; quote of, 88
Mondale, Walter, 177, 195, 211
Mondragon, Manuel, 10
Morris, Tom, 65-66, 88, 129; photo of, 89
Muir, John, 7
Multiple use, 8, 12-14, 62, 135, 141, 142, 191, 211; threat of, 99, 131, 133, 156-57. See also Exclusive use

Murphy, Charles, 57-58
Myers, Ralph, viii, 39
Mysticism, xii

N

Nadel, Michael, 160, 191
Nakai, Raymond, 135-36
Nash, Philleo, 57
National Committee for Restoration of the Blue Lake Lands to the Taos Indians, 128, 133, 138-39, 141, 153, 191, 201; fund-raising by, 161, 182, 202
National Congress of American Indians (NCAI), 149, 161, 166, 168, 181, 194; Albuquerque meeting of, 164-65, 175; Nixon and, 148, 151; support from, 88, 137, 141, 191
National Council of Churches (NCC), 125, 133; support from, 72, 90-91, 101,116-19, 124, 128, 137, 153, 191
National Council on Indian Opportunity (NCIO), 151, 152, 166, 172, 173, 174, 176, 191, 194, 197; Agnew and, 168-69, 175
National Educational Television, 203-4
National forests, 8, 10, 19
National Forest Service. *See* Forest Service
National parks, creation of, 7
National Wildlife Federation (NWF), 102-3, 133, 146
Naturalness, tenet of, 157
Navajos, 6
NCAI. *See* National Congress of American Indians
NCC. *See* National Council of Churches
NCIO. *See* National Council on Indian Opportunity
Newman, Wallace "Chief," 218; influence of, 148, 186
New Mexico Commission on Indian Affairs, 88, 149
New Mexico Council of Churches (NMCC), 90, 124-25
New Mexico Wildlife and Conservation Association, 103, 143, 145
New York Times, 3, 150, 193, 207, 215; editorial by, 4, 137; obituary from, 220; support from, 92-93, 96, 187
Nixon, Richard M., 150, 177-81, 193, 194, 196, 197, 200, 201, 205, 215, 220; Blue Lake and, 3-4, 170, 172, 177, 181, 216-19; H.R. 471 and, 165, 175, 181, 185, 186, 188-89, 195, 204; Indian policy of, 4, 148-49, 166, 168, 172-73, 186-87; NCAI and, 151; photo of, 178, 188; quote of, 216, 219
NMCC. *See* New Mexico Council of Churches
North House, 108; photo of, 75-76
NWF. *See* National Wildlife Federation

O

O'Connor, Representative, 38
Office of Interamerican Affairs, ix
O'Keeffe, Georgia, 23
OK Lumber Company, 36
O'Leary, Thomas, 191

Olson, Walter, 70, 74
Overgrazing. *See* Grazing

P

Pardo, Richard, 160
Parrish, Maxfield, 17
Pasztor, Laszlo, 166
Patterson, Brad, 169, 173, 185, 195
Payne, Mary Lou: photo of, 94
People's Institute, The, 23
Percy, Charles, 212
Perpetual easement, 113
Peterson, Helen, 107
"Petitioner's Findings of Fact and Brief," 79
Phillips, Bert: quote of, 10-11, 13, 14
Phipps, Joe, 124, 141
Pilgrimages, 121, 143, 145
Pinchot, Gifford, 6-9, 12, 49, 97, 211; drawing of, 8; Muir and, 7-8; multiple use and, 14
Plummer, F.G., 12
Pomeroy, Kenneth, 146
Poole, Rufus, 72, 73, 87, 111, 112, 114, 115, 119, 120, 122, 126, 127, 141; hiring of, 70-71; quote of, 86; withdrawal of, 116
Poole, Suzie, 71, 127, 141
Poor People's March, 136
Porter, Eliot, 128
Precedent, 131, 132, 134, 141, 146, 162, 190, 191 203, 205, 208-9, 212
Proctor, George, xi, 57, 66, 70; opposition from, 60-62, 187, 191
Public Law 194 (1928), 20
Public Law 91-550, 217-19
Public Law 93-638, 219
Public relations campaign, 59-60
Pueblo Lands Act (1924), 18
Pueblo Lands Board, ix, 18, 21, 76, 79; hearings of, 27-28
Pueblo Relief Bill of 1933, 27, 79

R

Rainer, John, 107, 149-50, 168, 175, 191; photo of, 149, 190
Range management, Forest Service and, 33-35
Ranger bill, 201-4, 207, 211, 212
Ravagli, Angelo: photo of, 25
Reed, Joan Huggins, xi, 59
Reich, Charles, 137
Religion: struggle for, 9, 17-19; suppression of, 6, 13, 16-18, 59
Religious argument, dubiousness of, 120-22
Religious attachment, 79-80, 97, 131, 132, 143
Religious Crimes Act, 16
Religious freedom, xii-xiii, 51, 96, 98, 99, 101-3, 117, 127, 131-33, 136, 137, 143, 155, 175, 207, 216; focusing on, 88, 91-94, 118, 135; violation of, 157
Religious privacy, 122, 156-57, 193
Reno, Phillip, 72
Reparations, suits for, 75-76
Republican Governors' Conference, 179
Republican National Committee (RNC), 165-66, 191
Republican party, 165-66, 171, 174
"Restoring a Shrine" (*Washington Post*), 96

Reversion clause, 176, 191, 202, 203
Reyna, Hilario, 76
Reyna, John, 88, 101; photo of, 94, 95, 97, 215
Reyna, John C., 93
Reyna, John J.: photo of, 84, 117
Reyna, Manuel: photo of, 190
Reyna, Tony, 136-37
Riegle, Don, 162
Rio Lucero watershed, 30
Rio Pueblo de Taos, 37; photo of, 10, 75, 108
Rio Pueblo watershed, 30, 38, 156, 157
Rixon, Theodore F., 11
Robertson, Robert, 173-75, 179, 185, 195, 196; photo of, 199
Rolstad, Bruce, 90-91, 124, 125
Romero, Abe, x, 52-53
Romero, Cesario, 76
Romero, Daisy: photo of, 215
Romero, Juan de Jesús, xiii, 4, 187, 190, 193, 194, 197, 200, 203, 211, 213, 214, 216, 218-20; birth of, 6; control by, 182-84; obituary of, 220; photo of, 5, 184, 188, 190; power of, 185, 189; quote of, 183-85, 192, 217
Romero, Pat, x
Romero, Querino, 166, 169, 183, 197, 213; photo of, 144, 170, 190; testimony of, 132, 133, 142-43
Romero, Richard, 98, 99, 122
Romero, Teofilo: photo of, 5
Roosevelt, Franklin, 26
Roosevelt, Theodore, ix, 8, 11, 12, 13, 14, 97, 131
Rosenthal, Abe, 150
Rule T-12, invoking, 35

S

"Sacred Lake of Taos, The" 109
Sacred watershed, 15, 19, 28, 46, 51, 106, 118; exclusive use of, 18, 20, 21, 59; Forest Service and, 20, 49; invasion of, 9-10, 44; return of, 39, 45, 68, 76, 83, 85, 93-94, 133. *See also* Blue Lake
Samora, Doroteo "Frank": photo of, xiii, 41
Sandburg, Carl, 17
Sandoval, Joe Sun Hawk, viii
Sandoval, Lupe, 159
San Juan-Chama Water Diversion, 163
San Juan Indians, 109-10
Santa Clara Pueblo, 14
Santa Fe New Mexican, 70, 120; editorial in, 60, 136; Ranger bill and, 201
Santistevan, Ernest, 191
Santo Domingo Pueblo, 55
Saylor, John, 135, 162, 163
Schaab, William, 127, 129, 130, 141, 146, 164, 165, 168, 169, 191, 197, 201, 202, 215; debt to, 134, 139, 153; photo of, 150, 190; quote of, 128, 132, 214; testimony of, 131-32, 142, 156, 159
Schifter, Richard, 46, 57, 58, 64, 66-68, 72-74, 79, 80, 85-87, 110, 114, 115, 126, 139; charges against, 111-13; quote of, 59, 61
Schlesinger, James R., 176

Seaman, Don, 85, 160
Section 4, 28, 30
Self-consciousness, developing, 69, 83-84
Self-determination, 149, 151-52, 169, 171, 174, 180, 185, 189, 212; H.R. 471 and, 188, 194, 195; Nixon and, 186-87, 194, 195
Senate Bill 48, 55
Senate Bill 750, 199, 201; hearings on, 196; introduction of, 152-53
Senate Bill 903, 55-56
Senate Bill 1624, 120, 140
Senate Bill 1625, 120, 140
Senate Bill 2914, 27
Senate Bill 3085; defeat of, 111; hearings on, 95-105; introduction of, 87, 91, 96; opposition to, 90-91, 95, 100-104; provisions of, 93; revision of, 110; support for, 88, 90-98, 101-3, 107, 109
Senate Investigating Committee, 27
Shrines, 79-80, 124; as campsites, 91-92; identification of, 118; threat to, 101
Sierra Club, 7, 102
Simpson, Milward, 96
Smith, M.E., 121
Soul on Ice (Cleaver), 136
Southern California Committee for the Restoration of Blue Lake, 182
South House, 108; photo of, 75
Sovereignty, tribal, 45
Speiser, Lawrence, 109, 191
Spraying, 104-5, 107, 184
Spy trip, 146, 157, 160
Squadron, Howard, 128-29
Squatters, 17, 18
Stacey, Alison, 42
"Statement by the Taos Pueblo Council on the Blue Lake Legislation," 122
Steiger, Congressman, 131
Steiner, Stan, 203
Stevens, Alden, 94, 111, 114, 115, 116
Stillman, John, 133
Straus, Jerry, 161, 165, 168, 169, 176, 179, 195, 197, 199, 202, 205, 21
Suazo, Gilbert, 189; photo of, 190
Subcommittee on Indian Affairs, 134, 182, 197, 199, 200; hearings of, 27, 95-105, 130-33, 140-43, 145-46, 154, 196; members of, 96
Summers, Harry, 121, 124
Swallow, Alan, ix

T
Taos County Commission, 90, 152, 163
Taos County Committee, 145-46
Taos Forest Preserve, 11-13
Taos Indians: appropriations for, 28;

conservation practices of, 11-12; financial problems for, 138-39, 202; ICC and, 43; Nixon and, 4, 149
Taos News, 66, 88, 124, 137, 163; Anderson in, 120; Blue Lake controversy and, 60; editorial in, 136; opposition from, 70; support from, 87, 92, 96
Taos Plaza: photo of, 15
Taos Pueblo: description of, 4, 6, 9, 23; map of, xviii, xix; title to, vii
Taos Soil and Water Conservation District, 191
Taos Soil Conservation District, 88
Taos Town Council, 63, 69, 88, 96, 161, 191
Termination, 45, 152, 186, 211
Timbering, 21, 110, 119, 122, 131, 138, 142, 159, 184; Anderson and, 104-5, 121; controversy over, 35-36, 56, 62-63, 99. See also Clear-cutting
Time magazine, 215
Tourism, 58, 59; ban on, 62; conflict over, 36-37; promoting, 28, 68
Tragar, George L., 121
Train, Russell, 154
Treaty of Guadalupe Hidalgo, 6, 76
Tribal Council, x, xi, 18, 37, 39, 42, 47, 52-53, 55, 68, 71, 85, 113, 127, 143, 152-53; Cacique and, 182-83; cooperation by, 88; division of, 73; Ellis and, 77; Forbes and, 116, 126; H.R. 471 and, 87, 154; Kelley and, 118; Martinez and, 45; Schaab and, 130
Tribal elders, testimony of, 79-81, 83
"Tribe Fights to Regain Church" (New York Times), 92-93
Trujillo, Cruz: photo of, 190, 215
Trujillo, Geronimo, 53; photo of, 89
Truman, Harry S., 4, 48
Trust title, 51, 68, 83, 97, 104, 110, 111; acquiring, 52, 99; argument for, 99; Collier and, 64-65; quest for, 18, 64-66, 69-70, 72-74, 76, 77, 83, 112-15, 183
Trust-title bill, 55, 65-66; opposition to, 56, 90, 101; support for, 101; Tribal Council and, 87
"TV Show Brings Cries of Anger from Taos" (New Mexican), 60
Twining, photo of, 11

U
Udall, Morris, 162
Udall, Stewart, 103, 110, 121, 122, 124-26, 129, 151, 153, 165; photo of, 95; quote of, 14, 155; support from, 94-96, 191; testimony of, 96-101, 130-31, 140-41
"Unholy alliance" telegram, 115, 126
United Pueblos Agency, 70

United States Geological Survey, 11
United States v. Sandoval, 17
Use-permit, 28, 30, 32-33, 47, 50, 51, 53, 55, 68, 74, 79; inadequacy of, 122; perpetual, 110, 113; protection of, 103, 114; renewal of, 67; special, 35; value of, 67, 80-81, 159-60
Utes, 109

V
Veterans of Foreign Wars, 90
Vincent, Craig, 65
Visitor permits, 20-22, 73-74, 122, 124, 142; issuing, 74, 157; withholding, 57, 59, 99
Voting issue, 42, 61, 65, 66, 73, 152

W
Walker, Johnny, 129
Walker, Preston, 121
Wallace, H.A., 28
Wannamaker, John, 128
Ward, C.D., 169, 171, 173, 175, 177, 185, 195, 196; photo of, 199; quote of, 176
Washington Post, 96, 207; editorial in, 4, 138
Washington Star, quote from, 200
"Water Is So Clear that a Blind Man Could See, The," 203-4
Water rights, xi, 19, 20, 155, 163-64, 202, 203
Waters, Frank: photo of, xiii, 25, 41; quote of, 39; support from, 59
Webb, Harry, 159
Wheeler, Burton K., 28
Wheeler Peak Wilderness Area, 100, 133; protecting, 103, 107, 110, 119
Wilderness, preservation of, 13, 19, 100, 121, 133, 137, 155
Wilderness Act, 95, 100, 103, 122
Wilderness Amendment, 98
Wilderness Protection Act, 110, 131
Wilderness Society, 103, 107, 160, 169, 191
Wilkie, Bruce, 191
Wilkinson, Cragun, and Barker (law firm), 161, 165
Winters, Esther: photo of, 206
Wood, Claude, 120-21, 187
Work, Hubert, 19
Wurzel, Alan, 72

Y
Younger-Hunter, Eve: photo of, 25
Younger-Hunter, John: photo of, 25

Z
Zimmerman, William, 45, 46, 102